FEAR GOD AND TAKE YOUR OWN PART

BY THEODORE ROOSEVELT

FEAR GOD
and
Take Your Own Part

By
Theodore Roosevelt

NEW YORK
GEORGE H. DORAN COMPANY

DEDICATION

This book is dedicated to the memory of

Julia Ward Howe

because in the vital matters fundamentally affecting the life of the Republic, she was as good a citizen of the Republic as Washington and Lincoln themselves. She was in the highest sense a good wife and a good mother; and therefore she fulfilled the primary law of our being. She brought up with devoted care and wisdom her sons and her daughters. At the same time she fulfilled her full duty to the commonwealth from the public standpoint. She preached righteousness and she practised righteousness. She sought the peace that comes as the handmaiden of well doing. She preached that stern and lofty courage of soul which shrinks neither from war nor from any other form of suffering and hardship and danger if it is only thereby that justice can be served. She embodied that trait more essential than any other in the make-up of the men and women of this Republic—the valor of righteousness.

v

BATTLE HYMN OF THE REPUBLIC

JULIA WARD HOWE

Mine eyes have seen the glory of the coming of
    the Lord;
He is trampling out the vintage where the grapes
    of wrath are stored;
He hath loosed the fateful lightning of His ter-
    rible swift sword,
His truth is marching on.

I have seen Him in the watch-fires of a hundred
    circling camps;
They have builded Him an altar in the evening
    dews and damps;
I can read His righteous sentence by the dim and
    flaring lamps,
His day is marching on.

I have read a fiery gospel, writ in burnished rows
    of steel:
"As ye deal with my contemners, so with you my
    grace shall deal;
Let the Hero, born of woman, crush the serpent
    with His heel,
Since God is marching on."

BATTLE HYMN OF THE REPUBLIC

*He has sounded forth the trumpet that shall
   never call retreat;*
*He is sifting out the hearts of men before His
   judgment-seat;*
*Oh, be swift, my soul, to answer Him! be jubi-
   lant, my feet,*
Our God is marching on.

*In the beauty of the lilies, Christ was born across
   the sea,*
*With a glory in His bosom that transfigures you
   and me;*
*As he died to make men holy, let us die to make
   men free,*
While God is marching on.

TO THE PEOPLE OF AMERICA

Over two months have gone by since this book was published and during those two months affairs have moved rapidly, and at every point the march of events has shown the need of reducing to practice every principle herein laid down.

The monotonous succession of outrages upon our people by the Mexicans was broken by a spectacular raid of Villa into American territory, which resulted in the death of half a dozen American soldiers and an equal number of civilians. We accordingly asked Carranza to permit us to assist him in hunting down Villa and Carranza grudgingly gave the permission. We failed to get Villa; we had to fight the Villistas and at one moment also the Carranzistas; we lost valuable lives, and at this time of writing the expedition is halted and it is announced at Washington that it is being considered whether or not it shall be withdrawn. We have not been able to scrape together the troops and equipment necessary to punish a single bandit. The professional pacificists and professional antipreparedness advocates are invited to consider these facts. We are told we have kept the peace in Mexico. As a matter of fact we have twice been at war in Mexico within the last two years. Our failure to prepare, our failure to take action of a proper sort on the Mexican border has not averted bloodshed; it has invited bloodshed. It has cost the loss of more lives than were lost in the Spanish War. Our Mexican failure is merely the natural fruit of the policies of pacificism and anti-preparedness.

Since the first edition of this book was published, President Wilson has notified Germany and has informed Congress that if Germany continues submarine warfare against merchant and passenger steamers as she has carried it on for the last year America will take action. Apparently the first step is to be the sundering of diplomatic relations. Such sunderance would, of course, mean nothing if the submarine war was continued. Merely to recall our Ambassador if men, women and children are being continually killed on the high seas and to take no further action would be about as effective as the conduct of a private individual who, when another man slapped his wife's face, retaliated by not bowing to the man. Therefore, either Germany will have to surrender on the point at issue, or this protest of ours will prove to have meant nothing, or else there must be a war. Fourteen months have elapsed since we sent our "strict accountability" note to Germany demanding that there be no submarine warfare that should endanger the lives of American citizens. She did not believe that we meant what we said and the warfare has gone on. If she now stops, it will be proof positive that she would have stopped at the very outset had we made it evident that we meant what we said. In such case the loss of thousands of lives of men, women and children will be at our doors for having failed to make it evident that we meant what we said. If she does not stop, then we shall have to go to war or back down; and in that case it must be remembered that during these fourteen months—and during the preceding seven months—we have not prepared in naval, military or industrial matters in the smallest degree. The peace-at-any-price men, the professional pacificists shrieked loudly that to prepare would be to invite war. The Administration accepted their view and has not prepared. The result is that we are near to war. The blindest can now see that had we, in August 1914 when the great war began, ourselves begun actively to prepare, we would now be in a position such that every one knew our words would be made good by our deeds. In such case no nation would dream of interfering with us or of refusing our demands; and each of the warring nations would vie with the others to keep us out of the war. Immediate preparedness at the outset of the war would have meant that there would never have been the necessity for sending the "strict accountability" note. It would have meant that there never would have been the murder of the thousands of men, women and children on the high seas. It would have meant that we would now be sure of peace for ourselves. It would have meant that we would now be ready to act the part of peacemaker for others.

THEODORE ROOSEVELT.

Sagamore Hill, April 24th, 1916.

INTRODUCTORY NOTE

This book is based primarily upon, and mainly consists of, matter contained in articles I have written in the *Metropolitan Magazine* during the past fourteen months. It also contains or is based upon an article contributed to the *Wheeler Syndicate,* a paper submitted to the American Sociological Congress, and one or two speeches and public statements. In addition there is much new matter, including most of the first chapter. In part the old matter has been rearranged. For the most part, I have left it unchanged. In the few instances where what I spoke was in the nature of prophecy as to what might or would happen during the last year, the prophecy has been fulfilled, and I have changed the tense but not the purport of the statements. I have preferred to run the risk of occasional repetition rather than to attempt rewriting certain of the chapters, because whatever of value these chapters have had lay in the fact that in them I was applying eternal principles of right to concrete cases which were of vital importance at the moment, instead of merely treating these eternal principles as having their place forever in the realm of abstract thought and never to be reduced to action. I was speaking to and for the living present about the immediate needs of the present.

INTRODUCTORY NOTE

The principles set forth in this book are simply the principles of true Americanism within and without our own borders, the principles which, according to my abilities, I have preached and, according to my abilities, I have practised for the thirty-five years since, as a very young man, I first began to take an active interest in American history and in American political life.

THEODORE ROOSEVELT.

Sagamore Hill, February 3, 1916.

CONTENTS

CONTENTS

FEAR GOD AND TAKE YOUR OWN PART

CHAPTER I

FEAR GOD AND TAKE YOUR OWN PART

READERS of Borrow will recognize in the heading of this chapter, which I have also chosen for the title of the book, a phrase used by the heroine of Lavengro.

Fear God; and take your own part! Fear God, in the true sense of the word, means love God, respect God, honor God; and all of this can only be done by loving our neighbor, treating him justly and mercifully, and in all ways endeavoring to protect him from injustice and cruelty; thus obeying, as far as our human frailty will permit, the great and immutable law of righteousness.

We fear God when we do justice to and demand justice for the men within our own borders. We are false to the teachings of righteousness if we do not do such justice and demand such justice. We must do it to the weak, and we must do it to the strong. We do not fear God if we show mean envy and hatred of those who are better off than we are; and still less do we fear God if we show a base arrogance towards and selfish lack of consideration for those who are less well off. We must apply the same standard of conduct alike to man and to woman, to rich man and to poor man, to employer and employee. We must organize our social and industrial life so as to secure a reasonable equality of opportunity for all men to show the stuff that is in them, and a reasonable division among those engaged in industrial work of the reward for that industrial work, a division which shall take into account all the qualities that contribute to the necessary success. We must demand honesty, justice, mercy, truthfulness, in our dealings with one another within our own borders. Outside of our own borders we must treat other nations as we would wish to be treated in return, judging each in any given crisis as we ourselves ought to be judged—that is, by our conduct in that crisis. If they do ill, we show that we fear God when we sternly bear testimony against them and oppose them in any way and to whatever extent the needs require. If they do well, we must not wrong them ourselves. Finally, if we are really devoted to a lofty ideal we must

16

in so far as our strength permits aid them if they are wronged by others. When we sit idly by while Belgium is being overwhelmed, and rolling up our eyes prattle with unctuous self-righteousness about "the duty of neutrality," we show that we do not really fear God; on the contrary, we show an odious fear of the devil, and a mean readiness to serve him.

But in addition to fearing God, it is necessary that we should be able and ready to take our own part. The man who cannot take his own part is a nuisance in the community, a source of weakness, an encouragement to wrongdoers and an added burden to the men who wish to do what is right. If he cannot take his own part, then somebody else has to take it for him; and this means that his weakness and cowardice and inefficiency place an added burden on some other man and make that other man's strength by just so much of less avail to the community as a whole. No man can take the part of any one else unless he is able to take his own part. This is just as true of nations as of men. A nation that cannot take its own part is at times almost as fertile a source of mischief in the world at large as is a nation which does wrong to others, for its very existence puts a premium on such wrongdoing. Therefore, a nation must fit itself to defend its honor and interest against outside aggression; and this necessarily means that in a free democracy every man fit for citizenship must be trained so that he can do his full duty to the nation in war no less than in peace.

Unless we are thorough-going Americans and unless our patriotism is part of the very fiber of our being, we can neither serve God nor take our own part. Whatever may be the case in an infinitely remote future, at present no people can render any service to humanity unless as a people they feel an intense sense of national cohesion and solidarity. The man who loves other nations as much as he does his own, stands on a par with the man who loves other women as much as he does his own wife. The United States can accomplish little for mankind, save in so far as within its borders it develops an intense spirit of Americanism. A flabby cosmopolitanism, especially if it expresses itself through a flabby pacifism, is not only silly, but degrading. It represents national emasculation. The professors of every form of hyphenated Americanism are as truly the foes of this country as if they dwelled outside its borders and made active war against it. This is not a figure of speech, or a hyperbolic statement. The leaders of the hyphenated-American movement in this country (who during the last eighteen months have been the professional German-Americans and Austro-Americans) are also leaders in the movement against preparedness. I have before me a little pamphlet, circulated by a "German-American" organization, consisting of articles written by a German-American for a paper which claims to be the leading German paper in Illinois. This pamphlet is a bitter attack upon the policy of preparedness for the United States, and a slanderous assault on those advocating this American policy. It is, therefore, an effort *in the interest of Germany* to turn the United States into a larger Belgium— an easy prey for Germany whenever Germany desires to seize it. These professional German-Americans and Pro-Germans are Anti-American to the core. They play the part of traitors, pure and simple. Once it was true that this country could not endure half free and half slave. To-day it is true that it can not endure half American and half foreign. The hyphen is incompatible with patriotism.

Patriotism should be an integral part of our every feeling at all times, for it is merely another name for those qualities of soul which make a man in peace or in war, by day or by night, think of his duty to his fellows, and of his duty to the nation through which their and his loftiest aspirations must find their fitting expression. After the *Lusitania* was sunk, Mr. Wilson stated in effect that such a time was not the right time to stir up patriotism. This statement is entirely incompatible with having a feeling of deep patriotism at any time. It might just as appropriately have been made by George Washington immediately after his defeat at the Brandywine, or by Abraham Lincoln immediately after the surrender of Fort Sumter; and if in either of these crises our leaders had acted on any such principle we would not now have any country at all. Patriotism is as much a duty in time of war as in time of peace, and it is most of all a duty in any and every great crisis. To commit folly or do evil, to act inconsiderately and hastily or wantonly and viciously, in the name of patriotism, represents not patriotism at all, but a use of the name to cloak an attack upon the thing. Such baseness or folly is wrong, at every time and on every occasion. But patriotism itself is not only in place on every occasion and at every time, but is peculiarly the feeling which should be stirred to its deepest depths at every serious crisis. The duty of a leader is to lead; and it is a dreadful thing that any man chosen to lead his fellow-countrymen should himself show, not merely so profound a lack of patriotism, but such misunderstanding of patriotism, as to be willing to say in a great crisis what President Wilson thus said at the time of the sinking of the *Lusitania*. This statement, coupled with his statement made about the same time as to being "too proud to fight," furnishes the clue to the Administration's policy both before and since. This policy made our great democratic commonwealth false to its duties and its ideals in a tremendous world crisis, at the very time when, if properly led, it could have rendered an inestimable service to all mankind, and could have placed itself on a higher pinnacle of worthy achievement than ever before.

Patriotism, so far from being incompatible with performance of duty to other nations, is an indispensable prerequisite to doing one's duty toward other nations. Fear God; and take your own part! If this nation had feared God it would have stood up for the Belgians and Armenians; if it had been able and willing to take its own part there would have been no murderous assault on the *Lusitania,* no outrages on our men and women in Mexico. True patriotism carries with it not hostility to other nations but a quickened sense of responsible good-will towards other nations, a good-will of acts and not merely of words. I stand for a nationalism of duty, to oneself and to others; and, therefore, for a nationalism which is a means to internationalism. World peace must rest on the willingness of nations with courage, cool foresight, and readiness for self-sacrifice to defend the fabric of international law. No nation can help in securing an organized, peaceful and justice-doing world community until it is willing to run risks and make efforts in order to secure and maintain such a community.

The nation that in actual practice fears God is the nation which does not wrong its neighbors, which does so far as possible help its neighbors, and which never promises what it cannot or will not or ought not to perform. The professional pacifists in and out of office who at peace congresses pass silly resolutions which cannot be, and ought not to be, lived up to, and enter into silly treaties which ought not to be, and cannot be, kept, are not serving God, but Baal. They are not doing anything for anybody.[1] If in addition these people, when the concrete case arises, as in Belgium or Armenia, fear concretely

[1] See the excellent little book called "Is War Diminishing?" by Woods and Baltzly. The authors deal, as they necessarily must if truthful deal, with the mischievous activities of those professional pacifists among whom Mr. Andrew Carnegie has attained an unhappy prominence: activities which in this country for the last five years have worked nothing but evil, and very serious evil, to our nation and to humanity at large, and to all genuine movements for the promotion of the peace of righteousness. The writers instance Mr. Nicholas Murray Butler as presenting in typical manner the shams and perversions of fact upon which the professional pacifists rely for their propaganda, and remark that these pacifists, "who pride themselves on having the superior moral point of view, openly disregard the truth," and ask "these professors of ethics, law and justice, these presidents of colleges, these moral educators, if morality is not necessarily bound up with truth." The pacifist movement in this country has not only been one of extreme folly and immorality, but has been bolstered by consistent and unwearied falsification of the facts, laudation of shallow and unprincipled demagogues, and condemnation of the upright public servants who fearlessly tell the truth.

to denounce and antagonize the wrongdoer, they become not merely passive, but active agents of the devil. The professional pacifists who applauded universal arbitration treaties and disarmament proposals prior to the war, since the war have held meetings and parades in this country on behalf of peace, and have gone on silly missions to Europe on behalf of peace—and the peace they sought to impose on heroes who were battling against infamy was a peace conceived in the interest of the authors of the infamy. They did not dare to say that they stood only for a peace that should right the wrongs of Belgium. They did not dare to denounce the war of aggression by Germany against Belgium. Their souls were too small, their timidity too great. They were even afraid to applaud the war waged by Belgium in its own defence. These pacifists have served morality, have shown that they feared God, exactly as the Pharisees did, when they made broad their philacteries and uttered long prayers in public, but did not lift a finger to lighten the load of the oppressed. When Mr. Wilson and Mr. Bryan made this nation shirk its duty towards Belgium, they made us false to all our high ideals; for they acted and caused this government to act in that spirit of commercial opportunism which refuses to do duty to others unless there is in it pecuniary profit for oneself. This combination of mean timidity and mean commercial opportunism is peculiarly odious because those practising it have sought to hide it by profuse outbursts of wordy sentimentality and loud professions of attachment to impossible and undesirable ideals. One of the besetting sins of many of our public servants (and of not a few of our professional moralists, lay and clerical) is to cloak weakness or baseness of action behind insincere oratory on behalf of impractical ideals. The true servant of the people is the man who preaches realizable ideals; and who then practises what he has preached.

Moreover, even as regards the pacifists who genuinely desire that this nation should fear God, it is to be remembered that if the nation cannot take its own part, the fact that it fears God will be of no practical consequence to any one. Nobody cares whether or not the feeling of the Chinese people is against international wrongdoing; for, as China is helplessly unable to take her own part, she is in practise even more helpless to take the part of any one else and to secure justice and mercy for any one else. The pacifists who are seeking to Chinafy the United States are not only seeking to bring the United States to ruin, but are also seeking to render it absolutely impotent to help upright and well-behaved nations which are oppressed by the military power of unscrupulous neighbors of greater strength.

The professional pacifists, the leaders in the pacifist movement in the United States, do particular harm by giving well-meaning but uninformed people who do not think deeply what seems to them a convincing excuse for failure to show courage and resolution. Those who preach sloth and cowardice under the high-sounding name of "peace" give people a word with which to cloak, even to themselves, their failure to perform unpleasant duty. For a man to stand up for his own rights, or especially for the rights of somebody else, means that he must have virile qualities: courage, foresight, willingness to face risk and undergo effort. It is much easier to be timid and lazy. The average man does not like to face death and endure hardship and labor. He can be roused to do so if a leader of the right type, a Washington or Lincoln, appeals to the higher qualities, including the stern qualities, of his soul. But a leader, or at least a man who holds a leader's place, earns praise and profit unworthily if he uses his gift of words to lull well-meaning men to sleep, if he assures them that it is their duty to do the easy and selfish thing, and furnishes them high-sounding phrases with which to cover ignoble failure to perform hard and disagreeable duties.

Peace is not the end. Righteousness is the end. When the Saviour saw the money-changers in the Temple he broke the peace by driving them out. At that moment peace could have been obtained readily enough by the simple process of keeping quiet in the presence of wrong. But instead of preserving peace at the expense of righteousness, the Saviour armed himself with a scourge of cords and drove the money-changers from the Temple. Righteousness is the end, and peace a means to the end, and sometimes it is not peace, but war which is the proper means to achieve the end. Righteousness should breed valor and strength. When it does breed them, it is triumphant; and when triumphant, it necessarily brings peace. But peace does not necessarily bring righteousness.

As for neutrality, it is well to remember that it is never moral, and may be a particularly mean and hideous form of immorality. It is in itself merely unmoral; that is, neither moral nor immoral; and at times it may be wise and expedient. But it is never anything of which to be proud; and it may be something of which to be heartily ashamed. It is a wicked thing to be neutral between right and wrong. Impartiality does not mean neutrality. Impartial justice consists not in being neutral between right and wrong, but in finding out the right and upholding it, wherever found, against the wrong. Moreover, submission to an initial wrong means that all protests against subsequent and lesser wrongs are hypocritical and ineffective. Had we protested, in such fashion that our protest was effective, against what was done in Belgium by Germany, and against the sinking of the *Lusitania* by Germany, we could have (and in such case we ought to have) protested against all subsequent and minor infractions of international law and morals, including those which interfered with our commerce or with any other neutral rights. But failure to protest against the first and worst offences of the strongest wrongdoer made it contemptible, and an act of bad faith, to protest against subsequent and smaller misdeeds; and failure to act (not merely speak or write notes) when our women and children were murdered made protests against interference with American business profits both offensive and ludicrous.

The pacifists have used all kinds of arguments in favor of peaceful submission to, or refusal to prepare against, international violence and wrongdoing, and among others the very ancient arguments based upon the supposed teaching of the New Testament against war. In the first place, as I have already pointed out, this argument is quite incompatible with accepting

27

the lesson taught by the action of the Saviour in driving the money-changers from the Temple; not to mention, incidentally, that the duty of preparedness has rarely been put in stronger form than by St. Luke in the direction that "He that hath no sword, let him sell his garment and buy one."

In the next place, the plea is merely an instance of the adroit casuistry that can twist isolated teachings of the Gospels in any required direction. As a matter of fact, the Gospels do not deal with war at all. During the period they covered there was no war in Judea, and no question arising from the need of going to war. The precepts and teachings upon which the pacifists rely apply not to war, but to questions arising from or concerning individual and mob violence and the exercise of the internal police power. In so far as sincere and logical pacifists are concerned, they recognize this fact. There are schools of pacifists who decline to profit by the exercise of the police power, who decline to protect not merely themselves, but those dearest to them, from any form of outrage and violence. The individuals of this type are at least logical in their horror even of just war. If a man deliberately takes the view that he will not resent having his wife's face slapped, that he will not by force endeavor to save his daughter from outrage, and that he disapproves of the policeman who interferes by force to save a child kidnapped by a black-hander, or a girl run off by a white-slaver, then he is logical in objecting to war. Of course, to my mind, he occupies an unspeakably base and loathsome position, and is not fit to cumber the world—in which, as a matter of fact, he exists at all only because he is protected by the maintenance by others of the very principle which he himself repudiates and declines to share.

Such a position I hold to be as profoundly immoral as it is profoundly unpatriotic. But, at least, the men holding it are trying logically to apply the principles which they profess to follow. Messrs. Bryan, Jordan, Ford, and the other professional pacifists, however, are either insincere in their denunciation of war, or else must announce that the same principle which makes them denounce a just war entered into for the sake of the welfare of the nation as a whole, also makes them denounce the man who, by force, endeavors to protect his daughter against infamy, or the woman who opposes her feeble strength to the brutality of the kidnapper of her child. Either these gentlemen, as regards their own families, approve of tame submission to kidnapping and white slavery, and disapprove of suppression of kidnapping and white slavery by

the police, or else they are either thoroughly
unintelligent or else thoroughly dishonest in their
denunciation of national preparedness and of
readiness to enter into just war on behalf either
of ourselves or of others.

Let us beware of confusing names with things.
The fuglemen of President Wilson have kept
praising him because, forsooth, he has "kept us
out of war." Every now and then one of them
reverses his praise, and says that in any event
President Wilson could not have gone to war,
because war can only be declared by Congress.
But as a matter of fact, President Wilson has
gone to war, both with Hayti and with Mexico.

This is a matter of deeds, not of words. When
our armed forces attack the chief seaport city
of a foreign country, as we did in the case both
of Mexico and of Hayti, and take it by violence,
after conflicts in which scores of our own men
and either scores or hundreds of our opponents
are killed and wounded, the act is one of war.
It may be successful war like that which Mr. Wilson nerved himself to wage with tiny Hayti—
for Mr. Wilson was not afraid of Hayti. It may
be utterly ineffective war, as in the case of Mr.
Wilson's little war with Mexico. But both were
wars; and each was waged without any Congressional action whatever. Mr. Wilson sent the
fleet down to Vera Cruz, and took it in order to

get a salute for the flag. The men wearing the
United States uniform, who carried out his command, suffered a considerable loss of life and
inflicted a greater loss of life. He then brought
our forces away without achieving the object
he had in view. His little war was an ignoble
war, and he was beaten in it. But it was a war.

Some of his defenders now say that, although
defeated in the avowed purpose of the war, he
succeeded as regards the unavowed purpose,
which was to drive out Huerta in the interests
of Villa. This is, of course, a confession that
their statements on behalf of Mr. Wilson are
untrue, that he has not kept the country at peace,
but has put it into a war, not to serve any public
purpose, but to gratify his personal feelings. It
is, of course, a statement absolutely incompatible with Mr. Wilson's own claim that he did not
intervene in Mexico. Therefore, these admirers
of Mr. Wilson come to his defence by vociferat-
ing what he asserts to be contrary to the truth.

As a matter of fact, in this case they are correct. Mr. Wilson has more than once interfered
—to use his own scholarly and elegant phrase-
ology, "butted in"—by making war in Mexico.
He never did it, however, to secure justice for
Americans or other foreigners. He never did
it to secure the triumph of justice and peace
among the Mexicans themselves. He merely did

31

it in the interest of some bandit chief, whom at the moment he liked, in order to harm some other bandit chief whom at the moment he disliked. Under such circumstances his methods of action, and his defence of his action, are worthy of a Byzantine logothete—but not of an American statesman who is true to the traditions of Washington and Lincoln, and an heir to the valor shown by the soldiers of Grant and of Lee.

Mr. Wilson has been President when the urgent need of the nation was for action. He has met the need purely by elocution. A friend, writing to me last Christmas Eve, remarked that he had just found in *Cymbeline* "in anticipation of the gentleman in the White House":

"Prithee have done,
 And do not play in wench-like words with that
 Which is so serious."

Peace is not a question of names. It is a question of facts. If murders occur in a city, and if the police force is so incompetent that no record is made of them officially, that does not interfere with the fact that murders have been committed and that life is unsafe. In just the same way, if lives are taken by violence between nations, it is not of the slightest consequence whether those responsible for the government of the nation whose citizens have lost their lives

do or do not assert that the nation is at peace.
During the last three years we have been technically at peace. But during those three years
more of our citizens have been killed by Mexicans, Germans, Austrians and Haytians than
were killed during the entire Spanish War. It
is true that the American citizens killed during
the past three years have been mostly non-combatants, including women and children, although
many men wearing the national uniform have
also been killed, some of them on American soil.
But the fact that women and children are killed
instead of full-grown men in uniform surely in-
creases rather than diminishes the horror. We
have had a great many more citizens killed during this time of alleged peace, and thanks to the
activities of the emissaries of foreign governments with the torch and the bomb on our own
soil, we have had much more American property
destroyed, than was the case during the open
war with Spain; and whereas, thanks to the abject quality of Mr. Wilson's tameness, no benefit
whatever, to us or to mankind at large, has
come from this loss of life and destruction of
property during the last three years, the short
war with Spain brought incalculable benefits to
Cuba, Porto Rico, the Philippines, not to speak
of ourselves.

On February 12th it will be a year since the

time when we notified Germany that in case any of our citizens were killed, we would hold her to a strict accountability; and during these eleven months the passenger ships sunk by German or Austrian submarines in defiance of our warning have included among others the *Falaba, Lusitania, Arabic, Hesperian, Ancona, Yasaka, Ville de la Ciotat* and *Persia*. They were British, Italian, Japanese and French. Many hundreds of Americans were among the passengers and a couple of hundred of these, including many women and children, were killed. The total deaths on these ships since March last amount to between 2,000 and 2,100. The campaign against them has been a campaign of sheer murder, on a vaster scale than any indulged in by any of the old-time pirates of the Indian Ocean and the Spanish Main. Now, the total number of lives of non-combatants, including many hundreds of women and children, thus taken exceeds many times over the aggregate in all the sea-fights of the War of 1812, both on the American and on the British side. It is over double the number of lives lost by the British navy in Nelson's three great victories, the Battle of Trafalgar, the Battle of the Nile and the Battle of the Baltic, combined. It much exceeds the total number of lives lost in the Union navy—and indeed in the Union and

Confederate navies combined—during the Civil War. That is, this nation has been "peaceful" during the past year, while peaceful ships on which its citizens were sailing lost a larger number of lives than we lost at sea in the entire War of 1812 and than we inflicted at sea in the War of 1812, a much greater loss than Farragut's fleet suffered in the aggregate in all its victories, a greater loss than Nelson's fleets suffered in his three great victories. If any individual finds satisfaction in saying that nevertheless this was "peace" and not "war," it is hardly worth while arguing with him; for he dwells in a land of sham and of make-believe. Of course, incidentally, we have earned contempt and derision by our conduct in connection with the hundreds of Americans thus killed in time of peace without action on our part. The United States Senator, or Governor of a State, or other public representative, who takes the position that our citizens should not, in accordance with their lawful rights, travel on such ships, and that we need not take action about their deaths, occupies a position precisely and exactly as base and as cowardly (and I use those words with scientific precision) as if his wife's face were slapped on the public streets and the only action he took was to tell her to stay in the house.

Our course toward foreign nations has com-

bined unworthy submission to wrongs against
ourselves, with selfish refusal to keep our word
and do right by others. Under the sixth article
of the Constitution treaties are "the Supreme law
of the land." The Hague Conventions were
treaties of this kind. They included a guaranty
from Germany that she would not violate the
territory of neutral nations (including the
territory of Belgium) and a guaranty by Belgium that if an attempt was made to violate
her territory she would fight to prevent the violation. Germany broke her solemn promise to
us, and offended against the Supreme law of
our land. Belgium kept her solemn promise made
by her to us, to Germany, to France, Russia and
England. We shirked our duty by failing to take
any action, even by protest, against the wrongdoer and on behalf of the wronged, by permitting
this violation of our law, of the law which we
guaranteed, of the "supreme law of the land,"
and by announcing through our President that
we would be "neutral in thought as well as in
deed" between the oppressor and the oppressed.

We have been equally signal in our remiss-
ness to prepare for our own defence. It is our
highest duty thus to prepare, and in manful fashion to pay the cost of preparation. Seven years
ago we were relatively to the rest of the world
far better prepared than ever before in our his-

tory. Our navy was in combined size and efficiency the second in the world. The Philippines had been pacified, Mexico was orderly and peaceful, and the Hague Conventions, if actively enforced and treated as binding by peaceful and law-abiding nations, would have regulated the conduct of war, circumscribed its limits, and minimized the chance of its occurrence. Under such conditions our regular army was of sufficient size (provided the work of improving its efficiency was steadily continued, as had been the case during the preceding seven years)—for the navy was our first and principal line of defence. Although as President I had called the attention of Congress and of the people to the Swiss system of universal service as a model for us as well as other democracies, there did not at that time seem any sufficient justification for military alarm. But what has happened during the last year and a half has forced all reasonably farsighted men to understand that we are living in a new world. We have let our navy deteriorate to a degree both shameful and alarming. We have shown by our own conduct when the Hague Conventions were violated that all such treaties are utterly worthless, as offering even the smallest safeguard against aggression. Above all, the immense efficiency, the utter ruthlessness, and the gigantic scale of the present military operations show that we need military preparedness on a scale never hitherto even dreamed of by any American statesman.

Eighteen months have gone by since the great war broke out. It needed no prescience, no remarkable statesmanship or gift of forecasting the future, to see that, when such mighty forces were unloosed and when it had been shown that all treaties and other methods hitherto relied upon for national protection and for mitigating the horrors and circumscribing the area of war were literally "scraps of paper," it had become a vital necessity that we should instantly and on a great and adequate scale prepare for our own defence. Our men, women and children— not in isolated cases, but in scores and hundreds of cases—have been murdered by Germany and Mexico; and we have tamely submitted to wrongs from Germany and Mexico of a kind to which no nation can submit without impairing its own self-respect and incurring the contempt of the rest of mankind. Yet during these eighteen months not one thing has been done. The President in his Message to Congress four months after the beginning of the war actually took ground against such preparedness. At this moment we are no stronger by one soldier or one sailor, by one cannon or by one ship, because of anything that has been done during these eighteen months in view of the frightful world calamity that has befallen. At last the popular feeling has grown to be such that the President has paid to it the tribute of advocating an inefficient and belated half-measure of preparedness. But even so, not one thing has yet been done. Everything is still in the future, and there is not the slightest sign that the urgency of the case has been recognized. Nine-tenths of wisdom is being wise in time. Never in the country's history has there been a more stupendous instance of folly than this crowning folly of waiting eighteen months after the elemental crash of nations took place before even making a start in an effort—and an utterly inefficient and insufficient effort—for some kind of preparation to ward off disaster in the future.

If President Wilson had shown the disinterested patriotism, courage and foresight demanded by this stupendous crisis I would have supported him with hearty enthusiasm. But his action, or rather inaction, has been such that it has become a matter of high patriotic duty to oppose him. No man can support Mr. Wilson without being false to the ideals of national duty and international humanity. No one can support Mr. Wilson without opposing the larger Americanism, the true Americanism. No man can support Mr. Wilson and at the same time be

39

really in favor of thoroughgoing preparedness against war. No man can support Mr. Wilson without at the same time supporting a policy of criminal inefficiency as regards the United States navy, of shortsighted inadequacy as regards the army, of abandonment of the duty owed by the United States to weak and well-behaved nations, and of failure to insist on our just rights when we are ourselves maltreated by powerful and unscrupulous nations.

It has been a matter of sincere regret to me to part company with so many German friends who believe that I have been unkind to Germany. It has also been a matter of sincere grief to me to find that my position has been misunderstood and misrepresented and resented by many upright fellow-citizens to whom in the past I have been devoted, but who have let their loyalty to Germany, the land from which they themselves or their forefathers came, blind them to their loyalty to the United States and their duty to humanity at large. I wish explicitly and emphatically to state that I do not believe that this is the attitude of any but a minority of American citizens of German birth or descent. Among my stanchest friends are many men of German blood, who are American citizens and nothing else. As I have elsewhere said, I could name an entire administration from the President down through every member of the Cabinet, every man of whom would be of German blood, but an American and nothing else; an administration which I and all those like me could follow with absolute confidence in dealing with this or any similar crisis.

The German element has contributed much to our national life, and can yet do much more in music, in literature, in art, in sound constructive citizenship. In the greatest of our national crises, the Civil War, a larger percentage of our citizens of recent German origin, than of our citizens of old revolutionary stock, proved loyal to the great ideals of union and of liberty. I am myself partly of German blood. I believe that this country has more to learn from Germany than from any other nation—and this as regards fealty to non-utilitarian ideals, no less than as regards the essentials of social and industrial efficiency, of that species of socialized governmental action which is absolutely necessary for individual protection and general well-being under the conditions of modern industrialism. But in this country we must all stand together absolutely without regard to our several lines of descent, as Americans and nothing else; and, above all, we must do this as regards moral issues. The great issues with which we must now deal are moral even more than material;

and on these issues every good American should be with us, without the slightest regard to the land from which his forefathers came.

As regards the German-Americans who assail me in this contest because they are really mere transported Germans, hostile to this country and to human rights, I feel not sorrow, but stern disapproval. I am not interested in their attitude toward me; but I am greatly interested in their attitude toward this nation. I am standing for the larger Americanism, for true Americanism; and as regards my attitude in this matter, I do not ask as a favor, but challenge as a right, the support of all good American citizens, no matter where born, and no matter of what creed or national origin. I do not in the least desire any support for or approval of me personally; but I do most emphatically demand such support and approval for the doctrines of the larger Americanism which I advocate.

When some fourteen months ago I published under the title of "America and the World War," a little volume containing what I had publicly said and urged during the first months of the war, I took substantially the ground that I now take. But there is infinitely more reason for taking such ground now.

At that time Germany had sinned against civilization by her conduct toward Belgium and her

method of carrying on the war, and I held it to
be our duty in accordance with our solemn covenant to take whatever action was necessary in
order to show that our nation stood for the right
and against the wrong, even when the wrong was
triumphant. But our duty is far stronger now.
For many months Germany has waged war
against us, the war being conducted by openly
authorized agents of Germany on the high seas
and within our land against our munition plants
by men who have been shown to be the direct
or indirect agents of Germany—and whom
as matter of fact no human being in his senses
denies to be such. What I say of Germany applies in less degree to Austria, which has become the instrument of Germany's ambition and
her agent in wrongdoing.[1]

[1] In a recent excellent pamphlet Mr. Gustav Bissing, who, like
myself, is an American of non-English blood (I believe mainly
German blood), speaks of the activities of the hyphenated professional German-Americans and Austrian-Americans in part
as follows: "Are we really a nation, a people, a fused product
of the melting-pot, or are we, after all, a polyglot conglomerate
of unfused nationalities? . . . What we need is a leader, one
who walks ahead, some one with prescience, imagination and
courage. The chord which is to reverberate in American ears
throughout the land must be struck by a master-musician not
afraid of the foreign vote. 'Gott erhalte Franz der Kaiser' and
'Die Wacht am Rhein' are both inspiring national anthems.
But just now I am longing for the simple strains of simon-pure
'Yankee Doodle.'" One of the best Americans I know—a man
both of whose parents were born in Germany—writes me from
South America as follows: "We of the U. S. are considered
here a more or less spiritless, invertebrate sort of humanity,
because of the insults we have accepted from Germany, and
our inaction in Mexico. At the present time it is far safer and
more pleasant for an American to remain home. No man's life

I preach antipathy to no nation. I feel not merely respect but admiration for the German people. I regard their efficiency and their devoted patriotism and steady endurance as fraught with significant lessons to us. I believe that they have permitted themselves to be utterly misled, and have permitted their government to lead them in the present war into a course of conduct which, if persevered in, would make them the permanent enemy of all the free and liberty-loving nations of mankind and of civilization itself. But I believe that sooner or later they will recover their senses and make their government go right. I shall continue to cherish the friendliest feelings toward the Germans individually, and for Germany collectively as soon as Germany collectively comes to her senses. No nation is always right, and very few nations are always wrong. It is our duty to judge each nation by its conduct in the given crisis which must at the moment be faced. Since this country became a nation, there have been occasions when it has so acted as to deserve the condemnation of

is safe in the hands of a man like Wilson! If the people of the U. S. A. don't overwhelmingly drive the peace-at-any-price party out of office at the next election, they will lose practically all standing in foreign countries, and will have to face the discontent and humiliation of their own most high-minded citizens. We do not need more wealth in the U. S. A. to-day; our crying need is manhood! The American people must awake to a realization of duty and put a stop to the abuses which now threaten our honor and our national integrity."

mankind—and as regards slavery its action was persevered in for many years. During the same period England, France, and Russia have each of them and all of them at one time or another so behaved as to merit from us condemnation and antagonism; and, at certain periods in our history, during the Napoleonic wars, for instance, and during our own Civil War, the attitude of the ruling classes in both France and England was unfriendly to our country. In 1898 Germany was hostile to us, and all the nations of Continental Europe followed suit, whereas England, and England alone, stood by us. In the Revolution France was our only real friend. During the time of the Civil War Russia was the only European nation which showed us any sympathy whatever.

When as a nation we displayed a purpose to champion international piracy in the interest of slavery we deserved to be condemned. But in the end we did well, and proved our worth by our endeavor, and when we championed orderly freedom in Cuba, the Philippines, and Panama, we deserved to be praised. In 1878 it was right to champion Russia and Bulgaria against Turkey and England. For exactly the same reasons we ought now to champion Russia and England and Servia against Turkey and Bulgaria. A century ago the sympathies of humanity ought to have been with the Germany of Koerner and Andreas Hofer against Napoleonic France; and to-day they ought to be with the Belgian and French patriots against the Germany of the Hohenzollerns. To oppose England now because in 1776 we fought England is as foolish and wicked as it would be now to oppose Germany because in that same Revolutionary War masses of German mercenaries fought against us. I have certainly never hesitated, and at this moment am not hesitating, to condemn my own country and my own countrymen when it and they are wrong. I would just as unhesitatingly condemn England, France, or Russia if any one of them should in the future behave as Germany is now behaving. I shall stand by Germany in the future on any occasion when its conduct permits me so to do. We must not be vindictive, or prone to remember injuries; we need forgiveness, and we must be ready to grant forgiveness. When an injury is past and is atoned for, it would be wicked to hold it in mind. We must do justice as the facts at the moment demand.

Abraham Lincoln, with his far-seeing vision and his shrewd, homely common sense, set forth the doctrine which is right both as regards individuals and as regards nations when he said: "Stand with anybody that stands right. Stand with him while he is right and part with him when he goes wrong. To desert such ground because of any company is to be less than a man, less than an American." As things actually are at this moment, it is Germany which has offended against civilization and humanity—some of the offences, of a very grave kind, being at our own expense. It is the Allies who are dedicated to the cause and are fighting for the principles set forth as fundamental in the speech of Abraham Lincoln at Gettysburg. It is they who have highly resolved that their dead shall not have died in vain, and that government of the people, by the people, and for the people shall not perish from the face of the earth. And we have stood aside and, as a nation, have not ventured even to say one word, far less to take any action, for the right or against the wrong.

To those persons who fifty years ago cried for peace without regard to justice or righteousness, for the peace of cowardice, Abraham Lincoln answered in words that apply to-day. These words appropriately answer the sinister or silly creatures—including especially the silly or sinister Americans—who now likewise demand a peace acceptable only to the fool, the weakling, and the craven—a peace that would consecrate triumphant wrong and leave right bound and helpless. Said Lincoln, "The issue before us is distinct, simple, and inflexible. It is an issue which can only be tried by war and settled by victory. The war will cease on the part of this government whenever it shall have ceased on the part of those who began it. . . . We accepted war rather than let the nation perish. With malice towards none, with charity for all, with firmness in the right as God gives us to see the right, let us strive on to finish the work we are in, and to do all which may achieve a just and lasting peace among all nations."

Surely, with the barest change of a few words, all that Lincoln said applies now to the war the Allies are waging on behalf of orderly liberty and self-government for the peoples of mankind. They have accepted war rather than let the free nations of Europe perish. They must strive on to finish the work they are in, and to achieve a just and lasting peace which shall redress wrong and secure the liberties of the nations which have been assailed.

We Americans must pay to the great truths set forth by Lincoln a loyalty of the heart and not of the lips only. In this crisis I hold that we have signally failed in our duty to Belgium and Armenia, and in our duty to ourselves. In this crisis I hold that the Allies are standing for the principles to which Abraham Lincoln said this country was dedicated; and the rulers of Germany have, in practical fashion, shown this to be the case by conducting a campaign against Americans on the ocean, which has resulted in the wholesale murder of American men, women, and children, and by conducting within our own borders a campaign of the bomb and the torch against American industries. They have carried on war against our people; for wholesale and repeated killing is war—even though the killing takes the shape of assassination of noncombatants, instead of battle against armed men.

It is a curious commentary on the folly of the professional pacifists among my fellow-countrymen that they should applaud a "peace" to be obtained by conceding triumph to these wrongdoers. It is a no less curious commentary on the attitude of the rulers of Germany that at the moment when they are forcing the Belgian people to aid in the manufacture of materials of war to be used against their own countrymen, they are also protesting against the United States manufacturing such materials for the use of those who are seeking to free Belgium from the dreadful brutality of which it has been the victim.

It is always hard to make a democracy prepare in advance against dangers which only the farsighted see to be imminent. Even in France there were well-meaning men, who but a few years ago did not realize the danger that hung over their land, and who then strove against adequate preparedness. In England, which was by no means in the same danger as France, there were far more of these men—just as there are far more of them in our own country than in England. Almost all these men, both in France and in England, are now doing everything in their power to atone for the error they formerly committed, an error for which they and their fellow countrymen have paid a bitter price of blood and tears. In our land, however, the men of this stamp have not learned these lessons, and with evil folly are endeavoring to plunge the nation into an abyss of disaster by preventing it from so preparing as to remove the chance of disaster. France has learned her lesson in the hard school of invasion and necessity; England has been slower to learn, because the war was not in her home territory; and our own politicians, and to a lamentably large degree our own people, are fatuously unable to profit by what has happened, because they lack the power to visualize either the present woe of others or the future danger to themselves.

France has shown a heroism and a loftiness of soul worthy of Joan of Arc herself. She was better prepared than either of her allies, perhaps because the danger to her was more imminent and more terrible, and therefore more readily understood; and since the first month of the war she has done everything that it was in human power to do. The unity, the quiet resolution, the spirit of self-sacrifice among her people—soldiers and civilians, men and women—are of a noble type. The soul of France, at this moment, seems purified of all dross; it burns like the clear flame of fire on a sacred tripod. Frenchmen are not only a gallant but a generous race; and France realizes that England and Russia are now both bearing their share of the burden in the same spirit that France herself has shown.

Russia's sufferings have been sore, but it is not possible to overestimate Russia's tremendous tenacity of purpose and power of endurance. Russia is mighty, and her future looms so vast that it is hardly possible to overstate it. The Russian people feel this to be their war. Russia's part in the world is great, and will be greater; it is well that she should stand valiantly and stubbornly for her own rights; and as a firm and ardent friend of the Russian people may I add that Russia will stand for her rights all the more effectively when she also stands for the rights of Finn and Pole and Jew; when she learns the lesson that we Americans must also learn—to grant every man his full rights, and to exact from each man the full performance of his duty.

The English navy was mobilized with a rapidity and efficiency as great as that of the German army. It has driven every warship, except an occasional submarine, and every merchant-ship of Germany off the seas, and has kept the ocean as a highway of life not only for England, but for France, and largely also for Russia. In all history there has been no such gigantic and successful naval feat accomplished as that which the seamen and shipwrights of England have to their credit during the last eighteen months. It was not originally expected that England would have to do much on the continent; and although her wisest sons emphatically desired that she should be ready to do more, yet this desire represented only a recognition of the duty owed by England to herself. To her Allies she has more than kept the promise she has made. She has given Russia the financial assistance that none but she could give; her money effort has been unparalleled in all previous history. Eighteen months ago no Frenchman would have expected that in the event of war England would do more than put a couple of hundred thousand men in France. She has already put in a million, and is training and arming more than double that number. Her soldiers have done their duty fearlessly and well; they have won high honor on the fields of horror and glory; they have shown the same gallantry and stubborn valor that have been so evident in the armies of France and Russia. Her women are working with all the steadfast courage and self-sacrifice that the women of France have shown. Her men from every class have thronged into the army. Her fisher folk, and her seafarers generally, have come forward in such numbers that her fleet is nearly double as strong as it was at the outset of the war. Her mines and war factories have steadily enlarged their output, and it is now enormous, although many of the factories had literally to build from the ground up, and the very plant itself had to be created. Coal, food, guns, munitions, are being supplied with sustained energy. From across the sea the free Commonwealths of Canada, Australia, New Zealand, and South Africa, and the Indian Empire, have responded with splendid loyalty, and have sent their sons from the ends of the earth to do battle for liberty and civilization. Of Canada I can speak from personal knowledge. Canada has faced the time that tries men's souls, and with gallant heroism she has risen level to the time's need. Mighty days have come to her, and she has been equal to the mighty days. Greatness comes only through labor and courage, through the iron willingness to face sorrow and death, the tears of women and the blood of men, if only thereby it is possible to serve a lofty ideal. Canada has won that honorable place among the nations of the past and the present which can only come to the people whose sons are willing and able to dare and do and die at need. The spirit shown by her sister-commonwealths is the same. High of heart and undaunted of soul the men and women of the British Islands and of the whole British Empire now front the crisis that is upon them.

Having said all this, let me point out, purely for the instruction of our own people, that, excepting always as regards her navy, England has been much less effective than she should have been in the use of her strength during these first eighteen months of war. This is because she had not prepared in advance, because she had not accepted the advice of Lord Roberts. If all her sons had been trained under a system of universal service, and if it had been clearly understood that in war time neither undue profit-making by capitalists nor striking by workingmen would be tolerated—for universal service means that each man is to serve the nation, and not himself, in whatever way is necessary—there would have been no invasion of Belgium, and no long-drawn and disastrous war. Nine-tenths of wisdom consists in being wise in time! Universal training in time of peace may avert war, and if war comes will certainly avert incalculable waste and extravagance and bloodshed and possible ultimate failure. Let us of the United States learn the lesson. Let us inaugurate a system of obligatory universal military training, and instill into our sons the spirit of intense and exclusive loyalty to the United States. Let ours be true Americanism, the greater Americanism, and let us tolerate no other. Let us prepare ourselves for justice and efficiency within our own border during peace, for justice in international relations, and for efficiency in war. Only thus shall we have the peace worth having.

Let this nation fear God and take its own part. Let it scorn to do wrong to great or small. Let it exercise patience and charity toward all other peoples, and yet at whatever cost unflinchingly stand for the right when the right is menaced by the might which backs wrong. Let it furthermore remember that the only way in which successfully to oppose wrong which is backed by might is to put over against it right which is backed by might. Wanton or unjust war is an abhorrent evil. But there are even worse evils. Until, as a nation, we learn to put honor and duty above safety, and to encounter any hazard with stern joy rather than fail in our obligations to ourselves and others, it is mere folly to talk of entering into leagues for world peace or into any other movements of like character.

The only kind of peace worth having is the peace of righteousness and justice; the only nation that can serve other nations is the strong and valiant nation; and the only great international policies worth considering are those whose upholders believe in them strongly enough to fight for them. The Monroe Doctrine is as strong as the United States navy, and no stronger. A nation is utterly contemptible if it will not fight in its own defence. A nation is not wholly admirable unless in time of stress it will go to war for a great ideal wholly unconnected with its immediate material interest.

Let us prepare not merely in military matters, but in our social and industrial life. There can be no sound relationship toward other nations unless there is also sound relationship among our own citizens within our own ranks. Let us insist on the thorough Americanization of the newcomers to our shores, and let us also insist on the thorough Americanization of ourselves. Let us encourage the fullest industrial activity, and give the amplest industrial reward to those whose activities are most important for securing industrial success, and at the same time let us see that justice is done and wisdom shown in securing the welfare of every man, woman, and child within our borders. Finally, let us remember that we can do nothing to help other peoples, and nothing permanently to secure material well-being and social justice within our own borders, unless we feel with all our hearts devotion to this country, unless we are Americans and nothing else, and unless in time of peace by universal military training, by insistence upon the obligations of every man and every woman to serve the commonwealth both in peace and war, and, above all, by a high and fine preparedness of soul and spirit, we fit ourselves to hold our own against all possible aggression from without.

We are the citizens of a mighty Republic consecrated to the service of God above, through the service of man on this earth. We are the heirs of a great heritage bequeathed to us by statesmen who saw with the eyes of the seer and the prophet. We must not prove false to the memories of the nation's past. We must not prove false to the fathers from whose loins we sprang, and to their fathers, the stern men who dared greatly and risked all things that freedom should hold aloft an undimmed torch in this wide land. They held their worldly well-being as dust in the balance when weighed against their sense of high duty, their fealty to lofty ideals. Let us show ourselves worthy to be their sons. Let us care, as is right, for the things of the body; but let us show that we care even more for the things of the soul. Stout of heart, and pledged to the valor of righteousness, let us stand four-square to the winds of destiny, from whatever corner of the world they blow. Let us keep untarnished, unstained, the honor of the flag our fathers bore aloft in the teeth of the wildest storm, the flag that shall float above the solid files of a united people, a people sworn to the great cause of liberty and of justice, for themselves, and for all the sons and daughters of men.

CHAPTER II

IN December last I was asked to address the American Sociological Congress on "the effect of war and militarism on social values." In sending my answer I pointed out that infinitely the most important fact to remember in connection with the subject in question is that if an unscrupulous, warlike, and militaristic nation is not held in check by the warlike ability of a neighboring non-militaristic and well-behaved nation, then the latter will be spared the necessity of dealing with its own "moral and social values" because it won't be allowed to deal with anything. Until this fact is thoroughly recognized, and the duty of national preparedness by justice-loving nations explicitly acknowledged, there is very little use of solemnly debating such questions as the one which the sociological congress assigned me—which, in detail, was "How war and militarism affect such social values as the sense of the preciousness of human life; care for child welfare; the conservation of human resources; upper-class concern for the lot of the masses; interest in popular education; appreciation of truth-telling and truth-printing; respect for personality and regard for personal rights." It seems to me positively comic to fail to appreciate, with the example of Belgium before our eyes, that the real question which modern peace-loving nations have to face is not how the militaristic or warlike spirit within their own borders will affect these "values," but how failure on their part to be able to resist the militarism of an unscrupulous neighbor will affect them. Belgium had a very keen sense of the "preciousness of human life" and of "the need for the care of child welfare and the conservation of human resources," and there was much "concern" by the Belgian "upper classes for the lot of the masses," great "interest in popular education and appreciation of truth-telling and truth-printing and a high respect for personality and regard for personal rights." But all these "social values" existed in Belgium only up to the end of July, 1914. Not a vestige of them remained in 1915. To discuss them as regards present-day Belgium is sheer prattle, simply because on August 4, 1914, Belgium had not prepared her military strength so that she could put on her frontiers at least half a million thoroughly armed and trained men of fighting spirit. In similar fashion the question of the internal reformation of China at this moment is wholly secondary to the question whether any China will remain to be reformed internally. A Chinese gentleman wrote me the other day that he had formerly been absorbed in plans for bringing China abreast of the modern movement, but that the events of the past year had shown him that what he really ought to be absorbed in was the question whether or not China would be able by military preparation to save itself from the fate of Korea. Korean "social values" now have to be studied exclusively through a Japanese medium. At this moment the Armenians, who for some centuries have sedulously avoided militarism and war, and have practically applied advanced pacifist principles, are suffering a fate, if possible, worse than that of the Belgians; and they are so suffering precisely and exactly because they have been pacificists whereas their neighbors, the Turks, have not been pacifists but militarists. They haven't the vestige of a "social value" left, to be "affected" by militarism or by anything else.

In the thirteenth century Persia had become a highly civilized nation, with a cultivated class of literary men and philosophers, with universities, and with great mercantile interests. These literary men and merchants took toward the realities of war much the same attitude that is taken

in our own country by gentlemen of the stamp
of Messrs. David Starr Jordan and Henry Ford.
Unfortunately for these predecessors of the modern pacifists, they were within striking distance
of Genghis Khan and his Mongols; and, as of
course invariably happens in such a case, when
the onrush came, the pacifists' theories were
worth just about what a tissue-paper barrier
would amount to against a tidal wave. Russia
at that time was slowly struggling upward
toward civilization. She had become Christian.
She was developing industry, and she was struggling toward individual freedom. In other
words, she was in halting fashion developing the
"social values" of which the foregoing extract
speaks. But she had not developed military efficiency; she had not developed efficiency in war.
The Mongols overwhelmed her as fire over-
whelms stubble. For two centuries the Russians
were trodden under foot by an alien dominion
so ruthless, so brutal, that when they finally
shook it off, all popular freedom had been lost
and the soul of the nation seared by torment and
degradation; and to this day the scars remain
on the national life and character. The chief
difficulties against which Russia has had to
struggle in modern times are due ultimately to
the one all-essential fact that in the early part
of the thirteenth century she had not developed

the warlike strength to enable her to hold her own against a militaristic neighbor. The Russian Jew of to-day is oppressed by the Russian Christian because that Christian's ancestor in the thirteenth century had not learned efficiency in war.

There are well-meaning people, utterly incapable of learning any lesson taught by history, utterly incapable even of understanding aright what has gone on before their very eyes during the past year or two, who nevertheless wish to turn this country into an occidental China—the kind of China which every intelligent Chinaman of the present day is seeking to abolish. There are plenty of politicians, by no means as well meaning, who find it to their profit to pander to the desire common to most men to live softly and easily and avoid risk and effort. Timid and lazy men, men absorbed in money-getting, men absorbed in ease and luxury, and all soft and slothful people naturally hail with delight anybody who will give them high-sounding names behind which to cloak their unwillingness to run risks or to toil and endure. Emotional philanthropists to whom thinking is a distasteful form of mental exercise enthusiastically champion this attitude. The faults of all these men and women are of a highly non-militaristic and unwarlike type; and naturally they feel great satisfaction in condemning misdeeds which are incident to lives that they would themselves be wholly unable to lead without an amount of toil and effort that they are wholly unwilling to undergo. These men and women are delighted to pass resolutions in favor of anything with a lofty name, provided always that no demand is ever made upon them to pay with their bodies to even the smallest degree in order to give effect to these lofty sentiments. It is questionable whether in the long run they do not form a less desirable national type than is formed by the men who are guilty of the downright iniquities of life; for the latter at least have in them elements of strength which, if guided aright, could be used to good purpose.

Now, it is probably hopeless ever to convince the majority of these men except by actual disaster that the course they follow is not merely wicked, because of its subordination of duty to ease, but from their own standpoint utterly shortsighted—as the fate of the Armenians and the Chinese of the present day shows. But I believe that the bulk of our people are willing to follow duty, even though it be rather unpleasant and rather hard, if it can be made clearly evident to them; and, moreover, I believe that they are capable of looking ahead, and of considering the ultimate interest of themselves and their children, if only they can be waked up to vital national needs. The members of Sociological Societies and kindred organizations, and philanthropists, and clergymen, and educators, and all other leading men, should pride themselves on furnishing leadership in the right direction to these men and women who wish to do what is right.

The first thing to do is to make these citizens understand that war and militarism are terms whose values depend wholly upon the sense in which they are used. The second thing is to make them understand that there is a real analogy between the use of force in international and the use of force in intra-national or civil matters; although of course this analogy must not be pushed too far.

In the first place, we are dealing with a matter of definition. A war can be defined as violence between nations, as the use of force between nations. It is analogous to violence between individuals within a nation—using violence in a large sense as equivalent to the use of force. When this fact is clearly grasped, the average citizen will be spared the mental confusion he now suffers because he thinks of war as *in itself* wrong. War, like peace, is properly a means to an end—righteousness. Neither war nor peace is in itself righteous, and neither should be treated as of itself the end to be aimed at. Righteousness is the end. Righteousness when triumphant brings peace; but peace may not bring righteousness. Whether war is right or wrong depends purely upon the purpose for which, and the spirit in which, it is waged. Here the analogy with what takes place in civil life is perfect. The exertion of force or violence by which one man masters another may be illustrated by the case of a black-hander who kidnaps a child, knocking down the nurse or guardian; and it may also be illustrated by the case of the guardian who by violence withstands and thwarts the black-hander in his efforts to kidnap the child, or by the case of the policeman who by force arrests the black-hander or white-slaver or whoever it is and takes his victim away from him. There are, of course, persons who believe that all force is immoral, that it is always immoral to resist wrongdoing by force. I have never taken much interest in the individuals who profess this kind of twisted morality; and I do not know the extent to which they practically apply it. But if they are right in their theory, then it is wrong for a man to endeavor by force to save his wife or sister or daughter from rape or other abuse, or to save his children from abduction and torture. It is a waste of time to discuss with any man a position of such folly, wickedness, and poltroonery. But unless a man is willing to take this position, he cannot honestly condemn the use of force or violence in war—for the policeman who risks and perhaps loses or takes life in dealing with an anarchist or white-slaver or black-hander or burglar or highwayman must be justified or condemned on precisely the same principles which require us to differentiate among wars and to condemn unstintedly certain nations in certain wars and equally without stint to praise other nations in certain other wars.

If the man who objects to war also objects to the use of force in civil life as above outlined, his position is logical, although both absurd and wicked. If the college presidents, politicians, automobile manufacturers, and the like, who during the past year or two have preached pacifism in its most ignoble and degrading form are willing to think out the subject and are both sincere and fairly intelligent, they must necessarily condemn a police force or a posse comitatus just as much as they condemn armies; and they must regard the activities of the sheriff and the constable as being essentially militaristic and therefore to be abolished.

There are small communities with which I am personally acquainted where the general progress has been such as really to permit of this abolition of the policeman. In these communities—and I have in mind specifically one in New England and one in the Province of Quebec—the constable and sheriff have no duties whatever to perform, so far as crimes or deeds of violence are concerned. The "social values" in these communities are not in any way affected by either the international militarism of the soldier or by the civil militarism of the policeman, and on the whole good results; although I regret to say that in each of the two communities I have in mind there have been some social developments that were not pleasant.

We ought all of us to endeavor to shape our action with a view to extending so far as possible the area in which such conditions can be made to obtain. But at present the area cannot, as a matter of plain fact, be extended to most populous communities, or even to ordinary scantily peopled communities; and to make believe that it can be thus extended is a proof, not of goodness of heart, but of softness of head.

As a matter of practical common sense it is not worth while spending much time at this moment in discussing whether we ought to take steps to abolish the police force in New York, Chicago, San Francisco, or Montreal, because no police force is needed in a certain Vermont town or a certain Quebec village. Such a discussion would not help us in the least toward an appreciation and development of the "social values" of any one of the big cities in question.

Exactly the same principle, only a fortiori, applies as regards war. On the whole, there is a much greater equality of intellectual and moral status among the individuals in a great civilized community than there is between the various nations and peoples of the earth. The task of getting all the policemen, all the college professors, all the business men and mechanics, and also all the professional crooks, in New York to abandon the reign of force and to live together in harmony without any police force would be undoubtedly very much easier than to secure a similar working agreement among the various peoples of Europe, America, Asia, and Africa. One of the commonest failings of mankind is to try to make amends for failure to perform the duty at hand by grandiloquent talk about something that is afar off. Most of our worthy pacifist friends adopt in this matter the attitude Mrs. Jellyby took towards foreign missions when compared with her own domestic and neighborhood duties. Instead of meeting together and passing resolutions to affect the whole world, let them deal with the much easier task of regulating their own localities. When we have discovered a method by which right living may be spread so universally in Chicago and New York that the two cities can with safety abolish their police forces, then, and not till then, it will be worth while to talk about "the abolition of war." Until that time the discussion will not possess even academic value.

The really essential things for men to remember, therefore, in connection with war are, first, that neither war nor peace is immoral in itself, and, secondly, that in order to preserve the "social values" which were enumerated in the quotation with which I began this chapter it is absolutely essential to prevent the dominance in our country of the one form of militarism which is surely and completely fatal—that is, the military dominion of an alien enemy.

It is utterly impossible to appreciate social values at all or to discriminate between what is socially good and socially bad unless we appreciate the utterly different social values of different wars. The Greeks who triumphed at Marathon and Salamis did a work without which the world would have been deprived of the social value of Plato and Aristotle, of Aeschylus, Herodotus, and Thucydides. The civilization of Europe, America, and Australia exists to-day at all only because of the victories of civilized man over the enemies of civilization, because of victories stretching through the centuries from the

days of Miltiades and Themistocles to those of
Charles Martel in the eighth century and those
of John Sobieski in the seventeenth century.
During the thousand years that included the ca-
reers of the Frankish soldier and the Polish king,
the Christians of Asia and Africa proved unable to wage successful war with the Moslem
conquerors; and in consequence Christianity
practically vanished from the two continents; and
to-day nobody can find in them any "social values" whatever, in the sense in which we use the
words, so far as the sphere of Mohammedan influence and the decaying native Christian
churches are concerned. There are such "social
values" to-day in Europe, America, and Australia only because during those thousand years the
Christians of Europe possessed the warlike
power to do what the Christians of Asia and
Africa had failed to do—that is, to beat back
the Moslem invader. It is of course worth while
for sociologists to discuss the effect of this European militarism on "social values," but only if
they first clearly realize and formulate the fact
that if the European militarism had not been
able to defend itself against and to overcome
the militarism of Asia and Africa, there would
have been no "social values" of any kind in our
world to-day, and no sociologists to discuss them.

The Sociological Society meets at Washington this year only because the man after whom the city was named was willing to go to war. If he and his associates had not gone to war, there would have been no possibility of discussing "social values" in the United States, for the excellent reason that there would have been no United States. If Lincoln had not been willing to go to war, to appeal to the sword, to introduce militarism on a tremendous scale throughout the United States, the sociologists who listened to this chapter, when it was read to them, if they existed at all, would not be considering the "social values" enumerated above, but the "social values" of slavery and of such governmental and industrial problems as can now be studied in the Central American republics.

It is a curious fact that during the thirty years prior to the Civil War the men who in the Northern and especially the Northeastern States gradually grew to take most interest in the anti-slavery agitation were almost equally interested in anti-militaristic and peace movements. Even a casual glance at the poems of Longfellow and Whittier will show this. They were strong against slavery and they were strong against war. They did not take the trouble to think out the truth, which was that in actual fact slavery could be abolished only by war; and when the time came they had to choose between, on the one hand, the "social values" of freedom and of union and, on the other hand, the "social value" of peace, for peace proved incompatible with freedom and union. Being men fit to live in a free country, they of course chose freedom and union rather than peace. I say men; of course I mean women also. I am speaking of Julia Ward Howe and Harriet Beecher Stowe just exactly as I am speaking of Longfellow and Lowell and Whittier.

Now, during the thirty years preceding the Civil War these men and women often debated and occasionally in verse or prose wrote about the effect of war on what we now call "social values." I think that academically they were a unit in saying that this effect was bad; but when the real crisis came, when they were faced by the actual event, they realized that this academic discussion as to the effect of war on "social values" was of no consequence whatever. They did not want war. Nobody wants war who has any sense. But when they moved out of a world of dreams into a world of realities they realized that now, as always in the past has been the case, and as undoubtedly will be the case for a long time in the future, war may be the only alternative to losing, not merely certain "social values," but the national life which means the sum of all "social values." They realized that

73

as the world is now it is a wicked thing to use might against right, and an unspeakably silly, and therefore in the long run also a wicked thing, to chatter about right without preparing to put might back of right. They abhorred a wanton or an unjust war and condemned those responsible for it as they ought always to be condemned; and, on the other hand, they realized that righteous war for a lofty ideal may and often does offer the only path by which it is possible to move upward and onward. There are unquestionably real national dangers connected even with a successful war for righteousness; but equally without question there are real national dangers connected even with times of righteous peace. There are dangers attendant on every course, dangers to be fought against in every kind of life, whether of an individual or of a nation. But it is not merely danger, it is death, the death of the soul even more than the death of the body, which surely awaits the nation that does not both cultivate the lofty morality which will forbid it to do wrong to others, and at the same time spiritually, intellectually, and physically prepare itself, by the development of the stern and high qualities of the soul and the will no less than in things material, to defend by its own strength its own existence; and, as I at least hope some time will be the case, also to fit itself to defend other nations that are weak and wronged, when in helpless misery they are ground beneath the feet of the successful militarism which serves evil. At present, in this world, and for the immediate future, it is certain that the only way successfully to oppose the might which is the servant of wrong is by means of the might which is the servant of right.

Nothing is gained by debate on non-debatable subjects. No intelligent man desires war. But neither can any intelligent man who is willing to think fail to realize that we live in a great and free country only because our forefathers were willing to wage war rather than accept the peace that spells destruction. No nation can permanently retain any "social values" worth having unless it develops the warlike strength necessary for its own defence.

CHAPTER III

WHERE THERE IS A SWORD FOR OFFENCE THERE MUST BE A SWORD FOR DEFENCE

THE professional pacifists who have so actively worked for the dishonor of the American name and the detriment of the American nation (and who incidentally have shown themselves the basest allies and tools of triumphant wrong) would do well to bear in view the elementary fact that the only possible way by which to enable us to live at peace with other nations is to develop our strength in order that we may defend our own rights. Above all, let them realize that a democracy more than any other human government needs preparation in advance if peace is to be safeguarded against war. So far as self-defence is concerned, universal military training and, in the event of need, universal military service, represent the highest expression of the democratic ideal in government.

Jefferson had been an apostle of peace who had declared "that peace was his passion," and his refusal to lead the nation in preparedness bore bitter fruit in the war of 1812. But at least he learned aright the lesson that was taught. In 1813 he wrote to Monroe:

"We must train and classify the whole of our male citizens and make military instruction a regular part of collegiate education. We can never be safe till this is done."

And in 1814 he went still further:

"I think the truth must now be obvious that we cannot be defended but by making every citizen a soldier, and that in doing this all must be marshaled, classed by their ages, and every service ascribed to its competent class."

President Monroe in his message to Congress of December 3rd, 1822, just ninety-three years ago, used expressions which without changing a word can be applied to the far more urgent needs of to-day. He said:

"The history of the late wars in Europe furnishes a complete demonstration that no system of conduct however correct in principle, can protect neutral powers from injury from any party; that a defenceless position and distinguished love of peace are the surest invitations to war, and that there is no way to avoid it other than by being always prepared and willing for just cause to meet it. If there be a people on earth whose more especial duty it is to be at all times prepared to defend the rights with which they are blessed, and to surpass all others in sustaining the necessary burthens, and in submitting to sacrifices to make such preparations, it is undoubtedly the people of these states."

The question of more real consequence to this nation than any other at this moment is the question of preparedness. The first step must be preparedness against war. Of course there can be no efficient military preparedness against war without preparedness for social and industrial efficiency in peace. Germany, which is the great model for all other nations in matters of efficiency, has shown this, and if this democracy is to endure, it must emulate German efficiency —adding thereto the spirit of democratic justice and of international fair play. Moreover, and finally, there can be no preparedness in things material, whether of peace or war, without also preparedness in things mental and spiritual. There must be preparedness of the soul and the mind in order to make full preparedness of the body, although it is no less true that the mere fact of preparing the body also prepares the soul and the mind. There is the constant action and reaction of one kind of preparation upon another in nations as in individuals.

But there are certain elementary facts to be grasped by this people before we can have any policy at all. The first fact is a thorough understanding of that hoary falsehood which declares that it takes two to make a quarrel. It did not take two nations to make the quarrel that resulted in Germany trampling Belgium into the mire. It is no more true that it takes two to make a quarrel in international matters than it is to make the same assertion about a highwayman who holds up a passer-by or a blackhander who kidnaps a child. The people who do not make quarrels, who are not offensive, who give no cause for anger, are those who ordinarily furnish the victims of highwaymen, black-handers and white-slavers. Criminals always attack the helpless if possible. In exactly similar fashion aggressive and militarist nations attack weak nations where it is possible. Weakness always invites attack. Preparedness usually, but not always, averts it.

The next fact to remember is that it is of no use talking about reform and social justice and equality of industrial opportunity inside of a nation, unless that nation can protect itself from outside attack. It is not worth while bothering about any social or industrial problem in the United States unless the United States is willing to train itself, to fit itself, so that it can be sure that its own people will have the say-so in the settlement of these problems, and not some nation of alien invaders and oppressors. Thanks to the weakness we have shown for five years, and to the fact that for a year and a half we have shown the "neutrality" of the Levite who passed by on the other side when he saw on the ground the man who had been wounded by robbers near Jericho (and at the least the Levite did not boast of his "neutrality"), the United States has not a friend in the world.

Again, the United States should make up its mind just what its policy is to be. Foolish people say that the Monroe Doctrine is outworn, without taking the trouble to understand what the Monroe Doctrine is. As a matter of fact, to abandon the Monroe Doctrine would be to invite overwhelming disaster. In its essence the Monroe Doctrine amounts to saying that we shall not permit the American lands around us to be made footholds for foreign military powers who would in all probability create out of them points of armed aggression against us. We must therefore make up our mind that we will police and defend the Panama Canal and its approaches, preserve order and safeguard civilization in the territories adjacent to the Caribbean Sea, and see that none of these territories, great or small, are seized by any military empire of the Old World which can use them to our disadvantage. A prime duty, of course, is to secure livable conditions in Mexico. To permit such conditions as have obtained in Mexico for the past five years is to put a premium upon European interference; for where we shirk our duty to ourselves, to honest and law-abiding Mexicans, and to all European foreigners within Mexico, we cannot expect permanently to escape the consequences.

The events of the past year have shown that all talk of preventing aggression from unscrupulous militaristic nations by arbitration treaties, Hague Conventions, peace agreements and the like at present represents nothing but empty declamation. No person outside of an imbecile asylum should be expected to take such talk seriously at the present time. Leagues to Enforce Peace and the like may come in the future; I hope they ultimately will; but not until nations like our own are *not* too proud to fight, and *are* too proud not to live up to their agreements. It is at best an evidence of silliness and at worst an evidence of the meanest insincerity to treat the formation of such leagues as possible until as a nation we do two things.

In the first place, we must make ready our own strength. In the next place, by our action in actually living up to the obligations we assumed in connection with the Hague Conventions, we must make it evident that there would be some reasonable hope of our living up to the onerous obligations that would have to be undertaken by any nation entering into a League to Enforce Peace. The Hague Conventions were treaties entered into by us with, among other nations, Belgium and Germany. Under our Constitution such a treaty becomes part of "the Supreme Law of the Land," binding upon ourselves and upon the other nations that make it. For this reason we should never lightly enter into a treaty, and should both observe it, and demand its observance by others when made. The Hague Conventions were part of the Supreme Law of our Land, under the Constitution. Therefore Germany violated the *Supreme Law of our Land* when she brutally wronged Belgium; and we permitted it without a word of protest.

Nearly eighteen months have gone by since with the outbreak of this war it became evident to every man willing to face the facts, that military and naval problems and international problems of every kind were infinitely more serious than we had had reason to believe, that treaties were absolutely worthless to protect any nation unless backed by armed force, and that the need of preparedness was infinitely more urgent than any man in this country had up to that time believed. The belief that public opinion or international public opinion, unbacked by force, had the slightest effect in restraining a powerful military nation in any course of action it chose to undertake was shown to be a pathetic fallacy. But any man who still publicly adheres to and defends that opinion at the present time is engaged in propagating not a pathetic, but an absolutely mischievous and unpatriotic fallacy. It is the simple and literal truth that public opinion during the last eighteen months has not had the very smallest effect in mitigating any atrocities or preventing any wrongdoing by aggressive military powers, save to the exact degree that there was behind the public opinion actual strength which would be used if the provocation was sufficiently great. Public opinion has been absolutely useless as regards Belgium, as regards Armenia, as regards Poland. No man can assert the contrary with sincerity if he takes the trouble to examine the facts.

For eighteen months, with this world-cyclone before our eyes, we as a nation have sat supine without preparing in any shape or way. It is an actual fact that there has not been one soldier, one rifle, one gun, one boat, added to the American Army or Navy so far, because of anything that has occurred in this war, and not the slightest step has yet been taken looking toward the necessary preparedness. Such national shortsightedness, such national folly, is almost inconceivable. We have had ample warning to organize a scheme of defence. We have absolutely disregarded the warning, and the measures so far officially advocated are at best measures of half-preparedness, and as regards the large aspect of the question, are not even that.

We should consider our national military policy as a whole. We must prepare a well-thought-out strategic scheme, planned from the standpoint of our lasting national interests, and steadily pursued by preparation and the study of experts, through a course of years. The navy is our first line of defence, but it must be remembered that it can be used wisely for defence only as an offensive arm. Parrying is never successful from the standpoint of defence. The attack is the proper method of efficient defence. For some years we have been using the Navy internationally as a bluff defensive force, or rather asserting that it would be so used and could be so used. Its real value is as an offensive force in the interest of any war undertaken for our own defence. Freedom of action by the fleet is the secret of real naval power. This cannot be attained until we have at our disposal an effective military establishment which would enable us when threatened to repel any force disembarking on our coast. This is fundamental. It is only by creating a sufficient army that we can employ our fleet on its legitimate functions. The schemes of the Navy must always be cor-

related with the plans of the Army, and both of
them with the plans of the State Department,
which should never under any circumstances undertake any scheme of foreign policy without
considering what our military situation is and
may be made. For reasons I give elsewhere I
believe that we should base our military and
naval program upon the retention and defence
of Alaska, Hawaii, the Panama Canal and all
its approaches, including all the points of South
American soil north of the Equator, and of
course, including the defence of our own coasts
and the islands of the West Indies. To free the
Navy we need ample coast defences manned by
a hundred thousand men, and a mobile regular
army of one hundred and fifty thousand men.
The proposed Administration program is a
make-believe program. It is entirely inadequate to our needs. It is a proposal not to do
something effective immediately, but to do something entirely ineffective immediately, and to
trust that the lack will be made good in succeeding years. Congress has never been willing to
carry out the plans advocated by the General
Board. Until 1911, however, the differences between what was needed and what was actually
appropriated for, although real, was not appallingly great. At the very time, however, when
the extraordinary development of navies abroad

rendered it imperative that we should enlarge our own program and treat it far more seriously than ever before, Congress stopped entirely the proper upbuilding of the Navy. At present what is needed is immediately to strain every nerve of the government so that this year we will begin work on half-a-dozen formidable fighting battleships and formidable speedy armed cruisers. Whether we begin them in public or private yards is of no earthly consequence compared with the vital importance of beginning on these ships somewhere at once—not next summer, but within thirty or sixty days. Frederick Palmer has recently shown that in the three squadron actions of this war the beaten side has behaved with the same skill and prowess shown by the victors but has been beaten purely because of the superiority of its opponent in the speed of the ships and in the range and power of the guns. He has furthermore shown that in these three squadron actions the defeated ships were in each case superior to any of our cruisers in speed and range and power of guns. In other words, our cruisers would be helpless against those of a first-rate power at the present time.

Our people need to remember that half-preparation is no preparation at all. A great many well-meaning people are of the same mind as a philanthropist who wrote me the other day to the effect that he believed in some preparedness, but not much. This is like building a bridge half way across a stream, but not all the way. I regret to state that this seems to be the attitude which our Government now takes as a substitute for its attitude of a year ago, when its view was that preparedness was "hysterical," immoral and unnecessary. The only proper attitude is that there shall be no preparedness at all that is not necessary, but that in so far as there is need for preparedness the need shall be fully met. Years ago I served as a deputy sheriff in the cattle country. Of course I prepared in advance for my job. I carried what was then the best type of revolver, a .45 self-cocker. I was instructed never to use it unless it was absolutely necessary to do so, and I obeyed the instructions. But if in the interest of "peace" it had been proposed to arm me only with a .22 revolver, I would promptly have resigned my job.

There are two immediately vital needs to be met:

1. That our navy shall at the earliest possible moment be made the second in the world in point of size and efficiency. We do not need to make it the first, because Great Britain is not a military power, and our relations with Canada are on a basis of such permanent friendliness that hostile relations need not be considered. But

the British Empire would, quite properly, be "neutral" if we were engaged in war with some great European or Asiatic power.

2. That our regular army shall be increased to at least a quarter of a million men, with an ample reserve of men who could be at once put in the ranks in the event of a sudden attack upon us; and provision made for many times the present number of officers; and in administration, provision made for a combination of entire efficiency with rigid economy that will begin with the abandonment of the many useless army posts and navy yards.

Neither of these needs is in any way met by the Administration's proposals. I am sincerely glad that the Administration has now reversed the attitude taken in the President's message to Congress of December, 1914, in which he advocated keeping this nation unprepared and helpless to defend its honor and vital interest against foreign foes. But I no less sincerely regret that the Administration has not thought out the situation and is not prepared to present a real and substantial plan for defence instead of a shadow program. During the last three years our navy has fallen off appallingly in relative position among the nations. The Administration now proposes a plan, to be followed mainly by the next Administration, which, if hereafter lived up to, would nominally replace the navy where it formerly was in ten years' time and really not until twenty years have passed—a plan which in reality, therefore, is merely an adroit method of avoiding substantial action in the present. This will not do. There should be no policy of adroit delay and make-believe action. Our government should make provision this year which will insure the regaining of our naval place at the earliest possible moment. The work should begin on a large scale at once. This is of the first importance.

But it is also vital to bring the army abreast of national needs. The proposed plan to create a rival national guard of half-trained or quarter-trained volunteers—for that is what the absurdly named "continental army" would amount to—if tried will prove very expensive, very detrimental to the existing national guard, and entirely useless from the standpoint of meeting the real needs of the country. It is thoroughly undemocratic, for it appeals to the "patriotism" of the employer to let his employees be trained to do his fighting! It would put a business premium on the unpatriotic employer who would not permit his men to take part in it. It would be much wiser to spend the money in increasing the size and efficiency of the national guard, and establishing national control over it—although this also would be a

mere half-measure, in no way going to the root
of things. The Administration has declined to
ask for the adoption of any of the military systems which have been so strikingly successful in
Switzerland, Australia, Argentina, not to speak
of Germany. Instead they, congenially, ask for
the system which England fatuously tried, and
which in the crisis proved worthless. Their proposed "continental army" has nothing in common
with Washington's continental army, which was
an army of regulars, whose efficiency was conditioned by service year in and year out in win-
ter and summer. It is nothing but the English
"territorial" army, reliance upon which by England was one of the main factors in securing that
unpreparedness for war for which England is
now paying so heavy a penalty—for the splendid
courage and self-sacrifice of the English who are
now fighting so gallantly can not wholly undo
the effects of the failure adequately to prepare in
advance. The best men among the Territorials
keenly realized the truth of the position taken by
that high-minded old hero, Lord Roberts, and in
1913 memorialized the English government in favor of a system of universal military service as
the only adequate method to secure effective
home defence. But the political leaders of England insisted upon blindly following the easy path
to disaster, the path down which, in imitation

of these blind leaders, our own American politicians now contentedly amble.

The proposed increase in the size of the regular army as outlined by the Administration is utterly inadequate to serve any real purpose. It is one of those half-measures which are of service, if at all, only from the political standpoint. Either we need to prepare or we do not. If we do, then we should prepare adequately. I should not regard as wise a proposal for doing away with the New York Fire Department—the wisdom of such a proposal being about on a par with the wisdom of the attitude of Messrs. Bryan, Ford, Jordan, and the rest of the professional pacifists, as regards what they are pleased to call "militarism." Yet it would not be materially less wise than a proposal to compromise, by, on the one hand, having fire engines, but, on the other hand, not fitting them to throw a stream of water higher than the second story. The military plans of the Administration are on a level with plans for the New York Fire Department which should provide only for second-story hose; they go on the theory that it is desirable to try to put out a fire a little, but not too much. Now, it is always wise either to let a fire alone or to deal with it thoroughly.

The unwisdom of being content with a sham in this case is shown by the opposition of the professional pacifists and peace-at-any-price leaders even to the shadow-plan of the Administration. They have been busily engaged in opposing it on the ground that it is "rushing into militarism," and that a standing army is an "instrument for aggression." Of course in reality the trouble with the Administration's plan is that the standing army it would provide would not even be an instrument for defence. As for "rushing into militarism," we are not even trickling in that direction. The proposal advocated by the real believers in national defence (as distinguished from those who support the Administration's plan) is to make the regular army, relatively to the United States, as large as the New York police force is relatively to the city of New York; for a quarter of a million men bears to the nation just about the proportion that the present police force does to New York City. Surely even hysteria cannot see "militarism" and "aggression" in such a proposal.

A few of the professional pacifists now support the Government's plan for a half preparation, for pretending to meet needs without meeting them. But the extreme pacifists can always be trusted to insist on the nadir of folly. They do not wish to see this nation even pretend to act with self-respect. It is natural that they should wage a sham battle with a sham, for all their utterances are those of men who dwell in a world of windy make-believe. Their argument is that we should have no preparedness whatever, that we should not prepare for defence, nor bear arms, nor be able to use force, and that this nation must "influence others by example rather than by exciting fear," and must secure its safety "not by carrying arms, but by an upright, honorable course." Of course such a position can be honestly held by a man of intelligence only if he also demands the abolition of the police force throughout the United States and announces that he will not resent the action of an offender who slaps the face of his wife or outrages his daughter. However, to argue with these gentlemen is to waste time, for there can be no greater waste of time than to debate about non-debatable things.

It seems literally incredible that any human being can take the position now taken by the professional pacifists, with the fates of Belgium and China before their eyes at this very moment. China has sought to influence others "by example" instead of by "exciting fear," and half her territory is in the possession of aliens. Belgium thought to secure her safety "by an upright honorable course" instead of by "carrying arms," and in consequence she has been trampled into dust. Probably there is not in all Belgium a man, a woman, or a child over six years old, who would consider the arguments of these pacifists against preparedness as other than peculiarly heartless jests. In China, however, among elderly mandarins of unusually conservative type, it is possible that they would be taken seriously.

I very earnestly hope that the ordinary citizens of this country, since their official leaders refuse to lead them, will themselves wake to their own needs and lead the should-be leaders. Let us at once take action to make us the second naval power in the world. Let us take the action this year, not the year after next. Do it now. The navy is our first line of defence. It is from the national standpoint literally criminal to neglect it.

As regards the army, first and foremost let us know the advice of the experts. Then provide a regular army of a quarter of a million men. Relatively to the nation this army would be no larger than the New York police force is relatively to the city of New York. On paper our present strength is 100,000, and we have in the United States a mobile army of only 30,000 men. We need 10,000 more men adequately to man our coast defences at home, and 5,000 additional adequately to man those abroad. We need 20,000 additional men to provide an adequate mobile army for meeting a raid on our overseas possessions. At home we should have a mobile army of 150,000 men, in order to guarantee us against having New York or San Francisco at once seized by any big military nation which went to war with us. A quarter of a million in the regular army is the minimum that will insure the nation's safety from sudden attack.

In addition we must provide backing for this regular army. Provide a real reserve of enlisted men. Provide as many officers, active and reserve taken together, as will enable us to officer a million and a half of men in the event of war. Meanwhile do everything possible for the national guard, providing the necessary Federal control to make it really efficient; and provide for many training camps like that at Plattsburg. Drop the undemocratic continental volunteer army which discriminates between employer and employed, which would help the unpatriotic employer who refused to do as his patriotic rival was glad to do, and which would result merely in the establishment of an inefficient rival to the national guard. Provide an adequate reserve of war material—this is of prime importance.

We should at once begin governmental encouragement and control of our munition plants. To make war on them is to make war on the United States; and those doing so should be treated accordingly and all who encourage them should be treated accordingly. The existing plants should be encouraged in every legitimate way, and provision made to encourage their continuance after the war. But it is most unfortunate that they are situated so near the seacoast. The establishment of munition plants further inland should be provided for, without delay. Pittsburg is as far east as any plant should by rights be placed. This whole matter of providing and regulating the output of munitions is one in which Germany should especially stand as our model. Let us study carefully what she has done, and then develop and adapt to our own needs the schemes which she has found successful, supplementing them with whatever additional measures our own experience may indicate as advisable. There should be a great plant in the southern iron fields —the iron fields whose development was rendered possible by the wise action of the United States Government in permitting the United States Steel Corporation to secure the Tennessee Coal and Iron Company, action which has since been passed on and approved by the Federal courts.

Steadily remember that ample material is useless unless we prepare in advance the highly trained personnel to handle it. This applies all the way through from battle cruisers and submarines to coast guns and field artillery and aeroplanes. We need the best types of sea-going submarines. We need an immense development of the Aviation Corps. I wonder how many of our people understand that at this time the total strength of the officers and men in the French Aviation Corps surpasses in number the total strength of the officers and enlisted men in the United States Army? As regards the army— strict economy should at once be introduced, and, as a preliminary, all useless army posts should be abandoned—just as economy in the navy should imply the abandonment of useless navy yards. A board of first-class army officers, and another of first-class navy officers, should be chosen and required to report, on purely military grounds, which posts should be kept and which abandoned; and their reports should be followed implicitly. However, we ought to have training posts for a mass of officers ready to lead our citizen armies in time of need; and these army posts and navy yards could be very advantageously used for this purpose.

These are the needs that can be and ought to be immediately met. But I believe with all my heart that we must adopt a system of universal service on the Swiss or Australian models, adapted of course to our own needs. This is the method of true democracy. In a free republic rights should only be allowed as corollaries to duties. No man has a right to vote who shirks his obligations to the state whether in peace or war. The full citizen must do a citizen's full duty; and he can only do his full duty if he fits himself to fight for the common good of all citizens in the hour of deadly peril of the nation's life. Manhood suffrage should mean manhood service in war just as much as in peace. People speak in praise of volunteers. I also praise the volunteer who volunteers to fight. But I do not praise the volunteer who volunteers to have somebody else fight in his place. Universal service is the only way by which we can secure real democracy, real fairness and justice. Every able-bodied youth in the land should be proud to, and should be required to, prepare himself thoroughly to protect the nation from armed aggression.

The question of expense is of wholly secondary importance in a matter which may well be of life or death significance to the nation. Five years hence it may be altogether too late to spend any money! We will do well at this time to adopt, with a slight modification, the motto popular among our forefathers a century ago: Millions for defence but not a cent for either tribute or aggression.

Fortunately we can, if we have sufficient good sense and foresight, not only successfully safeguard ourselves against attack from without, but can, and ought to, do it in such a manner as immeasurably to increase our moral and material efficiency in our everyday lives. Proper preparation for self-defence will be of immense incidental help in solving our spiritual and industrial problems.

In a country like ours a professional army will always be costly, for as regards such an army the Government has to go into the labor market for its soldiers, and compete against industrialism. Universal service, as an obligation on every citizen, is the only way by which to secure an economical and inexpensive army.

A democracy fit to be called such must do its own fighting, and therefore must make ready in advance. The poltroon and the professional pacifist are out of place in a democracy. The man fit for self-government must be fit to fight for self-government. Universal service means preparedness not for war but primarily against war. Such essentially democratic preparedness would render it less likely that war will come and certain that if it does come we shall avoid disgrace and disaster. Such preparedness would mean much for the soul of this nation. The efficiency of the average man in civil life would be thereby greatly increased. He would be trained to realize that he is a partner in this giant democracy, and has duties to the other partners. He would first learn how to obey and then how to command. He would acquire habits of order, of cleanliness, of self-control, of self-restraint, of respect for himself and for others. The whole system would be planned with especial regard to the conditions and needs of the farmer and the workingman. The average citizen would become more efficient in his work and a better man in his relations to his neighbors. We would secure far greater social solidarity and mutual understanding and genuine efficiency among our citizens in time of peace. In time of war we would put back of the navy and of the regular army the weight of the whole nation. With the navy and the very small regular army asked for, only a quarter of a million men, we would be able to meet sudden emergencies; and behind the army and navy would stand a people so trained and so fitted that if the demand was not merely to meet a sudden emergency but a great and long-continued strain, our citizens would be able to furnish within a reasonably short time the number of men necessary to meet this strain.

Universal military service as here indicated would be the best preliminary for fitting this nation for the kind of efficient industrialism, and efficiency of spiritual and moral patriotism from the standpoint of the commonwealth as a whole, which would make us able to parallel the extraordinary German achievements without loss of our own democratic spirit. It is our great duty to

combine preparedness for peace, efficiency in securing both industrial success and industrial justice, with preparedness against war. We need
not in servile fashion follow exactly the example
set abroad, but if we are wise we will profit by
what has been achieved, notably among great
industrial nations like Germany, in these matters.
Switzerland has shown that the most absolute
democracy, without one touch of militarism, can
develop high industrial efficiency in time of peace
and can adequately prepare against war while
at the same time securing a marked advance
among the citizens in their relations with one another, as regards the qualities of mutual respect,
of order, of regard for the law and for the rights
of the weak. We are the largest republic of the
world. Let us be ashamed to fall behind France,
a great republic, and Switzerland, a small but
gallant republic, and Australia, the great democracy of the South Seas, and Argentina and Chile
in our own hemisphere, in such matters as patriotism, as national efficiency, as the subordination of the individual to the socialized welfare of
the people as a whole.

The Administration, at this most critical
period of our history, when our people so need
the light, has refused to let them have the light,
by forbidding the professional officers to discuss
the problems which they are especially fitted to

discuss. It is treachery to the republic for statesmen—and for professional officers—to propose
and to acquiesce in unsound half-measures which
necessitate large continuing expenditures, but
which do not provide for adequate national defence.

I am told that "women oppose war," and therefore that, with illogical folly, they oppose preparedness against war. I appeal, as a lover of
peace, in the name of my wife and myself—the
father and mother of sons who would have to
go to war, and of daughters who in war would
work and suffer as much as the sons—to every
good man and good woman in this country. We
dread war; but we follow Washington and Lincoln in dreading some things worse than war.
Therefore we desire to prepare against war. I
wish every man and woman in the land would
read a piece in the November *Woman's Home
Companion* which my wife recently showed me.
The writer does not give her name. She says
she is "a plain old woman of seventy-three" who
lives "in a little country town in Kansas." She
tells of her husband, John, a skilled mechanic,
who went to war in '61, who later grew blind
from injuries received in the war, and whose life
was a hard, hard struggle. She says that she
would like to see everything done to keep war
away from us; that therefore she would like to

see "forts, submarines, a fine strong fleet, and then every boy raised to be a soldier," to see "every man in some farm, or factory, or business in peace times," but trained so as to be always ready to defend the nation if the call comes; and she "would include the girls, too"—which is quite right, for universal service does not mean that every man must fight, but that every man or woman must serve the country in the position in which he or she can render best service. She ends by saying: "I did raise my boy to be a soldier. If a million other mothers, if every mother in the country would do the same, we would be safe forever."

Universal service would be in every way beneficial to the state and would be quite as beneficial from the standpoint of those who consider the interest of the state in time of peace as from the standpoint of those who are interested in the welfare of the state in time of war. The normal tests of military efficiency are the very tests which would test a man's efficiency for industry and for the ordinary tasks of civil life. If a large percentage of men are unfit for military service it shows that they are also poorly fit for industrial work. A high percentage of infant mortality does not mean the weeding out of the unfit; it means the existence of conditions which greatly impair the vitality of even those who survive. Moreover, the moral effect is at least as great as the physical.

The fundamental evil in this country is the lack of sufficiently general appreciation of the responsibility of citizenship. Unfair business methods, the misused power of capital, the unjustified activities of labor, pork-barrel legislation, and graft among powerful politicians have all been made possible by, and have been manifestations of, this fundamental evil. Nothing would do more to remedy this evil than the kind of training in citizenship, in patriotism and in efficiency, which would come as the result of universal service on the Swiss or Australian models or rather on a combination of the two adapted to our needs. There should be military training, as part of a high-school education which should include all-round training for citizenship. This training should begin in the schools in serious fashion at about the age of 16. Then between the ages of 18 and 21 there should be six months actual and continuous service in the field with the colors.

Such universal training would give our young men the discipline, the sense of orderly liberty and of loyalty to the interests of the whole people which would tell in striking manner for national cohesion and efficiency. It would tend to enable us in time of need to mobilize not only troops but workers and financial resources and industry itself and to coördinate all the factors in national life. There can be no such mobilization and coördination until we appreciate the necessity and value of national organization; and universal service would be a most powerful factor in bringing about such general appreciation.

As a result of it, every man, whether he carried a rifle or labored on public works or managed a business or worked on a railway, would have a clearer conception of his obligations to the State. It would moreover be a potent method of Americanizing the immigrant. The events of the last eighteen months have shown us the gravity of the danger to American life of the existence of foreign communities within our borders, where men are taught to preserve their former national identity instead of entering unreservedly into our own national life. The hyphenated American of any type is a bad American and an enemy to this country. The best possible antiscorbutic for this danger is universal service.

Such a service would be essentially democratic. A man has no more right to escape military service in time of need than he has to escape paying his taxes. We do not beseech a man to "volunteer" to pay his taxes, or scream that it would be "an infringement of his liberty" and "contrary to our traditions" to make him pay them.

We simply notify him how much he is to pay, and when, and where. We ought to deal just as summarily with him as regards the even more important matter of personal service to the commonwealth in time of war. He is not fit to live in the state unless when the state's life is at stake he is willing and able to serve it in any way that it can best use his abilities, and, as an incident, to fight for it if the state believes it can best use him in such fashion. Unless he takes this position he is not fit to be a citizen and should be deprived of the vote. Universal service is the practical, democratic method of dealing with this problem. Rich boy and poor boy would sleep under the same dog tent and march shoulder to shoulder in the hikes. Such service would have an immense democratizing effect. It would improve the health of the community, physically and morally. It would increase our national power of discipline and self-control. It would produce a national state of mind which would enable us all more clearly to realize the necessity of social legislation in dealing with industrial conditions of every kind, from unemployment among men and the labor of women and children to the encouragement of business activities.

What I thus advocate is nothing new. I am merely applying to present day conditions the advice given by President George Washington when he submitted a plan for universal military training in his special message to Congress of January 21st, 1790. This plan advocated military training for all the young men of the country, stating that "every man of proper age and ability of body is firmly bound by the social compact to perform personally his proportion of military duty for the defence of the state," and that "all men of the legal military age should be held responsible for different degrees of military service," and that "the United States are to provide for arming, organizing and disciplining these men." This is merely another name for compulsory universal service, and the plan actually provided that no man of military age should vote unless he possessed a certificate showing that he had performed such service. Washington did not regard professional pacifists as entitled to the suffrage.

I advocate universal service because it would be a potent means of securing a quickened social conscience; because it would help us greatly industrially; and because it would put us where, if necessary, we shall be able to defend ourselves against aggression. This is part, and a vital part, of the doctrine of the larger Americanism. The prime work for this nation at this moment is to rebuild its own character. Let us find our own souls; let us frankly face the world situation to-day as it affects ourselves and as it affects all other countries. We must have a definite home policy and we must have a definite foreign policy. Let us, when we enter into treaties, speak the truth, be wary of making promises, and honorable in fulfilling them. Let us clearsightedly and after mature deliberation adopt a definite policy without and within our borders and then prepare ourselves to carry it through. Let us quit trying to fool ourselves by indulging in cheap self-assertion or even cheaper sentimentality. We must have a period of self-searching. We must endeavor to recover our lost self-respect. Let us show in practical fashion that we fear God and therefore deal justly with all men; and let us also show that we can take our own part; for if we cannot take our own part we may be absolutely certain that no one else will try to take it for us. A policy of unpreparedness and of tame submission to insult and aggression invites the kind of repeated insolence by foreign nations which in the end will drive our people into war. I advocate preparedness, and action (not merely words) on behalf of our honor and interest, because such preparedness and the readiness for such action are the surest guarantees of self-respecting peace.

The larger Americanism demands that we insist that every immigrant who comes here shall become an American citizen and nothing else; if he shows that he still remains at heart more loyal to another land, let him be promptly returned to that land; and if, on the other hand, he shows that he is in good faith and wholeheartedly an American, let him be treated as on a full equality with the native born. This means that foreign born and native born alike should be trained to absolute loyalty to the flag, and trained so as to be able effectively to defend the flag. The larger Americanism demands that we refuse to be sundered from one another along lines of class or creed or section or national origin; that we judge each American on his merits as a man; that we work for the well-being of our bodily selves, but also for the well-being of our spiritual selves; that we consider safety, but that we put honor and duty ahead of safety. Only thus shall we stand erect before the world, high of heart, the masters of our own souls, fit to be the fathers of a race of freemen who shall make and shall keep this land all that it seemed to the prophetic vision of the mighty men who founded it and the mighty men who saved it.

CHAPTER IV

AMERICA FIRST—A PHRASE OR A FACT?

THE present Administration, with its inveterate fondness for Ephraim's diet, and its conviction that phrase-making is an efficient substitute for action, has plumed itself on the sentence, "America First." In practice it has acted on the theory of "America Last," both at home and abroad, both in Mexico and on the high seas.

One of the first and most elementary duties of any nation worth calling either civilized or self-respecting is to protect its citizens from murder and outrage. For five years in Mexico, and for a year and a half on the high seas in connection with the great European war, the United States Government has signally and basely failed in the performance of this duty. The number of cases in which American men, women and children have been murdered on the high seas, first by German, and now by Austrian, submarines, and the number of cases in which American men have been murdered and American women raped in Mexico and in which American soldiers of the

United States, wearing the United States uniform, have been killed or wounded, and civilians, men, women and children, killed or wounded on American territory by Mexican soldiers, taken in the aggregate mount far up into the hundreds. The murders of Americans that have taken place within the last thirty days have been of peculiarly cold-blooded character. They have represented a contemptuous disbelief in President Wilson's willingness to do anything except write notes. The deaths of these men and women are primarily due to President Wilson's policy of timidity and weakness.

Not one effective step has been taken to put an end to these atrocities. Moreover, for five years the outrages on the persons and property of other foreigners in Mexico have been numerous; and innocent Mexicans have been butchered by scores of thousands; and in many thousands of cases Mexican girls and women have been submitted to the last extremity of infamy and outrage by the brutal bandits masquerading as military or civil leaders of the Mexican people. Our government has let these people procure ammunition with which to murder our own soldiers and their own peaceful citizens; and the President has actually proclaimed that they ought not to be interfered with in "spilling blood."

During the last year and a half unoffending,

peaceful and law-abiding neutral nations like Belgium, unoffending, industrious and law-abiding peoples like the Armenians, have been subjected to wrongs far greater than any that have been committed since the close of the Napoleonic Wars; and many of them are such as recall the days of the Thirty Years' War in Europe, and, indeed, in the case of the Armenians, the wars of Genghis Khan and Tamerlane in Asia. Yet this government has not raised its hand to do anything to help the people who were wronged or to antagonize the oppressors.

It is not an accident, it betokens a certain sequence of cause and effect, that this course of national infamy on our part began when the last Administration surrendered to the peace-at-any-price people, and started the negotiation of its foolish and wicked all-inclusive arbitration treaties. Individuals and nations who preach the doctrine of milk and water invariably have in them a softness of fiber which means that they fear to antagonize those who preach and practise the doctrine of blood and iron. It is true of our people, as once it was true of the fellow-countrymen of Ruskin when he said: "We have been passive where we should not have been passive, for fear. The principle of non-intervention, as now practised among us, is as selfish and cruel as the worst frenzy of conquest, and differs from it only by being not only malignant, but dastardly."

Professional pacifists of the stamp of Messrs. Bryan, Jordan and Ford, who in the name of peace preach doctrines that would entail not merely utter infamy but utter disaster to their own country, never in practice venture to denounce concrete wrong by dangerous wrongdoers. Professional pacifists attack evil only when it can be done with entire safety to themselves. In the present great crisis, the professional pacifists have confined themselves to trying to prevent the United States from protecting its honor and interest and the lives of its citizens abroad; and in their loud denunciations of war they have been careful to use language which would apply equally to terribly wronged peoples defending all that was dear to them against cynical and ruthless oppression, and to the men who were responsible for this cynical and ruthless oppression. They dare not speak for righteousness in the concrete. They dare not speak against the most infamous wrong in the concrete. They work hand in glove with these exponents of hyphenated Americanism who are seeking to turn this country into an ally and tool of alien militarism.

These professional pacifists, through President Wilson, have forced this country into a path of shame and dishonor during the past eighteen months. Thanks to President Wilson, the most powerful of democratic nations has refused to recognize the binding moral force of international public law. Our country has shirked its clear duty. One outspoken and straightforward declaration by this government against the dreadful iniquities perpetrated in Belgium, Armenia and Servia would have been worth to humanity a thousand times as much as all that the professional pacifists have done in the past fifty years.

The effect of our inaction in Mexico has been unspeakably dreadful. It has on the whole been surpassed in dishonor by the action of our government in reference to the great European War —remembering in both cases that supine inaction may under many conditions prove the very worst form of action. Fine phrases become sickening when they represent nothing whatever but adroitness in phrase-making, with no intention of putting deeds behind the phrases. For three years the United States Government has been engaged in sending notes and diplomatic protests and inquiries and warnings and ultimatums and penultimatums to Germany, to Mexico, to Austria; and not one of these notes really meant or achieved anything. These notes of Mr. Wilson resemble the "notes" of Mr. Micawber. The Micawber notes and the Wilson notes were of different kinds. But in value they were plainly on a par. The Micawber notes always went to protest; and Mr. Micawber always fondly believed that one could be sufficiently met by issuing another. Mr. Wilson has suffered from the same fond delusion.

During this period the Administration has failed to protect its naturalized citizens in their rights when they have behaved themselves; and yet when they have not behaved themselves has failed to insist on their performing their duties to the country to which they have sworn allegiance. It has permitted the representatives of the German and Austrian peoples and the German-Americans and Austro-Americans whose allegiance is to Germany or Austria and not to the United States to carry on within our border a propaganda of which one of the results has been the partial or entire destruction by fire or dynamite of factory after factory. Summary action of a drastic type would have put a stop to this warfare waged against our people in time of peace; but the Administration has not ventured to act. There has been a great alien conspiracy carried on against America on American soil, and it has been encouraged by the Administration's passivity.

The Austrian Ambassador, Dr. Dumba, wrote to the Austrian Minister of Foreign Affairs: "We can disorganize and hold up, if not entirely

prevent, the manufacture of munitions in Bethlehem and the Middle West, which is of great
importance, and amply outweighs the expenditure of money involved." Three months after
this was written, the threat was made good as
regards Bethlehem, and the *Germania Herald* in
Milwaukee expressed joy over the deed, saying
on November 12th: "We rejoice from the depths
of our heart over the destruction of these murderous machines." Ten days later a so-called
"German-American" mass meeting took place in
Milwaukee, and the same paper next day remarked with exultation: "Germany last night
spoke to her children on a foreign shore loudly
and distinctly." So she did. The president of
the meeting said that their purpose was "to
spread German ideals" throughout the country
(we have seen above how they were spread, with
the bomb and the torch) and that he and his fellows "considered the hyphen an honor." The
next speaker was quite as frank, saying: "We
are all German brothers together, no matter in
what country we may live." The men who make
and applaud such utterances are the enemies of
this country. Their insolence is rendered possible because this Administration is too afraid of
the political consequences to dare to uphold the
honor of the American flag or protect the lives
of American citizens.

Before recurring to the dreadful dereliction of duty to our own citizens I wish to speak another word as to the failure on our part to perform our duty toward neutral nations. On August 23rd, 1915, the New York *World,* recognized by common consent as President Wilson's special organ, published in detail certain secret papers obtained from the German Embassy as to the negotiations between the Embassy and President Wilson and as to the steps taken by the German representatives to engineer a pro-German campaign in the United States. I would not pay any heed to these statements if they had been from an anti-Administration paper; but they come, as I say, from the special organ of the Administration. Among other things this correspondence shows that an individual designated by the initials M. P., purporting to convey a special message from the President to the German Embassy, reported:

"1. The note to England will go in any event, whether Germany answers satisfactorily or not [the question of attacks by German submarines].

"2. Should it be possible to settle satisfactorily the *Lusitania* case, the President will bind himself to carry the protest against England through to the uttermost.

"3. The continuance of the difference with Germany over the *Lusitania* case is 'embarrassing' for the President in carrying out the protest against England.

"4. The President intimated his willingness to discuss the note to Germany [the note of July 21st which remains unanswered] with M. P., and eventually so to influence it that there will be an agreement for its reception and also to be ready to influence the press 'through a wink.'

"The President also openly declared that he could hardly hope for a positive statement that the submarine warfare would be discontinued."

Furthermore, the report was that the President, through M. P., "wishes to have the trend of the German note before the note is officially sent, and declares himself ready, before the answer is drafted, to discuss it with M. P. so as to secure an agreement for its reception."

Now, the action of the President since these exposures were made shows that M. P. either spoke by direction of the President or possessed the gifts of mind-reading and prophecy; for the agreement he purported to convey to the German Ambassador from the President has since been carried out to the letter. Germany has never made any atonement for the *Lusitania* case, but when England had destroyed its submarines around the British Isles, and when Germany was in consequence helpless to go on with this kind of warfare, it then consented to abandon it, eight

months after the President had first warned
them on the subject—during which eight months
it had sunk ship after ship in defiance of the
President's warning, treating with the contemptuous indifference they deserved the successive
notes which the President continued sending as
substitutes for action. As soon as the President
had received this make-believe concession, he did
what M. P. had assured the German Ambassador
would be done. He sent a strong note to England. This note was trumpeted as showing that
the President was taking the same action against
Germany as against England. The statement
was nonsense. Interference with commerce is
in no sense whatever comparable with the hein-
ousness of murder on the high seas. The controversy with Great Britain was a controversy as to
commerce, as to property. The controversy with
Germany was a controversy of humanity concerning the protection of innocent men, women
and children from murder on the ocean. President Wilson was making good the promise which
M. P. had alleged the President had forwarded
through him, and it was being done at the expense of humanity and at the expense of our rep-
utation for good faith and courage. All that
remains to be seen is whether Mr. Wilson will
now fulfill entirely the promise of M. P. to the
German Ambassador and carry out this policy

against England, on which he has embarked, "to the uttermost."

But this is not all. For a year and a quarter the President had not only kept silent over the hideous wrong inflicted on Belgium in and after the violation of its neutrality by Germany, but had publicly stated that as regards this violation of neutrality, this conflict between right and wrong, it was our duty to be "neutral not only in word, but in thought." There was no question as to what had been done. The Chancellor of the German Empire on August 3rd, 1914, stated that in invading Belgium, Germany had committed "a breach of international law" and had declined "to respect the neutrality of Belgium," and that he admitted "the wrong which we are now committing." Yet in spite of this declaration, and of our inaction, the President, through the Secretary of State, in his note to England used the following expressions: "The task of championing the integrity of neutral rights which have received the sanction of the civilized world against the lawless conduct of belligerents, the United States unhesitatingly assumes and to the accomplishment of that task it will devote its energies." It is literally astounding that any human being could have been guilty of the forgetfulness or effrontery of such a statement. As has been well said, it is odious hypocrisy to pose as the champion of neutral rights when the alleged champion ignores homicide, but is fearless about petty larceny. In his previous correspondence with Germany, President Wilson had informed Germany that if it acted as later it actually did act, he would hold it to "a strict accountability," and he showed by his subsequent conduct that in his view these words meant precisely and exactly nothing. By his previous conduct he has shown that this new announcement about "unhesitatingly championing the integrity of neutral rights" amounts to much less than nothing.

A year and a half ago I pointed out that it was the duty of the United States to "champion the integrity of the neutral rights" of Belgium (which had received the sanction of the Hague Conventions to which the United States was a signatory) against the "lawless conduct" of belligerent Germany. At that time the defenders of Mr. Wilson denounced me on the ground that I "wished neutrality violated" and wished the United States to ignore its own interests and meddle in something which was, financially speaking, not its own affair. Mr. Wilson himself publicly announced that it was not our duty to champion these neutral rights of Belgium against "the lawless conduct of belligerent" Germany, but that we should be neutral, "not only in word, but in thought." Yet now, a year later, Mr. Wilson repudiates his former position and himself expresses exactly my thought and my demand in practically exactly my language. Only—I meant what I said! Whereas Mr. Wilson's acts have shown that he did not mean what he said, so far as a nation of which he was afraid was concerned. The difference is that having caused our nation to shirk its duty to others, having caused it to shirk its duty when its own citizens were murdered, so long as the offender was a strong and ruthless nation, one with a large voting strength of its former citizens in this country, he now valiantly asserts, against a nation whose representatives have no voting strength in this country and which he believes can with impunity be defied, rights as regards cargoes of merchandise upon which he did not dare to insist when the point at issue was the slaughter of women and children; whereas I ask that we stand up for the wronged and the weak against the strength of evil triumphant, and that while we defend our property rights, we even more strongly defend the lives of our men and children, and the lives and honor of our women.

As regards Belgium, Mr. Wilson has played the part which 1900 years ago was played by the Levite towards the wayfarer who fell among thieves near Jericho. He now improves on the conduct of the Levite; for he comes to an understanding with the plunderer of the wayfarer and in his interest endeavors to browbeat the nations which (however mixed their motives) did in actual fact endeavor to play the part of the Good Samaritan towards unhappy Belgium.

Mr. Wilson, a year later, has finally adopted my principle about preparedness, although he has sought to apply it in a half-hearted and inefficient manner; a year after I denounced peace-at-any-price, he followed suit, quoting the verses of Ezekiel which for months I had been quoting; a year after I had attacked hyphenated Americanism Mr. Wilson followed suit—at least before the Colonial Dames; and now he accepts my doctrine of America's duty to neutral nations, which a year ago he stoutly opposed. But he applies it only as regards American dollars, and only in relation to nations who can be trusted not to be rude. I believe it should be applied as regards American dollars, but even more as regards American lives, and that it should first and most stoutly be asserted as regards the chief and most formidable offender.

Come back to the case of the *Lusitania!* When that ship was sunk scores of women and children, including American women and children, paid with their lives the penalty of a brutal and murderous attack by a warship which was acting in pursuance of the settled policy of the

German Government. President Wilson sat supine and complacent, making on the following night his celebrated statement about a nation "being too proud to fight," a statement that under the circumstances could only be taken as meaning that the murder of American women and children would be accepted by American men as justifying nothing more than empty declamation. These men, women and children of the *Lusitania* were massacred because the German government believed that the Wilson administration did not intend to back up its words with deeds. The result showed that they were right in their belief. Eight months have gone by since then. American ships were sunk and torpedoed before and afterward; other American lives were lost; and the President wrote other notes upon the subject; but he never pressed the *Lusitania* case; and the only explanation must be found in his fear lest the Germans might refuse to disavow their action. Even the disavowal in the case of the *Arabic* came only when the last possibility of profit to Germany by killings that extended to neutrals had vanished. President Wilson had done nothing beyond uttering prettily phrased platitudes about abstract morality without any relation to action.

On July 21st last in a formal note he asked of Germany a disavowal and promise of indemnity for the *Lusitania*. This was the note which M. P. purported to explain in the quotation above given. If the explanation he gave to the German Ambassador did not represent President Wilson's intentions, then there is absolutely no explanation of the fact that for six months after that note was sent there was no answer from Germany and no second demand made for an answer. The subject was renewed only when Germany found that her submarine warfare had failed, and that it was worth her while to pretend to abandon it if thereby she could get the United States to play her game against England, France and Belgium. Germany believed, seemingly with reason, that in return for a pretended concession to President Wilson, the latter would play Germany's game against England. And this movement was only halted (whether temporarily or not we can not now say) by the revelations in January of the complicity of the German Embassy in the plots against our munition plants.

Apparently President Wilson has believed that the American people would permanently forget their dead and would slur over the dishonor and disgrace to the United States by that basest of all the base pleas of cowardly souls, which finds expression in the statement: "Oh, well, anyhow the President kept us out of war!" The people who make this plea assert with quavering voices that they "are behind the President." So they are; well behind him. The farther away from the position of duty and honor and hazard he has backed, the farther behind him these gentry have stood—or run. "Stand by the President"—yes, while the President is right; and stand against him when he is wrong. In '56 and '60 the only way to stand by Lincoln was to stand against Pierce and Buchanan—as Lincoln did. If after the firing on Sumter, Lincoln had immediately in a speech declared that the friends of the Union might be "too proud to fight," and had spent the next four months in exchanging "firm" diplomatic notes with Jefferson Davis, he would have received the enthusiastic support of the ardent adherents of peace—and we would now have had no country.

The German press, which is sometimes appallingly frank, has with refreshing simplicity given us the exact German view when, in commenting on Mr. Wilson's note to England, the *Koelnische Volkszeitung* recently remarked: "If America had from the first energetically taken the position against Great Britain now adopted, there would have been no submarine war, no sinking of the *Lusitania* or the *Arabic*."

Evidently this German paper is in cordial agreement with M. P., and it will be impossible to desire better proof of the deliberate purpose with which the murderous assault on the *Lusitania* was contrived, and of the German belief that this murderous assault has achieved its purpose in terrorizing President Wilson into his present action about England, action which Dr. Dernburg, speaking not only for Germany, but for the hyphenated American voters of our own country, eulogizes as showing that Mr. Wilson is entitled to reward. So he is—except from Americans! But Dr. Delbrueck, also speaking for Germany, warns Mr. Wilson that his note against England must be followed by action if he hopes to retain German good will. The insolence with which the German government browbeats the timid folk at Washington is matched by the extreme cynicism of its brutality. It coerces wretched Belgians to make munitions with which to kill their own countrymen and protests against Americans making munitions to rescue Belgium from the murderers. And there are Americans so base as to advocate yielding to such threats and protests; while Mr. Henry Ford takes some of his fellow pacifists on a peace-junket to Europe, in the effort to bring about a peace more degrading to humanity than the worst war—a peace which would consecrate successful wrong, and trample righteousness in the dust.

As the direct result of our failure to act in the case of the *Lusitania,* came another hideous misdeed, the sinking of the *Ancona*. Over two hundred persons, most of them women and children, were murdered as a result of this submarine attack on a helpless passenger ship. Nine of those murdered were Americans. Of course, it is a matter of absolutely no consequence whether the deed was done by an Austrian or a German submarine. Remember the *Lusitania!* The deaths of these poor women and children on the *Ancona,* and on the various other ships that were sunk under similar circumstances, were due to the cowardice of our action, of the action of the American people through its Administration, in the case of the *Lusitania*. If our government had acted as it ought to have acted —as all of us who believe in American honor demanded that it should act, at the time—there would be no *Ancona* case now, no further murders of women and children on the high seas. And yet the Administration sat eagerly, nervously waiting for some pretext, some trivial excuse which would enable it to avoid action; and it acted at all only when the Austrian Government answered with such rude insolence as to force some action; and even then, the President did not dare act about the *Lusitania* case. The Austrian vote in this country is small and divided, and Austria cannot menace us in military manner. Neither statement applies to Germany and the professional German-Americans; and accordingly President Wilson turns from the first and most formidable offender, the offender of whom he is afraid, and seeks to distract attention by action against Austria, of whom he is much less afraid. About the *Lusitania* the President wrote note after note, each filled with lofty expressions and each sterile in its utter futility, because it did not mean action, and Germany knew it did not mean action. Then came the *Ancona* as the direct result of this policy of shuffling timidity and delay, just as the *Lusitania* itself was the direct result of the policy of "watchful waiting," that is, of shuffling timidity and delay, in Mexico. And after the sinking of the *Ancona* came the sinking of the *Persia,* and after the sinking of the *Persia* the proofs of the activity of Germany's official representative, Von Papen, in the campaign of murder and arson against our munition factories. I blame the Administration, but I blame even more the American people, who stand supine and encourage their representatives to permit unchecked the murder of women and children and other non-combatants rather than to take a policy which might, forsooth, jeopardize the life of some strong fighting man.

The Administration has recently devised a campaign button with a new campaign catch phrase—"safety first." It certainly expresses their attitude in putting honor and duty in the second place, or, rather, in no place at all. Safety first! This is the motto on which in a shipwreck those men act who crowd into the life-boats ahead of the women and children—although they do not afterward devise a button to commemorate this feat. There could be no more ignoble motto for a high-spirited and duty-loving nation. The countrymen of Washington and Lincoln, of Jackson and Grant, of Lee and Farragut, ought to hang their heads in shame at seeing their representatives in Washington thinking not about the slaughtered women and children, not about the wrongs done to the helpless and the dangers to our own people, but only about the best way to escape from the situation without being required to show either courage or patriotism. It is an evil day for a people when it permits its chosen representatives to practise the gospel of cowardice and of utter and selfish abandonment of duty. Let our countrymen remember that this policy of dishonor and discredit does not even secure the safety which it seeks. The policy of the Administration has not invited respect. It has invited murder. It has not secured peace—which, by the way, probably could have been secured by a policy of self-respecting strength and firmness. Peace is now in jeopardy, because weakness and timidity invite the constant repetition of actions which will in time goad any nation into war.

Nor is this all. Germany and Austria have not only been carrying on war against us on the high seas. They have carried on war against us here in our own land. They have, through their representatives, encouraged strikes and outrages in our factories. It has been published in the press that in their consulates and in the foreign papers controlled or influenced by these consulates the Administration's ruling about "dual citizenship" has been printed as a warning to immigrant workingmen that they were still citizens of their old countries and had to obey the directions of their former governmental representatives. Dr. Joseph Goricar, formerly Austro-Hungarian consul at San Francisco, has resigned because he declined to take part in the organized movement to destroy munition plants in this country. This movement is simply war; a war of assassination instead of open battle, but war nevertheless; and it is the direct result of the Administration's supine position.

Surely one of our first needs is self-defence against the conspirators of the torch and the bomb. The men who are engaged in this work are a great deal worse than ordinary alien enemies. The newspapers that apologize for their deeds or condone them should promptly be excluded from the mails. The men behind them, the high governmental authorities of Germany and Austria, are engaged in a much more vicious warfare in this country than if they were actually resorting to open force of arms. But President Wilson has been seeking to placate, not only these contemptuously hostile foreign nations, but also the men nominally citizens of this country, but really loyal to the foreign countries now hostile to us. He has by his actions encouraged these men to try to turn this country into a kind of polyglot boarding-house where any set of alien boarders may preach disloyalty and encourage treason and murder with impunity.

It is sickening to have to recapitulate the dreadful deeds that have been done during the last year and a quarter, while the United States sat tamely by. Miss Cavell was killed for deeds such as were committed by literally thousands of women, North and South, during the Civil War in this country; and if either Abraham Lincoln or Jefferson Davis had ever dreamed of putting any of these women to death, a deafening roar of execration would have gone up from the men of both sides. But there was no hesitation in killing Miss Cavell, and there was no disapprobation expressed by our Administration. Belgium was blotted out from the list of nations by an act which was a more flagrant instance of international wickedness than anything that has occurred since the close of the Napoleonic struggles; but this Administration did not venture to speak about it; and all the professional pacifists, the men of the stamp of Messrs. Bryan, Jordan and Ford, while with sobbing voices they called for peace, peace, did not venture even to allude to the outrage that had been perpetrated. Remember, there is not the slightest room for honest question either as to the dreadful, the unspeakably hideous, outrages committed on the Belgians, or as to the fact that these outrages were methodically committed by the express command of the German government, in order to terrorize both the Belgians and among neutrals those men who are as cold and timid and selfish as our governmental leaders have shown themselves to be. Let any man who doubts read the statement of an American eye-witness of these fearful atrocities, Mr. Arthur H. Gleason, in the New York *Tribune* of Nov. 25, 1915. Serbia is at this moment passing under the harrow of torture and mortal anguish. Now, the Armenians have been butchered under circumstances of murder and torture and rape that would have appealed to an old-time Apache Indian. The Administration can do nothing even if it wishes; for its timid silence about Belgium, its cringing fear of acting in the interests of our own citizens when killed by Mexicans in Mexico or by Germans and Austrians on the high seas, would render any wordy protest on its part a subject-matter for derision—and every one knows that it would not venture beyond a wordy protest.

But in the case of the Armenians some of the professional pacifists and praisers of neutrality have ventured to form committees and speak about—not act about—the "Armenian atrocities." These individuals did not venture to say anything about the Belgian atrocities; but they are willing to speak, although of course not to act, on behalf of Armenia. The explanation is simple. They were afraid of Germany; they were afraid of the German vote. But there is no Turkish vote, and they are not afraid of Turkey.

Under circumstances such as these it is the last note of unpatriotic folly for the pacifists of this country to chatter about peace, when they neither venture to stand up for righteousness nor to fight for real preparedness, so as to enable the United States to insure justice for itself and to demand justice for others. Mr. Taft accepts the presidency of the "League to Enforce Peace," and must of course know that unless the United States had an army of two or three million men it could do nothing at all toward "enforcing peace" in a crisis like the present world war; and yet, according to the press, he states that even a standing army of a couple of hundred thousand men means "militarism" and "aggression" and is to be opposed. This country will never be able to find its own soul or to play a part of high nobility in the world until it realizes the full extent of the damage done to it, materially and morally, by the ignoble peace propaganda for which these men and the others like them, whether capitalists, labor leaders, college professors, politicians or publicists, are responsible.

The United States has not a friend in the world. Its conduct, under the leadership of its official representatives, for the last five years and, above all, for the last three years, has deprived it of the respect and has secured for it the contempt of every one of the great civilized nations of mankind. Peace treaties and windy Fourth-of-July eloquence and the base materialism which seeks profit as an incident to the abandonment of duty will not help it now. For five years our rulers at Washington have believed that all this people cared for was easy money, absence of risk and effort, and sounding platitudes which were not reduced to action. We have so acted as to convince other nations that in very truth we *are* too proud to fight; and the man who is too proud to fight is in practice always treated as just proud enough to be kicked. We have held our peace when our women and children were slain. We have turned away our eyes from the sight of our brother's woe.

All of Mr. Henry Ford's companions, in the peace propaganda, led by gentlemen of the Bryan and Jordan type, could with profit study the thoughts expressed by Mr. E. S. Martin when he said:

"Nobody is much good who has not in him some idea, some ideal, that he cares more for than he does for life, even though it is life alleviated by the Ford motor.

"You help to make life pleasant, but war, Henry, helps to make it noble; and if it is not noble it does not matter a damn, Henry, whether it is pleasant or not. That is the old lesson of Calvary repeated at Mons and Ypres and Liége and Namur.

"Whether there are more people in the world or less, whether they are fat or lean, whether there are Fords or oxen, makes no vital difference; but whether men shall be willing to die for what they believe in makes all the difference between a pigsty and Paradise. Not by bread alone, Henry, shall men live."

If the people have not vision, they shall surely perish. No man has a right to live who has not in his soul the power to die nobly for a great cause. Let abhorrence be for those who wage wanton or wicked wars, who with ruthless violence oppress the upright and the unoffending. Pay all honor to the preachers of peace who put righteousness above peace. But shame on the creatures who would teach our people that it is anything but base to be unready and unable to defend right, even at need by the sternest of all tests, the test of righteous war, war waged by a high-couraged people with souls attuned to the demands of a lofty ideal.

Have these professional pacifists lost every quality of manhood? Are they ignorant of the very meaning of nobility of soul? Their words are an affront to the memory of Washington, their deeds a repudiation of the life-work of Lincoln. Are they steeped in such sordid materialism that they do not feel one thrill as they read Edward Everett Hale's "The Man Without a Country"? It is strange indeed that even their cold and timid hearts should be unstirred by Lowell's homely lines:

Better that all our ships an' all their crews
Should sink to rot in ocean's dreamless ooze,
Each torn flag wavin' challenge as it went,
An' each dumb gun a brave man's monu-
    ment,
Than seek sech peace ez only cowards crave;
Give me the peace of dead men or of brave.

CHAPTER V

DURING the past year the activities of our professional pacifists have been exercised almost exclusively on behalf of hideous international iniquity. They have struck hands with those evil enemies of America, the hyphenated Americans, and with the greediest representatives of those Americans whose only god is money. They have sought to make this country take her stand against right that was downtrodden, and in favor of wrong that seemed likely to be successful. Every man or woman who has clamored for peace without daring to say that peace would be a crime unless Belgium was restored to her own people and the repetition of such wrongdoing as that from which she has suffered provided against, has served the Devil and not the Lord. Every man or woman who in the name of peace now advocates the refusal on the part of the United States to furnish arms and munitions of war to those nations who have had the manliness to fight for the redressing of Bel-

138

gium's wrongs, is serving the Devil and not the Lord.

As for the hyphenated Americans, among the very many lessons taught by the last year has been the lesson that the effort to combine fealty to the flag of an immigrant's natal land with fealty to the flag of his adopted land, in practice means not merely disregard of, but hostility to, the flag of the United States. When two flags are hoisted on the same pole, one is always hoisted undermost. The hyphenated American always hoists the American flag undermost. The American citizen of German birth or descent who is a good American and nothing but a good American, and whose whole loyalty is undividedly given to this country and its flag, stands on an exact level with every other American, and is entitled to precisely the same consideration and treatment as if his ancestors had come over on the *Mayflower* or had settled on the banks of the James three centuries ago. I am partly of German blood, and I am exactly as proud of this blood as of the blood of other strains that flows in my veins. But—I am an American, and nothing else!

The German-Americans who call themselves such and who have agitated as such during the past year, have shown that they are not Americans at all, but Germans in America. Their action has been hostile to the honor and the interest of this country. The man who sings "Deutschland über Alles" means exactly what he sings. He means that he puts Deutschland above the American flag, above the honor of the United States, and above the well-being of Americans as a whole.

The Americans of German origin have been a peculiarly valuable element in our population. I believe that they are, in overwhelming proportion, thoroughgoing Americans. As I have said, I am partly of German blood. A large number of my closest friends, a large number of the men whom I most respect and honor in American life, are Americans of German parentage or descent or of German birth. One such American, a descendant of one of Blucher's colonels, sat in my Cabinet; and he sat beside another American, a descendant of one of Napoleon's brothers. But each was an American and nothing else! The scientific book of which I was proudest, I wrote in partnership with a close friend, a naturalist who was with me in Africa; he is of German parentage; but he is an American and nothing else. The man who was closest to me politically during the ten years of my service as Governor and President was of German parentage; but he was absolutely straight American. Some of the best men in my regiment, including

my orderly and one captain, were of German
birth or descent; but they were Americans, pure
and simple. Among the clergymen, philanthropists, publicists, good citizens of all kinds, with
whom I work in heartiest sympathy, an unusually
large proportion are of German descent and
some of German birth. I get on with these men
and women exactly as well as I do with the men
and women of Colonial American descent. But
I get on with them because they are Americans
and nothing else.

I stand for the American citizen of German
birth or descent, precisely as I stand for any
other American. But I do not stand at all for
the German-American, or any other kind of
hyphenated American. When I was President I
was brought into close contact with many officers
of the army and navy. Col. George Washington
Goethals has done the best work done by any
American of recent years. He is of Dutch parentage. But he is no more a Dutch-American
than I am. He is just plain American. Among
my military and naval aides were Lee, Grant,
Sheridan and Osterhaus, all descended from
generals who fought in the Union or Confederate Armies. Two of them were of old Revolutionary stock, Scotch or English. The grandfather of the third was born in Ireland, and the
grandfather of the fourth in Germany. But they

were all Americans and nothing else. General Wood, of Revolutionary stock, started Cuba on the road to self-government; General Barry, of Irish parentage, commanded the army that rescued Cuba from revolution; and one was exactly as good an American as the other. Among the admirals upon whom I leaned were Dewey, Evans, Taylor, and Cameron Winslow, of Revolutionary stock; and O'Neil and Schroeder, one of Irish and the other of German descent; and the last two were exactly as good Americans as the other four. It would have been a crime as well as a calamity to endeavor to divide all these and all the other fine and gallant officers of our army and navy on lines of birth or national origin or creed. It is no less a crime and a calamity to attempt to divide our citizens as a whole along such lines.

There was never a better American than Jacob Riis, who was born in Denmark and whom I always thought about the best American I ever knew. The Americans in whom I believe include Jews and Catholics and Protestants. They include men of old native American descent and other men of recent German, English, French, Irish, Italian, Scandinavian, Magyar and Slavonic descent; but all are Americans entitled to be treated as such, and claiming to be nothing else. I as emphatically condemn opposition to a good

American who happens to be of German birth or descent, because of that fact, as I condemn action by such a man designed to serve not the United States, but some foreign power. I speak against the German-American who seeks to use his American citizenship in the interest of a foreign power and who thereby shows himself an unworthy American. I should speak exactly as quickly against the American of English or French or Scandinavian or Irish descent who was guilty of similar conduct. The following letter which I recently wrote explains itself:

"—— I am very sorry but I cannot sign that appeal. I do not approve of it. You are asking Americans to proclaim themselves Anglo-Americans, and to sympathize with England on the ground that England is the mother-land, and in order to make what you call 'hands across the sea' a matter of living policy. I do not believe that this is the right attitude for Americans to take. England is not my mother-land any more than Germany is my father-land. My mother-land and father-land and my own land are all three of them the United States. I am among those Americans whose ancestors include men and women from many different European countries. The proportion of Americans of this type will steadily increase. I do not believe in hyphenated Americans. I do not believe in German-Americans or Irish-Americans; and I believe just as little in English-Americans. I do not approve of American citizens of German descent forming organizations to force the United States into practical alliance with Germany because their ancestors came from Germany. Just as little do I believe in American citizens of English descent forming leagues to force the United States into an alliance with England because their ancestors came from England. We Americans are a separate people. We are separated from, although akin to, many European peoples. The old Revolutionary stock was predominantly English, but by no means exclusively so; for many of the descendants of the Revolutionary New Yorkers, Pennsylvanians and Georgians have, like myself, strains of Dutch, French, Scotch, Irish, Welsh and German blood in their veins. During the century and a quarter that has elapsed since we became a nation, there has been far more immigration from Germany and Ireland and probably from Scandinavia than there has been from England. We have a right to ask all of these immigrants and the sons of these immigrants that they become Americans and nothing else; but we have no right to ask that they become transplanted or second-rate Englishmen. Most emphatically I myself am not

an Englishman-once-removed! I am straight
United States!

"In international matters we should treat each
nation on its conduct and without the slightest
reference to the fact that a larger or smaller
proportion of its blood flows in the veins of our
own citizens. I have publicly and emphatically
taken ground for Belgium and I wish that the
United States would take ground for Belgium,
because I hold that this is our duty, and that
Germany's conduct toward Belgium demands
that we antagonize her in this matter, and that
we emphatically and in practical shape try to see
that Belgium's wrongs are redressed. Because
of the British attitude toward Belgium I have
publicly and emphatically approved of her attitude, that is of Great Britain's conduct in living
up to her obligations by defending Belgium, even
at the cost of war. But I am not doing this on
any ground that there is any 'hands across the
sea' alliance, explicit or implicit, with England.
I have never used in peace or in war any such
expression as 'hands across the sea,' and I emphatically disapprove of what it signifies save in
so far as it means cordial friendship between us
and every other nation that acts in accordance
with the standards that we deem just and right.
On this ground all Americans, no matter what
their race origins, ought to stand together. It is

not just that they should be asked to stand with any foreign power on the ground of community of origin between some of them and the citizens of that foreign power. [Signed Theodore Roosevelt.]"

We of America form a new nationality. We are by blood, and we ought to be by feeling, akin to but distinct from every nationality of Europe. If our various constituent strains endeavor to keep themselves separate from the rest of their fellow-countrymen by the use of hyphens, they are doing all in their power to prevent themselves and ourselves from ever becoming a real nationality at all.

An American who is loyal to this great American nation has two duties, and only two, in international matters. In the first place, he is bound to serve the honor and the interest of the United States. In the second place, he is bound to treat all other nations in accordance with their conduct at any given time, and in accordance with the ultimate needs of mankind at large; and not in accordance with the interests of the European nation from which some or all of his ancestors have come. If he does not act along these lines, he is derelict in his duty to his fellow-citizens and he is guilty of betraying the interests of his country.

As for the persons who base their actions upon

greed in such a crisis as this, little needs to be said. The beef baron or the representative of the cotton interests who wishes to ignore the butchery of our women and children, and the sinking of our ships by German submarines, and to take sides against the Allies so that he may make money by the sale of cotton and beef, is faithless to every consideration of honor and decency. It is entirely fitting that the sheer materialist should on such an issue stand shoulder to shoulder with the professional pacifist, the peace-at-at-any-price man, and with his sinister brother, the hyphenated American. These men by their actions seek to condone the murder of American men, women and children and the trampling of Belgium into bloody mire. They are false to the cause of humanity. They come perilously near being treasonable to this country. It is hard to decide which is the most abject quality; the greed of the mere materialists or the short-sighted cowardice of the professional pacifists. As for the hyphenated American, he endeavors to serve his foreign Fatherland without exposing his own wretched carcass to the danger which would come to him if he served in the trenches beside his fellow-countrymen who have stayed at home —and who at least pretend to no divided allegiance.

I am not willing to admit that this nation has

no duty to other nations. Yet the action of this Government during the past year can only be defended on the assumption that we have no such duty to others.

Of course, it is a defensible, although not a lofty, position to deny that there is such a duty. But it is wholly indefensible to proclaim that there is such a duty and then in practice to abandon it. It is a base thing to propose to pass all-inclusive arbitration treaties, and to pass the thirty-odd all-inclusive commission peace treaties that actually have been passed during the last two years, and yet not to dare to say one word when the Hague Conventions which we have already signed are violated by the strong at the expense of the weak. I agree with the abstract theory of the men responsible for all these various treaties; for this theory is to the effect that America owes a duty to the world, to humanity at large. I disagree with their practice, because I believe that we should in fact perform this duty, instead of merely talking about it in the abstract and then shamefully abandoning it the moment it becomes concrete.

As a nation, during the past eighteen months we have refused to prepare to defend our own rights by our own strength. We have also refused to say one word against international wrongdoing of the most dreadful character. We have refused to carry out the promises we made in the Hague Conventions. We have been guilty of all these mean sins of omission, we are officially told, in the hope that the Administration may secure the empty honor of being a go-between when the belligerents decide to make peace. The actions of the Administration have tended to create such conditions that the "peace" shall be in the interest of the wrongdoer, and at the expense of his helpless victim. It is not right that this nation should be asked thus to shirk its duty to itself and to others in order to secure such a worthless function for any person whatsoever. Our plain duty was to stand against wrong, to help in stamping out the wrong, to help in protecting the innocent who had been wronged. This duty we have ignobly shirked. Nor is there any immediate probability that the empty honor which the Administration seeks will be granted to it. If it were, then doubtless there would be shallow Americans who would trumpet the fact as somehow creditable to America. But there is not another nation by which the United States under such conditions would be treated as having played any part excepting that of a dupe; or else the part of a cold and selfish intriguer, willing to sacrifice the welfare of humanity to the gratification of personal vanity.

Let our people keep their eyes fixed on the case

of Belgium. Belgium had faithfully observed
her international obligations. She had fulfilled
her duties in a spirit of loyal impartiality. She
had neglected no opportunity to maintain her
neutrality and to cause it to be respected by others. The attack upon her independence by Germany was a flagrant violation of the law of nations and a crime against humanity. It has been
carried out with inhuman severity. There has
been no more abhorrent spectacle in history than
the revenge visited upon Belgium for her daunt-
less defence of national rights and international
obligations. In all the grim record of the last
year this is the overshadowing accomplishment
of evil. The American who defends the action
taken against Belgium, or who fails to condemn
it, is unworthy to live in a free country, or to as-
sociate with men of lofty soul and generous tem-
per. Deep though the hurts are which have been
inflicted upon civilization by the sacrifice of millions of lives among the bravest and best of the
men of Europe, yet deeper and more lasting is
the wound given by the blow struck at international law and international righteousness in the
destruction of Belgium. This crime of Germany
was a crime against international good faith, a
crime against the soul of international law and
fair dealing. It is to this act of unforgivable
treachery that every succeeding infamy is to be

traced; from terrorism and indiscriminate slaughter on land to terrorism and indiscriminate massacre of non-combatants at sea. And this crime of Germany has been condoned by the recreant silence of neutral nations, and above all by the recreant silence of the United States and its failure to live bravely up to its solemn promises.

I am not speaking now of the hideous atrocities committed in Belgium and Northern France, as shown in such reports as that of the committee of which Lord Bryce was Chairman. I am not now speaking of the killing of non-combatants, including scores of women and children, in England and Italy, by air-craft and sea-craft. I deal only with facts as to which there is no dispute. In its broad outlines, what has occurred in the invasion of Belgium is not susceptible of dispute. The action being taken at this moment in Belgium is spoken of as follows by the *Norddeutsche Allgemeine Zeitung* in replying to German critics who were actually asserting that Belgium was being too mercifully treated. The German defence of Germany's "merciful" action in Belgium is as follows (condensed; the italics are my own):

"The German government is acting in Belgium with the object of preventing the safety and health of our army from being imperiled by famine and disease behind it. For this reason the

German government has gladly consented to food being supplied to the starving population by neutral countries *in order to insure that our own troops shall not suffer privation.* No more coal will be allowed to be taken from Belgian mines than will suffice for *the bare needs of the shivering people* and enable the industrious laboriously to exist. It is the right of the conqueror and our duty toward our own army to enable the conquered territory to produce the sums which without prejudice to a later war indemnity are withdrawn from the country in the shape of contributions. We demand at present from Belgium a payment of one hundred and twenty millions of dollars to be made in instalments within one year. *This sum represents the limit of the present capacity of the country,* which has been grievously affected by the war. The loss suffered by Belgium thus far through actual destruction is estimated at a value of more than a billion and a quarter of dollars. To this figure we have to add the contribution, *and the whole amount must be earned by Belgium."*

And the ignoble pacifists of the United States are at this moment agitating to prevent any export of arms and munitions to be used in redeeming the country which is suffering such hideous oppression! There was a period when Americans were proud of standing for Kossuth and for

Garibaldi, when they subscribed for those who had suffered from wrong in Ireland or Poland, when they sympathized with patriots wrongfully oppressed in any land. The Americans of a bygone generation who possessed such sympathies should turn in their graves at the thought that alleged believers in peace now advocate action in the interest of these oppressors who have trampled on the bodies and seared the souls of the men, women and children of peaceful and unoffending Belgium.

If no duty had been expressly imposed upon the United States in this matter, we ought nevertheless to have acted in accordance with the generous instincts of humanity. But as a matter of fact such a duty was expressly imposed upon us by the Hague Conventions. The Convention, signed at The Hague October 18th, 1907,[1] begins by saying that "His Majesty the German Emperor, King of Prussia," and the other signatory

[1] See pp. 133-140 of "The Hague Conventions and Declarations" [1915], edited by James Brown Scott. Dr. Scott is our foremost international lawyer. He is the head of the division of International Law of the Carnegie Endowment for International Peace. He has practically proved that he is a believer in the peace of righteousness; for he was an enlisted man in the American army in the Spanish War, having left his position as Dean of the Los Angeles Law School, now the Law School of the University of Southern California, in order to serve his country.

powers, including France, Belgium, Russia and the United States, have resolved to conclude a Convention laying down clearly the rights and duties of neutral powers in case of war on land. Article 1 runs: "The territory of neutral powers is inviolable." Article 5 states that a neutral power "must not allow belligerents to move troops across its territory." Article 10 states that "the fact of a neutral power resisting even by force attempts to violate its neutrality cannot be regarded as a hostile act." Article 7 states that "a neutral power is not called upon to prevent the export or transport on behalf of one or other of the belligerents of arms, munitions of war or in general of anything which could be of use to an army or a fleet." This Convention was ratified by Belgium on August 8th, 1910; by France on October 7th, 1910; by Germany, the United States and Russia on November 27th, 1909. It has been alleged by individuals anxious to excuse us for failure to act in accordance with our duty under this Convention that article 20 recites: "The provisions of the present Convention do not apply except between contracting powers and then only if all the belligerents are parties to the Convention." In the first place this objection would be merely technical, even if in some other area of the war a belligerent who was not a party to the Convention was concerned;

for of course the Convention must be construed with common sense. But even if it is construed in the most technical manner, it applies to the action taken by Germany in Belgium. This action was taken on August 3d and 4th, 1914. Germany was then at war only with France and Russia, both of which were signatories to this convention. Belgium was a signatory. The United States was a signatory. Germany was not at war at that time with Servia or Montenegro or England; nor was Austria at war with Belgium. When Germany violated the Hague Convention to which we were one of the signatory powers all of the belligerents in the case were signers of the Hague Convention. The case is technically no less than morally complete.

A treaty is a promise. The signing powers make promises each to the others and each to each of the others in such a case as this. Germany had promised France, Belgium, the United States and Russia that it would treat the territory of a neutral power (in this case Belgium) as inviolable. Germany violated this promise. Belgium had promised Germany, the United States, France and Russia that it would not permit such violation of its neutrality as Germany committed. Belgium kept its promise. Germany had promised that if a neutral power (Belgium) resisted by force such an attempt as it, Germany, made to violate its neutrality, Germany would not regard such an act as hostile. Germany broke this promise. When Germany thus broke her promises, we broke our promise by failing at once to call her to account. The treaty was a joint and several guarantee, and it was the duty of every signer to take action when it was violated; above all it was the duty of the most powerful neutral, the United States.

Germany promised that she would not call upon any neutral power to prevent the export or transport of arms or munitions of war on behalf of any belligerent. Germany broke this promise when she made precisely such a demand upon us. This was a flagrant act of bad faith on the part of Germany. It is especially flagrant in view of the fact, testified to me by one of the representatives at the Hague Conferences, and well known to all connected with the Hague Conferences, that this article was insisted upon by Germany. Mr. Charles Noble Gregory, the Chairman of the Standing Committee on international law of the American Bar Association, in a capital piece setting forth the right of our citizens to sell munitions of war to any belligerent power, mentions the same fact. He states that one of our Hague representatives told him that the chief interest of the German delegates seemed to be in securing this article, because the Krupp works at Essen were the chief purveyors of munitions of war to foreign powers.

A representative of a great American arms manufactory informed me recently that they had been about to abandon their work prior to the beginning of this war, because the Germans systematically endeavored to undersell them in every country. It has been the settled policy of Germany to drive all other countries out of the business of manufacturing arms and supplies because, of course, if this were once substantially accomplished, the rest of the world would be completely helpless before Germany; and Germany has made it evident that she knows no such thing as international morality and looks upon all other nations, including the United States, merely as possible prey. The Americans who are now striving to prevent the sale of munitions of war to the countries endeavoring to secure the redress of Belgium's wrongs, that is, the Allied Powers, are playing the game of a ruthlessly militaristic and anti-American Germany against their own country as well as against the interests of humanity at large. They are profoundly unpatriotic from the standpoint of the interests of the United States. They are committing the gravest possible offence against the cause of international right and of the interest of humanity.

It was Germany which for decades supplied

Turkey with the means of keeping the Christians of her European and Asiatic provinces in a state of dreadful subjection. It was Germany which established the artillery in the Belgian forts— and, as one of the men engaged in the work informed a friend of mine, the German War Office was then furnished with blue-prints of what had been done and of the neighboring geography, so as to enable the German armies to take the forts with the least possible delay and damage. Essen has been the center of military supplies to belligerents and has exported on an enormous scale to belligerents in all the modern wars, making vast profits from this traffic even in the late Balkan wars. Germany has consistently followed this course, even when one of the belligerents alone had access to her markets and the other, with which she was nominally in sympathy, had no such access. This was shown in the Boer War. Among the supplies furnished by Germany to Great Britain for use against the Boers were 108 fifteen pounder quick-firing guns and 54,000 rounds of ammunition for them; 65,000 hundredweight of swords, cutlasses, bayonets and arms of other sorts; 8,000,000 rounds of small-arms' ammunition and 1,000,500 of metal cartridge cases other than small-arms' ammunition; and some 27,000 hundredweight of cordite, gunpowder, dynamite and the like. In short,

Germany has thriven enormously on the sale of arms to belligerents when she was a neutral; she insisted that such sale be sanctioned by the Hague Conventions; she, so far as possible, desires to prevent other nations from manufacturing arms; and if she is successful in this effort she will have taken another stride to world dominion. The professional pacifists, hyphenated Americans, and beef and cotton-Americans; in short, all the representatives of American mollycoddleism, American greed, and downright treachery to America, in seeking to prevent shipments of munitions to the Allies, are playing the game of a brutal militarism against Belgium and against their own country.

Of course, if sales of munitions are improper in time of war, they are precisely as improper in time of peace, for in time of peace they are made only with a view to possible war. To prohibit them is to put a premium upon aggressive nations manufacturing their own ammunition, for it is the non-aggressive nations that do not conduct great manufactories for munitions of war. On November 13, 1870, Goldwin Smith, who was in ardent sympathy with the Germans in their contest with France of that year, wrote to his friend, Max Müller, upholding the propriety of the action of the United States in selling munitions of war to France, the right to do which had been insisted upon by President Grant. He stated that the Americans were acting in accordance with the right view of international law in refusing to prohibit such sales of arms. His letter runs in part: "If this were done, a great disadvantage would be given against the interests of civilization to the Powers which during peace employed their revenues in arming themselves for war instead of endowing professors. A moral and civilized people which had been benefiting humanity would be assailed by some French Empire which had been collecting chassepots, and when it wants to provide itself with the means of defence international law would shut up the gunshops."

In our existing treaties with Germany the right to such shipment of arms is explicitly affirmed, as it has also been in the Hague Convention from which I have above quoted. The American government has always maintained the right of its citizens to ship arms to belligerents. President Washington, through his Secretary of State, Thomas Jefferson, and his Secretary of the Treasury, Alexander Hamilton, took this position when France protested against the sale of arms to England in 1793, the answer being that "the exporting from the United States of warlike instruments and military stores is not to be interfered with." President Lincoln, through his Secretary of State, William H. Seward, took this view in 1862, when Mexico complained of the export of military supplies from the United States for the benefit of the French *Protec-* Lincoln and Secretary Seward sympathized with Mexico but explicitly informed Mexico that Mexico could not "prescribe to us what merchandise we shall not sell to French subjects because it may be employed in military operations against Mexico." President Grant and Secretaries of State Henry Clay, Bayard, Blaine, Olney and John Hay are among the high officials who have publicly taken the same position.

At this time to alter such a rule during the pendency of a state of war to the benefit of one of the warlike powers would be to place the United States on the side of that power—of the wrongdoing power—and to make it in effect itself a belligerent. The position was correctly stated on January 25, 1915, by President Wilson through Secretary of State Bryan in a published letter which recites that "the duty of a neutral to restrict trade in munitions of war has never been imposed by international law or by municipal statute. It has never been the policy of this government to prevent the shipment of arms or ammunition into belligerent territory;" and in response to the German protest it was stated that our right to export munitions of war to belligerents was settled and assured and it was declared that our government holds "that any change in its own laws of neutrality during the progress of a war which would affect unequally the relations of the United States with the nations at war would be an unjustifiable departure from the principles of strict neutrality by which it has sought to direct its actions."

A great expert on international law has said "that a system under which a peaceful commercial state may not, when attacked, use her cash and her credits in international markets to equip herself for defence is intolerable and in every way pernicious. Rules which interfere with such a right would tend to give the victory in war to the belligerent best prepared at the outset and therefore to make it necessary for peaceful nations to be in a constant state of over-preparedness." Under the German proposal a well behaved state which was not armed to the teeth could not, if wantonly attacked, be allowed to equip herself for defence. The American professional pacifists, in accepting the German position in this matter, are, as usual, playing into the hands of the Powers that believe in unprincipled aggression. The United States, if suddenly assailed by some great military power, would suffer incalculably from the application of the doctrine thus advanced by our silly professional pacifists.

The warlike and aggressive nation chooses the moment of attack and is fully equipped in advance. If the nation assailed cannot replenish her supplies from outside, she must always maintain them in time of peace at the highest point or else expose herself to ruin. The professional pacifists, the cotton-Americans, the beef barons and the German-Americans—in other words, the hyphenated Americans, the greedy materialists and all the mollycoddles of both sexes—advocate the prohibition of the shipment of munitions to the Allies who are engaged in fighting Belgium's battles. They thereby take a stand which, not merely in the concrete case of the moment but in all future cases, would immensely benefit powerful and aggressive nations which cynically disregard the rules of international morality at the expense of the peaceful and industrial nations which have no thought of aggression and which act toward their neighbors with honorable good faith.

From the standpoint of international law, as I have shown above, we have the absolute right to make such shipments. Washington and Lincoln, in fact all our Presidents and secretaries have peremptorily refused to allow this right to be questioned. The right has been insisted upon by Germany in her own interest, more strongly than by any other nation, up to the beginning of the present war. It has been exercised by Germany herself on a larger scale than by any other nation up to the time that she herself went to war.

From the standpoint of morality the justification is even more clear. Selling arms to a belligerent may be morally either very right or very wrong. This depends absolutely upon the justice of the cause in which the arms are to be used. This is as true in international as in private matters. It is moral and commendable to sell arms to a policeman in order that he may put down black-handers, white-slavers, burglars, highwaymen and other criminals who commit acts of violence. It is immoral to sell arms to those who are committing or intend to commit such acts of violence. In the same way it is thoroughly immoral in any way to help Germany win a triumph which would result in making the subjugation of Belgium perpetual. It is highly moral, it is from every standpoint commendable, to sell arms which shall be used in endeavoring to secure the freedom of Belgium and to create a condition of things which will make it impossible that such a crime against humanity as its subjugation by Germany shall ever be repeated, whether by Germany or by any other power.

CHAPTER VI

PEACE INSURANCE BY PREPAREDNESS AGAINST WAR

IN the 33d chapter of the great prophet Ezekiel, the first six verses run as follows:

1. Again the word of the Lord came unto me, saying:

2. Son of man, speak to the children of thy people and say unto them, When I bring the sword upon a land, if the people of the land take a man of their coasts and set him for the watchman;

3. If when he seeth the sword come upon the land, he blow the trumpet and warn the people;

4. Then whosoever heareth the sound of the trumpet and taketh not warning, if the sword come and take him away, his blood shall be upon his own head;

5. He heard the sound of the trumpet and took not warning, his blood shall be upon him. But he that taketh warning shall deliver his soul.

6. But if the watchman see the sword come and blow not the trumpet and the people be not warned; if the sword come and take any person

from among them, he is taken away in his iniquity; but his blood will I require at the watchman's hand.

I very heartily commend these verses to the prayerful consideration of all those in high political office, whether Presidents, Secretaries of State, or leaders of the Senate and the House at Washington; and to all male and female college presidents, clergymen, editors and publicists of pacifist tendency; and above all to the sometimes-well-meaning souls who have fallen victims to the habit of prolonged and excessive indulgence in attending universal peace meetings and giving, and listening to, lectures on immediate universal peace and disarmament.

Five years have gone by since Mexico, which had made no preparedness whatever against foreign war, was thrown into a violent civil war, attended with circumstances which made it our duty to take action, a duty which during the five years we, in our turn, have sedulously avoided fulfilling in efficient fashion. Eighteen months have passed since the great world war that centers in Europe burst out with, as its first result, the hideous destruction of the Belgian people—a destruction primarily due to the fact that Belgium had not prepared against war as Switzerland had prepared. The United States, in connection with The Hague treaties, had undertaken certain obligations to Belgium and to both neutral and belligerent powers. With criminal timidity we have failed to fulfill these obligations. We have also failed to stand up for the rights of our own people in any efficient fashion, even when our men, women and children were murdered on the high seas. We have earned, and have richly deserved, the contemptuous dislike of all the nations of mankind by the course we have followed for a year as regards the great world war, and for five years as regards Mexico. Worst of all, we have utterly failed, even with the lesson of the last year writ in blood and fire before our eyes, to take steps to protect ourselves from such horrors.

It is we ourselves, it is the American people, who are responsible for the public sentiment which permits unworthy action on the part of our governmental representatives. The peace propaganda of the past ten years in this country has steadily grown more noisy. It received an enormous impetus when five years ago, by the negotiation of peace-at-any-price or all-inclusive arbitration treaties, and in the last year by the ratification of the thirty odd peace-at-any-price arbitration-commission treaties, it was made part of our national governmental policy. It is the literal truth to say that this peace-at-any-price propaganda has probably, on the whole, worked more mischief to the United States than all the crookedness in business and politics combined during the same period. It has represented more positive deterioration in the American character. Millions of plain Americans, who do not have the opportunity to know the facts or to think them out for themselves, have been misled in this matter. They are not to blame; but the leaders and organizers of that movement, its upholders and apologists on the stump and in the pulpit and in the press, are very greatly to blame. Really good and highminded clergymen, capable of foresight and brave enough to risk being misrepresented, have stood steadfastly against the odious creed which puts peace ahead of righteousness. But every cheap man in the pulpit, like every cheap demagogue on the stump, has joined in the "peace-at-any-price" cry.

Some of the men and women who uphold the cause of the professional pacifists are actuated by good motives. The same statement can be made of some of the Tories in the Revolutionary War, of some of the Copperheads in the Civil War. But the fact remains in this case, as in the case of the Copperheads and the Tories, that the sum of the activities of the men and women thus engaged was purely mischievous and represented evil to America and evil to the cause of international justice and right. Wilkes Booth was an honest man; when he assassinated Lincoln he was doubtless sincere in the belief that he was doing right; and great courage was needed to perform the evil feat. Yet surely Wilkes Booth did a worse deed than the most corrupt politician or businessman of his time. In exactly the same way the man who preaches peace at any price, non-resistance to all wrong, disarmament and the submission of everything to arbitration, no matter how sincere and honest he may be, is rendering a worse service to his fellow-countrymen than any exponent of crooked business or crooked politics.

The deification of peace without regard to whether it is either wise or righteous does not represent virtue. It represents a peculiarly base and ignoble form of evil. For this reason it is a positive detriment to international morality for any man to take part in any of these universal peace-at-any-price or all-inclusive arbitration movements. Nor is this all. A movement right in itself may be all wrong if made at the wrong time. Even the proposal for a world peace of righteousness, based on force being put back of righteousness, is inopportune at this time.

There are far more pressing and immediate duties. First and foremost, the United States must seriously prepare itself against war, and show itself able to maintain its rights and make its weight felt in the world. Next, it must abandon both the policy of poltroonery—the policy we have practised as regards the *Lusitania* and Mexico—and the policy of recklessly making promises which neither can nor ought to be kept —the policy we practiced in the proposed all-inclusive arbitration treaties five years ago, and, above all, in the unspeakably silly and wicked thirty all-inclusive arbitration-commission treaties actually negotiated under the present Administration. Our people should note well the fact that these treaties were in principle promptly repudiated by the very President who had negotiated them as soon as Mr. Bryan asked that the principle be concretely applied in the case of the *Lusitania*.

When we are prepared to make our words good and have shown that we make no promises which we are not both ready and willing to back up by our deeds, then, and not until then, we shall be able with dignity and effect to move for the establishment of a world agreement to secure the peace of justice. Such agreement must explicitly state that certain national rights are never to be arbitrated because the nations are to be protected in their exercise; that other matters shall be arbitrated; and that the power of all the nations shall be used to prevent wrong being done by one nation at the expense of another. To put peace above righteousness is wicked. To chatter about it, without making ready to put strength behind it, is silly.

But all this is for the future, and it is beating the air to talk about it at present. "Ephraim feedeth on wind"—and wind is not a substantial diet. A nation which is "too proud to fight" is a nation which is sure to be kicked; for every fighting man or nation knows that that particular kind of "pride" is merely another name for abject cowardice. A nation helplessly unable to assert its own rights; a nation which for five years has refused to do its duty in Mexico and yet is unwilling to see other nations do their duty there; a nation which without the utterance of one word of protest has seen The Hague Conventions which it signed torn to pieces and thrown to the winds; a nation which has not ventured beyond empty words when its ships were sunk and its citizens, men, women and children, slain on the high seas, is in no position to help the cause of either peace or justice, and would excite merely derision if it proposed at this moment the creation of a "World League for Peace."

The six great powers of Europe have sent their best and their bravest by the million to die for the right as God gave them to see the right. All their finest young men are at the front.

Some of them are fighting for good, some for evil; but all are fighting for what they think to be good, and all are showing splendid and heroic qualities. We excite only derision when under these circumstances we permit foolish people, men and women, in the name of America to prattle in meaningless words about the kind of peace that brave men and high-minded women will always scorn. The all-insistent duty of the moment for America is two-fold. First, we must prepare ourselves against disaster by facing the fact that we are nearly impotent in military matters, and by remedying this impotence. Second, we must seriously and in good faith, and once for all, abandon the wicked and foolish habit of treating words as all-sufficient by themselves, and as wholly irrelevant to deeds; and as an incident thereto we must from now on refuse to make treaties which cannot be, and which will not be, lived up to in time of strain.

As regards the last matter, promise and performance, we Americans must rid ourselves of the habit of salving our vanity, when down at bottom we know we are not behaving well, by using fine words to excuse ourselves from effort which ought to be made, and to justify ourselves in avoiding risk which ought to be accepted. There are persons who are against preparedness for war and who believe in the avoidance of national duty, who nevertheless are honest in their belief and who may not be cowardly or weak, but only foolish and misguided; and there are hundreds of thousands of good and reasonably brave men and women who simply have not thought of the matter at all and who are misguided by their leaders. But of most of these leaders it is not possible to take so charitable a view. The fundamental characteristic of the peace-at-any-price men is sheer, downright physical or moral timidity. Very many of the leaders among the men who protest against preparedness and who are hostile to manly action on our part—hostile to the insistence in good faith upon the observance of The Hague Conventions and upon respect for the lives and property of our citizens in Mexico and on the high seas—are easily cowed by any exhibition of ruthless and brutal force, and never venture to condemn wrongdoers who make themselves feared. This fact might just as well be faced. To it is due the further fact that the professional pacifist usually turns up as the ally of the most cynical type of international wrong-doer.

This has been made evident by the attitude of the great bulk of the men and women who have shrieked loudest for peace during the last eighteen months. It has been made evident by the men who have joined in the Peace Conferences, Peace

Dinners and Peace Voyages during that time, and by the women of the same type who on this side of the water, or after traveling to the other side of the water, have advocated a peace without honor or justice. These men and women have demanded peace in terms that would not merely disregard righteousness, but that would crown unrighteousness with success. They have not ventured to make one protest against any concrete act of wrongdoing; they have not ventured to raise their voices in denunciation of the iniquity wrought by Germany against Belgium, the most wanton, the most hideous wrong, and the wrong on the largest scale, that had been perpetrated for over a century. Some of the women in question were abroad, actively engaged in exciting contempt and derision for themselves and their country by crying for peace without justice and without redress of wrongs, at the very time that the *Lusitania* was sunk.

American women and children were at the time being slain on the high seas; Belgian women and children, French women and children, in Belgium and Northern France, were at the same time suffering the last extremities of infamy and outrage; English women and children, in unfortified towns, were being killed by the bombs of German war vessels and aircraft; and our own women in Mexico had been subjected to nameless infamies.

But these amiable peace prattlers had not one word of effective sympathy for any of the women and children who had suffered these dreadful fates. All they did was to utter silly platitudes, which were of comfort to the wrongdoers, and which, in so far as they had any effect, confounded right and wrong and put a premium upon wrongdoing by making it evident that, if successful, it would escape condemnation; because the condemnation was so uttered as, if anything, to bear more heavily on those who resisted wrong than upon those who inflicted wrong. There is no meaner moral attitude than that of a timid and selfish neutrality between right and wrong.

Such action does not represent righteousness. At best it represents folly. Often it represents cowardice. Always it represents unrighteousness. Not the smallest particle of good has come from the peace propaganda of the last ten years as carried on in America. Literally, this agitation of the professional pacifists during these ten years has not represented the smallest advance toward securing the peace of righteousness. It has, on the other hand, represented a very considerable and real deterioration in the American character. I do not think it is a permanent deterioration. I think that we shall recover and become heartily ashamed of our lapse from vi-

rile manliness. But there has been a distinct
degeneracy in the moral fiber of our people owing
to this peace propaganda, a distinct increase in
moral flabbiness, a distinct increase in hysteria
and sentimental untruthfulness.

Not once in a thousand times is it possible to
achieve anything worth achieving except by labor, by effort, by serious purpose and by the
willingness to run risk. The persons who seek
to persuade our people that by doing nothing, by
passing resolutions that cost nothing, and by
writing eloquent messages and articles that mean
nothing, and by complacently applauding elocution that means less than nothing, some service is
thereby rendered to humanity, are not only rendering no such service, but are weakening the
spring of national character. This applies to the
publicists and politicians who write messages and
articles and make speeches of this kind; it applies
to the newspaper editors and magazine writers
who applaud such utterances; and most of all it
applies to those of our people who insist upon the
passage of treaties that cannot and will not be enforced, while they also inveigh against preparedness, and shudder at action on behalf of our
own rights.

Let no man propose a treaty unless he has reduced it to concrete terms; has proposed it in
these concrete terms to his fellows, and has de-

termined whether, when thus made concrete, it ought to be and will be observed. Take a few illustrative cases. The ultra-pacifist movement, the peace-at-any-price movement, has seemingly been as strong on the Pacific slope as on the Atlantic seaboard and in the interior. Congressmen and editors have made speeches and written articles in which they have advocated disarmament, and have demanded treaties by which the United States would agree to arbitrate everything. Worthy people, silly people, have encouraged schoolboys solemnly to debate such questions.

Now let these congressmen and editors face facts and be frank and truthful. When they applaud the passage of the thirty all-inclusive arbitration-commission treaties that the Administration has passed during the last year or so, do they mean that they wish, if the Japanese take Magdalena Bay or the Germans St. Thomas, to discuss the matter through a commission for a year without taking any action? Do they mean that when American women are raped in Mexico or American men murdered in our own territory by Mexicans firing across the line, or when the American flag is insulted and dishonored, we shall appoint a commission to discuss the matter for a year before taking action? Do they mean that if a French or English submarine sinks a ship crowded with non-combatants, as the Germans sank the *Lusitania,* and if American women and children are again drowned wholesale on the high seas, we shall appoint a commission to talk about it for a year and bind ourselves to take no action prior to that time?

If they do mean these things, if our people mean these things, then let them honestly say so. From my standpoint such action would be inconceivably base and cowardly. Nevertheless, it is at least possible to accept the mental integrity of the man taking it, if he announces from the beginning that such is his intention. But it is absolutely and grossly improper to take it unless the concrete case to which the general principle is to apply is thus set nakedly forth at the outset and we agree to abide by action in such concrete case.

Again, there are Pacific slope editors and public men who have excitedly applauded that phase of the peace-at-any-price propaganda in accordance with which it is proposed that we shall bind ourselves to arbitrate all questions, including those of national honor and vital national interest. The movement has been strong even in California. Now, do these public men and editors who champion this form of peace movement in California, Oregon and Washington mean that we shall in good faith submit to outsiders for arbitration the question whether or not there shall be an unlimited immigration of Asiatics to our shores? Do they mean that a court containing judges from Japan, Siam, China, Venezuela, Colombia and Ecuador, as well as from the European powers, shall say whether or not we have a right to decide what immigrants shall come to our shores and here establish citizenship?

The Californian who does not believe in arbitrating the question whether there shall be such unlimited immigration of Asiatics to California is guilty of the grossest bad faith when he champions or fails to condemn such proposals, when he votes for or approves of the thirty-odd peace-commission treaties recently passed by the present Administration and the all-inclusive arbitration treaties proposed by the preceding Administration. I hold that to arbitrate the question whether we should or should not allow the unlimited immigration of Asiatics to our shores would be a dreadful wrong. It is an almost equally serious wrong to conclude a treaty specifically binding us to accept such arbitration, and then to repudiate the treaty.

All this applies to the movement for inaugurating at this time a "World League for Peace," of which the decrees are to be backed by force. Before we make such a League for the future, let us in the present live up to our engagements under The Hague Conventions and without delay protest on behalf of Belgium. If we are not willing to undergo the modest risk implied in thus keeping the promise we have already made, then for heaven's sake let us avoid the hypocrisy of proposing a new world league, under which we would guarantee to send armies over to coerce great military powers which decline to abide by the decisions of an arbitral court. Above all, let us avoid the infinite folly, the discreditable folly, of agitating for such an agreement until we have a naval and military force sufficient to entitle us to speak with the voice of authority when fronted with great military nations in international matters. Let us not live in a realm of childish make-believe. Let us not make new and large promises in a spirit of grandiloquent and elocutionary disregard of facts unless and until we are willing by deeds to make good the promises we have already made but have refrained from executing; until we are willing to demand of our government that it live up to The Hague Conventions, and, above all, that it defend our own rights.

Now, the fact that these male and female professional peace enthusiasts who have screamed so busily for peace during the past year have been afraid to make any concrete protest against wrong is doubtless due primarily to sheer fear on their part. They were afraid of the trouble and effort implied in acting about Mexico. Above all, they are afraid of Germany. Those of them who are politicians are afraid of the German-American vote; for these professional pacifists have no sense of national honor and are great encouragers of hyphenated Americanism. But in addition they are terrorized, they are cowed, by the ruthless spirit of German militarism. The Berlin *Lokal Anzeiger* spoke as follows after the sinking of the *Lusitania:*

> We do not wish to gain the love of the Americans, but we desire to be respected by them. The loss of the *Lusitania* will earn that respect for us more than a hundred battles won on land.

Of course, when the *Lokal Anzeiger* spoke of inspiring "respect" in America, what it really meant was that it would inspire fear. The murder of women and children does not inspire respect; but, unfortunately, it may inspire fear. As a matter of fact, I think it did inspire fear among our pacifists. There are plenty of Americans like myself who immensely admire the efficiency of the Germans in industry and in war, the efficiency with which in this war they have subordinated the whole social and industrial activity of the state to the successful prosecution of the war, and who greatly admire the German people, and regard the German strain as one of the best and strongest strains in our composite American blood; but who feel that the German Government, the German governing class has in this war shown such ruthless and domineering disregard for the rights of others as to demand emphatic and resolute action (not merely words unbacked by action) on our part. Unfortunately, this ruthless and brutal efficiency has, as regards many men of the pacifist type, achieved precisely the purpose it was intended to achieve.

As part of her program, Germany has counted on the effect of terrorism upon all men of soft nature. The sinking of the *Lusitania* was intended primarily as terrorism; just as the use of poison gas in the trenches (a use defensible only if one also defends the poisoning of wells and the torture of prisoners) was intended as terrorism. The object—terrorization—has not been achieved as regards the fighting men of England, France, Belgium, Russia, Italy and Servia. But it has had a distinct effect in cowing timid persons everywhere. I do not believe it would have any effect in cowing the bulk of our people if our people could be waked up to what has happened; but I have no question that it has had a very great effect in cowing that noisy section of our people which has talked loudest about peace at any price. The people who say of the present Administration that "at any rate, it has kept us out of war with Mexico or Germany;" the people who say that we ought not to act about the *Lusitania;* the people who say we ought not to have acted on behalf of Belgium, include in their ranks all of the persons who are cowed by Germany, who are afraid of what Germany would do if we stood up for our own rights or for the rights of other and weaker peoples. Recently, in certain circles, some popularity has been achieved by a song entitled "I Didn't Raise My Boy To Be a Soldier" —a song which ought always to be sung with a companion piece entitled "I Didn't Raise My Girl To Be a Mother." The two would stand on precisely the same moral level. This hymn, in condemnation of courage, has been sung in music halls, and even in schools, with applause. Think of such a song being sung by or of the mothers, sisters and wives of the men who fought under Washington in the Revolution, or of the men who fought under Grant and Lee in the Civil War! Those who applaud such a song are wholly out of place at any patriotic celebration on Decoration Day or the Fourth of July; and most assuredly men of this abject type will be easily affected by terrorism.

The sinking of the *Lusitania,* the destruction of Louvain, the shooting of the Belgians who rallied to the defence of their flag precisely as the men of Lexington and Bunker Hill once rallied to the defence of theirs, the merciless thoroughness of the exploitation of the civilian population of Northern France and Belgium, the utter ruthlessness shown in dealing not only with men but with women and children—all this has undoubtedly cowed and terrorized the average American pacifist, the average peace-at-any-price man in the United States. It has cowed the type of man who cheers such a song as "I Didn't Raise My Boy To Be a Soldier." It has terrorized the type of man who makes speeches and writes editorials or newspaper or magazine articles on behalf of disarmament, on behalf of universal arbitration, and against the Monroe Doctrine. There is a Dr. Jeykll and Mr. Hyde in nations as in individuals; and sheer terrorism is often found working hand-in-hand with flabby and timid international pacifism for the undoing of righteousness and for the deification of the most brutal form of successful militarism.

Mrs. Wharton has sent me the following German poem on the sinking of the *Lusitania,* with her translation:

PREPAREDNESS AGAINST WAR

THE HYMN OF THE LUSITANIA

(*Translated from the German.*)*

The swift sea sucks her death-shriek under
As the great ship reels and leaps asunder.
Crammed taffrail-high with her murderous
    freight,
Like a straw on the tide she whirls to her
    fate.

A warship she, though she lacked its coat,
And lustful for lives as none afloat,
A warship, and one of the foe's best
    workers,
Not penned with her rusting harbor-shirk-
    ers.

Now the Flanders guns lack their daily
    bread,
And shipper and buyer are sick with dread,
For neutral as Uncle Sam may be
Your surest neutral's the deep green sea.

Just one ship sunk, with lives and shell,
And thousands of German gray-coats well!
And for each of her gray-coats, German
    hate
Would have sunk ten ships with all their
    freight.

* *Poem reprinted by courtesy of N. Y. Herald.*

Yea, ten such ships are a paltry fine
For one good life in our fighting line.
Let England ponder the crimson text:

TORPEDO, STRIKE! AND HURRAH FOR THE
NEXT!

This is not a pleasant poem. I do not envy
the person who could write with this exultation
of the death of women and children. It is a
manifestation of the policy of blood and iron
which should be pondered carefully by those
who, with voices of quivering timidity, are advocating our submission to such policies. Be it
remembered, moreover, that bad though it is to
do such a deed, it is even more contemptible to
submit to it. The policy of milk and water is
an even worse policy than the policy of blood
and iron. To sink a hundred American men,
women and children on the *Lusitania,* in other
words, to murder them, was an evil thing; but
it was not quite as evil and it was nothing like as
contemptible as it was for this nation to rest satisfied with governmental notes of protest couched
in elegant English, and with vaguely implied
threats which were not carried out. When a
man has warned another man not to slap his
wife's face, and the other man does it, the gentleman who has given the warning does not meet

the situation by treating elocution as a substitute for action.

Mr. Bryan resigns the foremost position in the American Cabinet and immediately addresses a large meeting of Germans, where he was very properly received with uproarious applause as a faithful servant of the present German government, as a man who, however amiable his intentions, had in actual fact stood against the honor and interest of America. Now, if Mr. Bryan were a German, the German government would not for one moment permit him to make the kind of address against Germany that the Germans applauded him for making against his own country and ours. The success of the German policy of blood-and-iron largely depends upon their possible rivals and opponents adopting a policy of milk-and-water. The blood-and-iron statesman of one nation finds in the milk-and-water statesman of another nation the man predestined through the ages to be his ally and his tool.

A number of persons, including especially the ultra-pacifists, have strongly objected to the statement that this country should have acted on behalf of Belgium, and have done this on the ground that we have declared as a nation that we did not intend to be drawn into "entangling alliances" in Europe. Yet the same persons now advocate our going into a league to enforce the results of universal arbitration, which, of course, represents the "entangling" of ourselves in a foreign alliance on the largest possible scale. It also represents an agreement on our part to wage offensive war on behalf of others, although many of the persons favoring such an agreement are opposed to the very moderate policy of making us fit to protect our own rights in defensive war. It is idle to make promises on behalf of a movement for world peace unless we intend to live up to them. If so, the first step is to live up to the promises we have already made, and not to try to sneak out of them on the ground that to fulfill them means to abandon our "policy of refusal to be entangled in foreign alliances."

This attitude of the ultra-pacifists is merely another illustration of the necessity of subordinating elocution in advocacy of universal world peace to action (not merely elocution) to meet more immediate and vital needs. It is utterly useless to advocate our entering into such a proposed league until we have prepared in military fashion to make our action effective and until we have seriously resolved to live up to our promises—and, as a consequence, to make but few promises. Therefore, at this moment all agitation for such a league merely offers an opportunity for the people who want to talk and to do nothing else. It gives them the chance to avoid the performance of immediate duty by empty elocution for something which is in the remote future and which cannot possibly be achieved until the immediate duty has been effectively performed. In my book, "America and the World War," I have outlined the only possibly feasible plan for securing world peace that has yet been propounded. But it is waste of time to advocate such a plan until we have adopted and put into effect a policy of national military preparedness, and until we take the trouble to find out what treaties—promises—mean, and to refuse to make them unless they are to be kept. To enter into the proposed "League of Peace" would mean that we promised, under certain conditions, to undertake offensive war on behalf of others. It would be ludicrous to make such a promise until we have shown that we are willing to undertake defensive war on behalf of ourselves.

In 1814, a little over a century ago, in the course of the War of 1812, a small British army landed in Chesapeake Bay. It defeated twice its number of "free-born American citizens," without training and discipline, who "had leaped to arms," as Mr. Bryan says, or become "an armed citizenry," as Mr. Wilson puts it. It then burned the public buildings at Washington. The "armed citizenry"—upon whose potentiality President

Wilson relied as an excuse for signal failure to make any preparation to do our duty by adequate preparation in view of the terrible world war now going on and of the situation in Mexico—fled with such unanimity and rapidity that only a score or so lost their lives. Thereupon the remainder, together with all the American editors and public men who for years had been screaming for peace and announcing that there was no need of preparing against war, instead of expressing their hearty shame and repentance for the national failure to prepare, became hysterical in attacking—with words only—the hostile army for having burned Washington. The British army a century ago was as profoundly indifferent to this attack as the war lords of Germany to-day are to our prattle about the *Lusitania* or the resolutions of our peace societies, and the boasts of our political orators on the Fourth of July. Such indifference was, and is, entirely justifiable. It was not a nice thing to burn the public buildings of Washington; but it was an infinitely worse thing for this country, after two years of war, to be utterly unable to protect its capital. It was not a nice thing to kill our women and children on the *Lusitania;* but it was an even meaner and more contemptible thing for us to fail to act with instant decision thereon—and had we so acted in the case of the

Gulflight, a few days previously, the *Lusitania* would never have been sunk.

Every right-minded man utterly despises a coward in private life. Cowardice is the unpardonable sin in a man. A corrupt man can be reformed. Many a corrupt man, both in politics and business, has been reformed within the past score of years, has realized the evils of corruption and is now a first-class citizen. In the same way a coward who appreciates that cowardice is a sin, an unpardonable sin if persevered in, may train himself so as, first to *act* like a brave man, and then finally to *feel* like and therefore to *be* a brave man. But the coward who excuses his cowardice, who tries to cloak it behind lofty words, who perseveres in it, and does not appreciate his own infamy, is beyond all hope. The peace-at-any-price people, the universal and all-inclusive arbitration people, and most of the men and women who have taken the lead in the pacifist movement in this country during the last five or ten years, are preaching international cowardice.

Sometimes these professional pacifists preach such cowardice openly. At other times they preach the utter flabbiness and feebleness, moral and physical, which inevitably breeds cowardice. It is a dreadful thing to think that in the event of war brave men would have to shed their blood; it is a worse thing to think that these feeble folk would purchase their own ignoble safety by the blood of others. The men and women guilty of such preaching and such practice are thoroughly bad citizens. The worst of them, of course, are those in the colleges, and those who profess to speak for the colleges; for to them much has been given and from them much should be expected. The college boys who adopt the professional pacifist views, who make peace leagues and preach the doctrines of international cowardice, are unfitting themselves for any career more manly than that of a nursemaid. A grown-up of the professional pacifist type is not an impressive figure; but the college boy who deliberately elects to be a "sissy" should be replaced in the nursery and spanked.

It is to be regretted that we do not learn history aright. Allusion has been made above to the War of 1812. Had Washington or men who carried out Washington's policy been in charge of our government during the first fifteen years of the nineteenth century, there would probably have been no war with Great Britain in 1812, or if there had been we would have been completely and overwhelmingly successful. But the great opponent of Washington's ideals, Thomas Jefferson, gave the tone to our governmental policies during that time. He announced that his "passion was peace"—not as strong an expression as "being too proud to fight," but sufficiently noxious. He and his followers declined to prepare a regular army and refused to upbuild the Navy. The very Congress that declared war on Great Britain declined to increase our Navy. Yet if at that time we had had an efficient navy of twenty battleships or an efficient mobile regular army of twenty thousand men, the war would not have taken place at all or else it would have ended in complete and sweeping victory the summer it was declared.

We trusted, however, to the "armed citizenry" of whom Mr. Wilson speaks and to the voluntary efforts of "the million men who spring to arms between dawn and sunset," described in Mr. Bryan's oratory. We trusted to the few frigates prepared by the men of Washington's school before the Jeffersonians came to power. These frigates did their duty well and but for them it is possible that our country would have broken in pieces under the intolerable shame of our failure on land. Nevertheless, our small cruisers could produce only a moral and not a material effect upon the war. On land for two years we were unable to do anything effective at all. When the war had begun, it was too late to make efficient preparations; and in any event we did not try. We raised a body of over a hundred thousand militiamen under the volunteer system. These militiamen were gathered in camps where they sickened of various diseases; but we were never able to get them against the foe in any numbers, except on one or two occasions, such as at Bladensburg. Mind you, they were naturally good enough men. The individuals who ran at Bladensburg were the sons of the men of Yorktown, the fathers of the men of Gettysburg. What they needed was preparation by long training in advance; training in the field, not merely in an armory or on a drill ground.

The same thing was true of our Civil War. In 1861 both of the contending armies at Bull Run could have been beaten with ease by a European army of regulars half the size of either. In 1863 there was not an army in Europe which could have contended on equal terms with either of the armies that fought at Gettysburg. In 1814, after two years of exertion, Brown, Scott, and a few other officers like them on the northern frontier, developed a tiny army as good as could be found anywhere, and Andrew Jackson, a real military genius, performed the same feat for the few thousand Tennesseeans and Louisianians whom he commanded at New Orleans.

But the War of 1812 was not a victorious war for us. At best it is possible to call it a draw. It was a thoroughly discreditable war from the standpoint of our people as a whole. The land officers I have named above, and a few thousand troops, not more than ten thousand all told, who served under them, did well. So did the officers and crews of our tiny navy and the shipwrights who built the ships. These men, and a very few others, deserved the highest credit. We of to-day owe them much. It is only because of their existence that Americans can think of the War of 1812 without unmixed shame. But the bulk of our people, and the politicians, from the President down, who represented our people, made a wretched showing in that war; and because of this showing the Union came very near splitting up. If history were rightly taught, this fact would be brought out clearly in our schools; and the pacifists, the peace-at-any-price men, the men who shirk preparedness and who chatter about the efficacy of salvation to be secured by diluted moral mush, would not have the clear field they now have.

Men cannot and will not fight well unless they are physically prepared; and they cannot and will not fight if, through the generations, they elaborately unfit themselves by weakening their own moral fiber. China furnishes the greatest example, and a living and contemporary example. Mr. Bryan recently announced that instead of war, which he regarded as outworn, he wished to try "persuasion." Evidently he was under the impression that persuasion was something new in the annals of history. Let Mr. Bryan and his fellow pacifists read history; and, if they won't read history, let them at least look at affairs that are contemporary. A sillier falsehood has never been uttered than the falsehood that "war settles nothing." War settled the independence of this country; war settled the question of union, and war settled the question of slavery. Pacifists pretend to speak in the interests of morality. It is a poor thing for professed moralists to rest their case on a falsehood, which they must know to be a falsehood. Many of the greatest events of history have been settled by war. Many of the greatest advances in humanity have been due to successful wars for righteousness.

Christianity is not the creed of Asia and Africa at this moment solely because the seventh century Christians of Asia and Africa, in addition to being rent asunder among themselves by bitter sectarian animosities—and sectarian intolerance and animosity stand for most that is evil in Christianity—had trained themselves not to fight, whereas the Moslems were trained to fight. Christianity was saved in Europe solely because the peoples of Europe fought. If the peoples of Europe in the seventh and eight centuries, and on up to and including the seventeenth century, had not possessed a military equality with, and gradually a growing superiority over, the Mohammedans who invaded Europe, Europe would at this moment be Mohammedan, and the Christian religion would be exterminated. Wherever the Mohammedans have had complete sway, wherever the Christians have been unable to resist them by the sword, Christianity has ultimately disappeared. From the hammer of Charles Martel to the sword of Sobieski, Christianity owed its safety in Europe to the fact that it was able to show that it could and would fight as well as the Mohammedan aggressor.

China is the great living example of unpreparedness, of pacifism, of the peace-at-any-price spirit, of the effort to preserve territory and national self-respect by "persuasion" and not by the sword. In consequence the English, the French, the Russians, the Japanese, control one-half of the territory of China, and the remaining territory, under the pressure of Japan, is at this moment losing all right to be considered an independent and self-respecting people. Well-meaning persons who treat peace pageants, peace parades, peace conferences and minor movements of similar nature as of consequence, are guilty of an error which makes their conduct foolish. Those of them who champion the exaltation of peace above righteousness and the abandonment of national power of self-defence—without which there never has been and never will be either national heroism or national manliness—will do well to study China.

It is mere gong-beating, it is the mere sounding of tom-toms and rattles, for our people to get together in conference at the present time and declare for universal peace and announce that they wish a world league by which they will agree to arbitrate everything and enforce the result by arms. Of course in no event should we agree to arbitrate everything. But the prime point to be considered at the moment is that until we show that we possess force, that we are willing to use it when necessary, and that we make no promises save those that ought to be and will be carried out, we shall be utterly useless to do anything for righteousness, whether through these leagues or in any other fashion.

Every peace body, whether religious or humanitarian, philosophic or political, and all advocates of peace, whether in public or private life, work nothing but mischief, and, save in so far as mere silliness prevents it, very serious mischief, unless they put righteousness first and peace next. Every league that calls itself a Peace League is championing immorality unless it clearly and explicitly recognizes the duty of putting righteousness before peace and of being prepared and ready to enforce righteousness by war if necessary; and it is idle to promise to wage offensive war on behalf of others until we have shown that we are able and willing to wage defensive war on behalf of ourselves. The man who fears death more than dishonor, more than failure to perform duty, is a poor citizen; and the nation that regards war as the worst of all evils and the avoidance of war as the highest good is a wretched and contemptible nation, and it is well that it should vanish from the face of the earth.

If our people really believed what the pacifists and the German-fearing politicians advocate, if they really feared war above anything else and really had sunk to the Chinese level—from which the best and bravest and most honorable Chinamen are now striving to lift their people—then it would be utterly hopeless to help the United States. In such case, the best thing that could befall it would be to have the Germans, or the Japanese, or some other people that still retains virility, come over here to rule and oppress a nation of feeble pacifists, unfit to be anything but hewers of wood and drawers of water for their masters.

But I do not for one moment admit that the American people has sunk or will sink to such a level. We are foolish and shortsighted and we permit the prattlers to misrepresent us. But at bottom the heart of this people is sound. We celebrate Decoration Day and Independence Day on the 30th of May and the 4th of July. We believe in the men of the Revolution, in the men of the Civil War and in the women who did "raise their sons to be soldiers" for the right. We know that in itself war is neither moral nor immoral, that the test of the righteousness of war is the object and purpose for which it is waged. Therefore, it is worth while for our people seriously to consider the problems ahead of them; and the first problem is the problem of preparedness.

The prime and all-important lesson to learn is that while preparedness will not guarantee a nation against war, unpreparedness eventually insures not merely war, but utter disaster. Take what has happened in the last twelve months at home and abroad. Preparedness has saved France from the unspeakable shame that befell it in 1870. Every Frenchman holds his head higher now than any Frenchman has held it in forty-five years. England suffers because she has not prepared. If her army had been prepared as Lord Roberts wished it to be prepared, if she had had universal military service on the German model, if she had copied the admirable

German efficiency, military, industrial and social (and had then, unlike Germany, applied it with regard for, instead of with disregard for, the rights of others), she would have been able to rescue Belgium and France from invasion and her own position would now be absolutely assured. She was well prepared from a naval point of view and so was able to protect herself on the ocean. But, when she guaranteed Belgium's neutrality, she abandoned her sea frontier and pushed her land frontier forward to the German border beyond Liége. She failed to realize this fact—just as we have failed to realize that our own moral frontier is not our own seaboard, but is overseas, in Alaska and Hawaii and the Panama Canal Zone.

But Belgium, when compared with Switzerland, offers the most complete example. In many respects Belgium a year ago stood strikingly near to where the United States stands today. She had not been quite as shortsighted as we have shown and are now showing ourselves to be; but she had been very shortsighted. She was an absolutely peaceful and exceedingly prosperous country. She had a great industrial population. For many years the wiser among her people, including especially, by the way, the wisest representatives of the labor element, the Socialists and others, had preached preparedness, so that the country might be saved from invasion by its great military neighbors. But her international policy was determined by the pacifists and peace-at-any-price men, the men and women who said that it was "immoral to fight" and that "war settled nothing," and the other men and women who said that nobody would ever attack Belgium because she was peaceful, and never committed aggression, and that all that was necessary to national well-being was business prosperity, and attention to measures of internal reform. These persons were successful in preventing any adequate preparation. Only a very inadequate one had been attempted and that only during the last year or two. This inadequate preparation was directly responsible for disaster so overwhelming as to wipe out what had been built up by generations of patient industry.

Switzerland meanwhile, the most peaceful country in Europe, had energetically taken full measures for her self-defence. Switzerland had an army of 400,000 men, highly efficient. Belgium, according to her population, on the same basis would have had an army of 700,000 men. If she had had such an army and had acted precisely as Switzerland acted, Belgian territory would now be in Belgian hands and the line of western war in Europe, representing what has been for fourteen months a stalemate, would have left Belgium on the right instead of on the wrong side; and she would have been free instead of trodden down and wasted under an appalling tyranny. No one acquainted with recent German military history, and with German military plans for the past twenty years, doubts for a moment that the German invasion would have taken place as quickly through Switzerland as through Belgium if it had been safe. But Belgium's army was only about one-sixth the size of the Swiss army. The small Belgian army fought valiantly; the conduct of the Belgian people during the last eleven months has been above all praise; and they have rendered mankind their debtor by their heroism. But the heroism came too late to be of avail. It was too late to prepare, or to make good the lack of preparedness, when once the Germans crossed the border. Switzerland had prepared in advance and Switzerland is at peace now, while the soil of Belgium has been trodden into bloody mire. The physical nature of the two countries has nothing to do with the difference. A century ago, Napoleon's armies treated Switzerland as cavalierly as Germany to-day treats Belgium; and for the same reason; because Switzerland was then utterly unprepared.

Let our people take warning. Look at what has happened in Asia at the same time. Japan was prepared; Japan was ready to fight. With trivial loss she has made enormous gains and now dominates China. China was not ready to fight; she had not prepared. In natural resources, in territory, in population, she many times over surpassed Japan; but she had committed the cardinal sin of neglecting to prepare; and she now is at Japan's mercy and her very existence is a matter of doubt.

The most certain way for a nation to invite disaster is to be opulent, self-assertive and unarmed. A nation can no more prepare for self-defence when war actually threatens than a spoiled college "sissy" of the pacifist type can defend himself if a young tough chooses to insult him; and unlike the sissy, the nation cannot under such conditions appeal to the police. Now and then to insure a house means that some scoundrel burns the house down in order to get the insurance. But we do not in consequence abandon insurance against fire. Now and then a nation prepares itself for a war of aggression. But this is no argument against preparedness in order to repel aggression. Preparedness against war is the only efficient form of national peace insurance.

CHAPTER VII

UNCLE SAM'S ONLY FRIEND IS UNCLE SAM

OVER forty years ago Charles Dickens wrote as follows of the United States: "In these times in which I write it is honorably remarkable for protecting its subjects wherever they may travel with a dignity and a determination which is a model for England." Ulysses Grant was then President of the United States. Like Washington and Lincoln and Andrew Jackson, he was an American who was not too proud to fight. Those of my countrymen who are still faithful to the old American tradition cannot but feel with bitter shame the contrast between the conditions Charles Dickens thus described and the conditions at the present moment.

The policy of watchful waiting, a policy popular among governmental chiefs of a certain type ever since the days of Ethelred the Unready and for thousands of years anterior to that not wholly fortunate ruler, has failed, as of course it always does fail in the presence of serious difficulty and of a resolute and ruthless foe. We have tried every possible expedient save only the application of wisdom and resolution. It has been said that we have not tried war; but this statement can be made only by those who are inexact in their terminology. Of course, if any one's feelings are soothed by saying that when we took Vera Cruz, suffered a loss of a hundred and twenty men killed and wounded and in return killed and wounded several hundred Mexicans, we were waging peace and not waging war, why there is no particular objection to this individual gaining whatever comfort is afforded by using words which misdescribe facts. But this is all the comfort he can gain. As a natural result of the impression created on foreigners by our conduct in Mexico, we were forced to hostile action in Haiti and a number of our men and our opponents were killed and wounded. Apparently we "waged peace" in Haiti, much as we "waged peace" in Mexico—and in Mexico the end of the war or peace or whatever it was that we waged was that we withdrew without getting the result which our Government had announced that it would get when it took Vera Cruz.

We of the United States have had a twofold duty imposed on us during the last year. We have owed a duty to ourselves. We have owed a duty to others. We have failed in both.

Primarily both failures are due to the mischievous effects of the professional pacifist agitation which became governmental nearly five years ago when the then Administration at Washington sought to negotiate various all-inclusive arbitration treaties under which we abandoned the right to stand up for our own vital interest and national honor. Very reluctantly we who believe in peace, but in the peace of righteousness, have been forced to the conclusion that the most prominent leaders of the peace agitation of the past ten years in this country, so far as they have accomplished anything that was not purely fatuous, have accomplished nothing but mischief. This result of the activities of these professional pacifist agitators has been due mainly to the fact that they have consistently placed peace ahead of righteousness, and have resolutely refused to look facts in the face if they thought the facts were unpleasant.

It is as foolish to ignore common sense in this matter as in any other matter. It is as wicked to exalt peace at the expense of morality as it is to exalt war at the expense of morality. The greatest service that Lincoln rendered to the cause of permanent peace and to the greater cause of justice and of righteousness was rendered by him when, with unshaken firmness, he accepted four years of grinding warfare rather

than yield to the professional pacifists of his day
—the Copperheads. Washington's greatest service to peace was rendered by similar action on
his part. And be it remembered that never in
history have two men rendered greater service to
the only kind of peace worth having for honorable men and women than was rendered by these
two heroes who did not shrink from righteous
war.

Failure to perform duty to others is merely
aggravated by failure to perform duty to ourselves. To pay twenty-five million dollars
blackmail to Colombia does not atone for our
timid refusal to do our duty by Belgium. It
merely aggravates it. Moreover, it should always be remembered that in these matters the
weak cannot be helped by the weak; that the brutal wrongdoer cannot be checked by the coward
or by the fat, boastful, soft creature who does
not take the trouble to make himself fit to enforce his words by his deeds. Preparedness
means forethought, effort, trouble, labor.
Therefore soft men, selfish, indolent men, men
absorbed in money-getting, and the great mass
of well-meaning men who shrink from performing the new duties created by new needs, eagerly
welcome a political leader who will comfort them,
and relieve their secret sense of shame, by using

high-sounding names to describe their shortcomings.

An adroit politician can unquestionably gain many votes in such fashion, if he exalts unpreparedness as a duty, if he praises peace and advocates neutrality, as both in themselves moral —even although the "peace" and "neutrality" may be conditioned on the failure to do our duty either to others or to ourselves. Such a politician, if he excels in the use of high-sounding words, may win votes and gain office by thus pandering to men who wish to hear their selfishness, their short-sightedness or their timidity exalted into virtues. But he is sapping the moral vitality of the people whom he misleads.

It has been an evil thing that this nation, which for five years has been strutting as the champion of peace and holding conferences to denounce war and praising its wealthy citizens for founding peace leagues, has contented itself with these futile activities and has not dared to strike a blow, has not dared even to say a word for righteousness in the concrete, while wrong has been at least temporarily triumphant during the past eighteen months. It is an even worse thing that during this last eighteen months we have wholly failed to prepare to defend our own homes from disaster.

Nor can we, the people of the United States,

escape blame for ourselves by putting it upon our public servants. Unquestionably the Administration has been guilty of culpable indifference to the honor and the interest of the nation during the last year and a half; but it has been guilty in this fashion precisely because it could count upon popular support; and therefore the ultimate blame rests on the people, that is, on us. It may well be that political gain will come to the politicians who appeal to what is selfish and timid in the hearts of our people, and who comfort soft self-indulgence by praising it as virtuous. A correspondent from Virginia, who has always been opposed to me politically, writes: "The most depressing feature of the present situation is that the great majority of the American people strongly approve of the stand of President Wilson and the other apostles of Buchananism. Every one is so satisfied with his money-making and comforts, the moving-picture shows, and his automobile that there is horror at the thought of death and of need and hunger and fatigue. There is a self-righteous disposition to regard heroism as wickedness, and to consider all soldiers as wicked and immoral. 'Peace with honor' is on the lips of many when the brutal alternatives are war with honor or peace with everlasting shame and dishonor. The Administration is thoroughly terrorized by the Germans. The people of this section are for peace at any price." This may be the general sentiment of the American people, and if so, then those who pander to it will profit politically. But they will win profit for themselves by helping to debase their fellow-countrymen.

When the world war broke out over a year ago, it was simply inexcusable for this people not at once to begin the work of preparation. If we had done so, we would now have been able to make our national voice felt effectively in helping to bring about peace with justice—and no other peace ought to be allowed. But not one thing has been done by those in power to make us ready. On the contrary, in his message to Congress of December, 1914, the President elaborately argued in favor of keeping ourselves unprepared, expressing the hope that, if we thus preserved immunity from hatred by keeping ourselves beneath contempt, we might create a situation where he would be employed as a go-between, as the man to fetch and carry among the warring powers when the time for peace negotiations arrived.

The attitude of the German-American press in this country toward the subsequent notes of the President to Germany throws the true light on this fond anticipation. These hyphenated American newspapers have shown that their entire loyalty is to that portion of the compound term which precedes the hyphen, and that they translate the term German-American as meaning that they are Germans who use their position in America as a means for endeavoring to force America to sacrifice its own honor and the interests of mankind in order to serve the German Government. The professional German-Americans here, acting, as has been shown by President Wilson's ardent supporters in New York, with the connivance of the Administration, and by the direct instigation of the German Government, have deliberately campaigned against the United States, have exulted in the German atrocities, and have openly stated that the support of the German-American vote was conditioned upon the Administration's attitude toward Germany, and that Germany would let President Wilson play a part in the peace negotiations only if he actively or passively helped Germany in the war. He has found them hard taskmasters; and they have so angered his other masters, the American people, that the latter have forced him to belated and half-hearted action. After eighteen months he has begun feebly to advocate an imperfect preparedness. After mere conversation for seven months over the *Lusitania* with Germany he finally becomes angry with Austria over the *Ancona*—for Austria is weaker than Germany and it is safer to be angry with her. But he takes no action about the various other ships which were sunk—there was little popular excitement about these ships.

Men are not to be seriously blamed for failure to see or foresee what is hidden from all but eyes that are almost prophetic. The most far-seeing Americans, since the days of Washington, have always stood in advance of popular feeling in the United States so far as national preparedness against war is concerned. But on the other hand not a few of the leaders have been much less advanced than the people they led. And under right leadership the people have always been willing to grapple with facts that were fairly obvious. They have refused to do this when the official leadership was wrong.

Twenty years after the Civil War we had let our Army and Navy sink to a point below that of any third-class power in Europe. Then we began to build up the Navy. The Navy is more important to us than any other branch of the service; and gradually our people grew to appreciate this. In 1898 came the Spanish War. We did badly; but the Spaniards did worse. As that profound philosopher who writes under the name of "Mr. Dooley" put it: "We were in a dream; but the Spaniards were in a trance." However, as a result we did bring our Navy up to

the fourth or fifth position among the navies of
the big powers, and we did raise our Army until
it was capable of being expanded to a hundred thousand. But immediately that the war
was over Congress, probably, I regret to say, re-
flecting popular indifference, sagged back.*

In 1901, under the malign leadership of cer-

---

* Certain adherents of the Administration, in endeavoring
untruthfully to defend it, have actually asserted that while
I was President I did not myself do enough to upbuild the
Army and Navy! Of course these individuals know perfectly well that the criticism aimed at me while I was President was invariably because I was supposed to be too militaristic, and my critics always condemned me for endeavoring to force Congress to go farther than it was willing to go
in building up the Army and Navy. During my term in the
Presidency the Navy was increased threefold in strength
and at least sixfold in efficiency; the Army was certainly
doubled in efficiency. I did my best to get Congress to do
much more than it would do. I accomplished the very
utmost that by appeal and argument I could get the people
to support. Beginning with my first message to Congress,
on December 3d, 1901, and in every year in my subsequent
messages, I at length and in detail argued for "preparedness
in advance," for "forethought and preparation," in building
up our naval and military forces, in favor of training "for
years" in advance our crews, for "no cessation in adding to
the effective units of the fighting fleet," for a general staff,
for keeping only the military posts and navy yards demanded
by military needs, etc., etc. I repeated these arguments in
dozens of speeches in every quarter of the Union. My messages to Congress and these speeches, in which I so often
and at such length argued for full preparedness in advance,
are open to any one who has access to a public library.

tain men on the Senate Naval Committee, Congress actually stopped making any appropriation whatever for fighting ships. During the succeeding eight years, however, the interrupted work was resumed. The Navy was steadily built up in numbers and still more in efficiency; shooting and fleet maneuvering on a large scale were for the first time treated as they should have been treated; and the result was that in 1909 our fleet stood second among the fleets of the world and was in shape to guarantee us against the aggression of any foreign power. This was then our first duty; and it had been accomplished. Meanwhile the efficiency of the Army had likewise been greatly increased, as was shown by the contrast between the handling of the expeditionary force to Cuba under General Barry and the handling of the army corps under General Shafter six or eight years previously. But very properly the men who were alive to the need of national defence had to devote their chief attention to the Navy; and it was impossible to get the public to consider both our real military and our real naval needs.

Then came the awful cataclysm of the present world war. During the years 1913 and 1914 our Navy deteriorated with frightful rapidity. This was partly due to the way it was handled in connection with our absurd and humiliating little make-believe war with Mexico. Our ships were not maneuvered and were never trained in fleet or squadron gunnery during these two years; and in consequence of this, among other causes, our fleet now stands certainly not higher than fifth among the nations in point of efficiency and is not fit at this moment to defend us from serious attack.

The events of the last year have shown that all who believed that the most frightful wrong-doing by warlike nations could be averted by the opinion of civilized mankind as a whole have been utterly in error. What is happening in this year 1916 shows that not the slightest particle of advance in international morality has been made during the century that has elapsed since the close of the Napoleonic wars. This failure is quite as much due to the misconduct of the pacifists as to the misconduct of the militarists. The milk-and-water statesmanship of the American Government during the past year has been a direct aid to the statesmanship of blood-and-iron across the water; it may not be as wicked, but it is far more contemptible. The United States has signally and culpably failed to keep its promises made in the Hague Conventions, and to stand for the right. Instead, it has taken refuge in the world-old neutrality between right and wrong which is always so debasing for the man practising it. As has been well said, such a neutral is the ignoblest work of God.

There was much excuse for a general failure of Americans to understand the danger to America prior to what happened in this world war. But now there is no excuse whatever. Now, thanks to our own feeble shirking of duty, we know that if any great nation menaces us, no matter how innocent of offence we may be, we have absolutely nothing to expect from other nations. Most assuredly the neutrality we have kept between right and wrong when Belgium was trodden under foot will be repaid us if our turn comes. Small blame will attach to the nations which grinningly quote our own neutral proclamations and say that they themselves intend in their turn to be neutral not only in deed but even in thought, if any European or Asiatic military power concludes to take from us the Panama Canal or Hawaii or Porto Rico or to seize and hold for ransom New York or San Francisco. Moreover, this war has made it evident that armies of hundreds of thousands of men can be transported not only across the narrow but across the broad seas. England's great navy has made the ocean a barrier to her foes, and a highway for herself, and it is only Britain's navy which has saved her from utter disgrace.

Let us profit alike by Belgium's heroic example

in the present, and by the terrible fate brought on her by her lack of forethought and preparedness in the past. At present, in spite of the shattering disasters of the last year and a quarter, and although only a tiny fraction of her territory is left unconquered, Belgium's army is stronger and more efficient than ever before. It numbers about 120,000 fighting men, with over 400 guns and thousands of machine guns and in addition first-class services of aviation, food supply, sanitation, manufacture of ammunition and the like. There are fourteen centers for the drilling of recruits, and excellent schools for the officers. The morale of the army is extraordinary. I know of nothing finer in history than the way in which this army has been raised and maintained by the Belgian nation in the midst of a cataclysm well-nigh unparalleled in the history of nations. But this cataclysm, this frightful and crushing disaster to Belgium, occurred precisely because no such effort was put forth before the event. The splendid heroism of the present can only repair a small part of the horrible damage due to the unpreparedness of the past. Belgium has suffered the last extremities of woe; and she would have gone almost unscathed if before the war came she had prepared an army as strong relatively to her then strength as the present army is strong relative to her present weakness.

England, during the first year of the war, afforded a lamentable example of the punishment that will surely in the end befall any nation which fails to take its duties seriously and to prepare herself thoroughly in advance by universal military training of her citizens, and by a high standard of loyal social efficiency, for the evil day when war may come on the land. Her navy did admirably from the beginning—thanks to men like Lord Fisher, who built it up, and to Prince Louis of Battenberg, who mobilized it in the nick of time, with an efficiency comparable to that which marked the mobilization of the German army. Her soldiers at the front behaved splendidly. But the English people as a whole did not appear to advantage when compared, for instance, with the French, until more than a year had gone by. This was true of their capitalists. It was still more true of their workingmen—compare their striking workmen with the French workingmen, who toiled night and day, and exchanged brotherly greetings with the generals at the front. It was true of their men in Parliament and the press who opposed universal military service. Over a year passed before they began to produce the instruments and munitions of war in a way at all comparable with what was being done in France and Germany. Her people have as a whole volunteered in magnificent manner; but those who wished to shirk their duty were permitted to shirk their duty, and this was a thoroughly evil thing. Now, eighteen months after the outbreak of the war, her people are working with extraordinary resolution and patriotism, but it is not possible wholly to undo the evil done by the lack of preparedness in advance.

If there were no lesson in this for us, I certainly should not dwell on the fact. The important point for us to remember is that if England did not do as well as she ought to have done, she did infinitely better than we would have done; and moreover she has learned her lesson and is doing well, whereas we have not learned our lesson, and our national leaders, executive, legislative, and non-official, from Mr. Wilson and Mr. Bryan to such Congressmen as Messrs. Kitchin and Hay, are still acting in a way that brings dishonor to the American name and that is fraught with the gravest peril to the future of the nation. Capital books have been inspired by this war; Owen Wister's "Pentecost of Calamity," for instance; but in its practical teachings the best book that this war has produced is Oliver's "Ordeal by Battle." I wish that every American would read Mr. Oliver's book and would realize that everything there said as to both the shortcomings and the needs of the English people applies with far greater force to the American people at the present time. Col. Arthur Lee, M.P., in an address to his constituents which all Americans should read, has clearly placed before the British people the vital needs and duties of the hour. Our politicians and our self-styled humanitarians and peace lovers, if they would read this address with open minds, would profit much.

Most certainly we should avoid with horror the ruthlessness and brutality and the cynical indifference to international right which the Government of Germany has shown during the past year, and we should shun, as we would shun the plague, the production in this country of a popular psychology like that which in Germany has produced a public opinion that backs the Government in its actions in Belgium, and cheers popular songs which exult in the slaughter of women and children on the high seas. But if we value the heritage bequeathed to us by Washington and saved for us by Lincoln, we will at once begin the effort to emulate the German efficiency, efficiency which is not only military but also social and industrial.

We in America claim that a democracy can be as efficient for defence as an autocracy, as a despotism. It is idle to make this claim, it is idle to utter windy eloquence in Fourth of July speeches, and to prate in public documents about our greatness and our adherence to democratic principles and the mission we have to do good on the earth by spineless peacefulness, if we are not able, if we are not willing, to make our words count by means of our deeds. Germany stands as the antithesis of democracy. She exults in her belief that in England democracy has broken down. She exults in the fact that in America democracy has shown itself so utterly futile that it has not even dared to speak about wrongdoing committed against others, and has not dared to do more than speak, without acting, when the wrong was done against itself. She openly exults in and counts upon the fact that the professional German-Americans are disloyal to the United States. She uses the politicians who are afraid of the German-American vote.

Every professional pacifist in America, every representative of commercialized greed, every apostle of timidity, every sinister creature who betrays his country by pandering to the anti-American feeling which masquerades under some species of hyphenated Americanism—all these men and women and their representatives in public life are at this moment working against democracy. If the democratic ideal fails, if democracy goes down, they will be primarily to blame. For democracy will assuredly go down if it once be shown that it is incompatible with national security. The law of self-preservation is the primary law for nations as for individuals. If a nation cannot protect itself under a democratic form of government, then it will either die or evolve a new form of government.

I believe that our people will realize these facts. I believe that our people will make democracy successful. They can only do so if they show by their actions that they understand the responsibilities that go with democracy. The first and the greatest of these responsibilities is the responsibility of national self-defence. We must be prepared to defend a country governed in accordance with the democratic ideal or else we are guilty of treason to that ideal. To defend the country it is necessary to organize the country in peace, or it cannot be organized in war. A riot of unrestricted individualism in time of peace means impotence for sustained and universal national effort toward a common end in war time. Neither businessman nor wage-worker should be permitted to do anything detrimental to the people as a whole; and if they act honestly and efficiently they should in all ways be encouraged. There should be social cohesion. We must devise methods by which under our democratic government we shall secure the socialization of industry which autocratic Germany has secured, so that business may be encouraged and yet controlled in the general interest, and the wage-workers guaranteed full justice and their full share of the reward of industry, and yet required to show the corresponding efficiency and public spirit that justify their right to an increased reward. But the vital fact to remember is that ultimately it will prove worse than useless to have our people prosper unless they are able to defend this prosperity; to fight for it.

Let us, then, make up our minds to prepare; and make up our minds just what we want to prepare to do. We have the Panama Canal. Many of our Congressmen have in the past consistently opposed the upbuilding of the navy and the fortification of the Panama Canal. These men may mean well, but their action has represented an unworthy abandonment of national duty; and they have shown themselves to be the most dangerous enemies of this republic, men unfit to be trusted in public life in any position whatsoever. If the American people wish to support such public servants, then let them instantly abandon the Canal, giving it back to Panama or turning it over to Japan or Germany or England or any other people whose ruling class is composed of men and not of eunuchs. Let them also abandon the Monroe Doctrine; let them abandon all pretense of protecting life and property in Mexico. In short, let us take the position of the China of the Occident and await with helpless weakness the day when our territory will be divided among more competent peoples.

But if we intend to play our part as a great nation and to be prepared to defend our own interests and to do good to others, let us decide what we want to do and then make ready to do it. South of the Equator, that is, south of the line of approaches on each side to the Panama Canal, we need no longer bother about the Monroe Doctrine. Brazil, Chile, the Argentine, are capable themselves of handling the Monroe Doctrine for all South America, excepting the extreme northern part. Consider the case of Argentina, for instance. In Argentina, as in Switzerland, they have universal military service. This has been of enormous use to them industrially and socially. It has also given them at present an army of close to half a million men, although they have not one-tenth the population of the United States. Argentina is far more fitted to defend its own territory from a sudden attack by a powerful enemy than is the United States. We would do well to sit at her feet and learn the lesson she can thus teach us.

Therefore we need bother with the Monroe

Doctrine only so far as the approaches to the Panama Canal are concerned, that is, so far as concerns the territories between our southern border and, roughly speaking, the Equator. We do not have to bother about the Monroe Doctrine and Canada, for during the past year Canada has shown herself infinitely more efficient than we are.

This Administration was elected on the specific promise to give freedom to the Philippines. The United States must keep its promises. No greater service has been rendered by any people to another during the past hundred years than we have rendered to the Philippines—and than we have rendered to Cuba also. In February, 1909, when the battle-fleet returned from its voyage around the world, the United States was in point of military, that is, primarily naval, efficiency in such shape that there was no people that would have ventured to attempt to wrong us; and under such circumstances we could afford to keep the Philippines and to continue the work that we were doing. But since then we have relatively to other powers sunk incalculably from a military standpoint; we are infinitely less fitted than we were to defend ourselves. Above all, we have promised the Filipinos independence in terms which were inevitably understood to be independence in the immediate future; and we have begun to govern them weakly.

Such indecision in international conduct shows that this people ought not to undertake the government of a distant dependency, and this both from military reasons and because of the need of keeping promises that have been made. Let us, then, as speedily as possible, leave the Philippines; and as the Philippines desire us to leave we would be quit of all moral obligations for them, and would under no circumstances be obliged to defend them from other nations.

There remain Alaska, Hawaii, our own coasts, and the Panama Canal and its approaches, as the military problem with which we should grapple; and with this problem we should grapple in the manner already set forth in this book.

A democracy should not be willing to hire somebody else to do its fighting. The man who claims the right to vote should be a man able and willing to fight at need for the country which gives him the vote. I believe in democracy in time of peace; and I believe in it in time of war. I believe in universal service. Universal service represents the true democratic ideal. No man, rich or poor, should be allowed to shirk it. In time of war every citizen of the Republic should be held absolutely to serve the Republic whenever the Republic needs him or her. The pacifist and the hyphenated American should be sternly required to fight and made to serve in the army and to share the work and danger of their braver and more patriotic countrymen; and any dereliction of duty on their part should be punished with the sharpest rigor. The man who will not fit himself to fight for his country has no right to a vote in shaping that country's policy. As for the woman who approves the song, "I Did Not Raise My Boy To Be a Soldier," her place is in China —or by preference in a harem—and not in the United States. But she is all right if she will change the song into "I Did Not Raise My Boy To Be the *Only* Soldier." Every woman who has not raised her boy to be a soldier at need has in unwomanly fashion striven to put a double burden on some other boy whose mother had a patriotic soul. The much-praised "volunteer" system means nothing but encouraging brave men to do double duty and incur double risk in order that cowards and shirks and mere money-getters may sit at home in a safety bought by the lives of better men.

The United States has—and deserves to have —only one friend in the world. This is the United States. We have ourselves treated the Hague Conventions as scraps of paper; and we cannot expect any one else to show the respect for such treaties which we have lacked. Our safety and therefore the safety of democratic institutions rests on our own strength and only on our own strength. If we are a true democracy, if we really believe in government of the people by the people and for the people, if we believe in social and industrial justice to be achieved through the people, and therefore in the right of the people to demand the service of all the people, let us make the Army fundamentally an army of the whole people.

This will be carrying out the democratic ideal. The policy advocated for Britain by Lord Roberts was really the necessary complement to the policy advocated for Britain by Lloyd-George. In a democracy service should be required of every man, in peace and in war; we should guarantee to every man his rights, and require from each man the full performance of his duties. It may well be that in the end we shall find it worth while to insist that all our young men, at their entrance to manhood, perform a year's industrial service—in the harvest fields, in city sanitation, on the roads, anywhere. Such service would be equally beneficial to the son of the millionaire and to the boy who grows up in the crowded quarters of our great cities or out on lonely farms in the back country.

This is for the future. As for the present, it is certain that a half year's military service would be a priceless boon to these young men themselves, as well as to the nation. It would tend to social cohesion. We would gain a genuine citizens' army, and we would gain a far higher type of citizenship. Our young men, at the outset of their lives, would be trained—not merely to shoot and to drill, which are only small parts of military training—but to habits of bodily endurance and moral self-mastery, to command and to obey, to act on their own initiative and to understand and promptly execute orders, to respect themselves and to respect others, and to understand that they are to serve their country with deeds and not words only. Under such conditions the young American would enter manhood accustomed to take pride in that disciplined spirit of orderly self-reliance combined with ability to work with others, which is the most essential element in the success of a great, free, modern democracy.

CHAPTER VIII

THE SOUND OF LAUGHTER AND OF PLAYING CHILDREN HAS BEEN STILLED IN MEXICO

A N astonishing proof of the readiness of many persons to pay heed exclusively to words and not at all to deeds is supplied by the statement of the defenders of this Administration that President Wilson has "kept us out of war with Mexico" and has "avoided interference in Mexico." These are the words. The deeds have been: first, an unbroken course of more or less furtive meddling in the internal affairs of Mexico carried to a pitch which imposes on this nation a grave responsibility for the wrong-doing of the victorious factions; and, second, the plunging of this country into what was really a futile and inglorious little war with Mexico, a war entered into with no adequate object, and abandoned without the achievement of any object whatever, adequate or inadequate.

To say that we did not go to war with Mexico is a mere play upon words. A quarter of the wars of history have been entered into and carried through without any preliminary declaration of war and often without any declaration of war at all. The seizure of the leading seaport city of another country, the engagement and defeat of the troops of that country, and the retention of the territory thus occupied for a number of months, constitute war; and denial that it is war can only serve to amuse the type of intellect which would assert that Germany has not been at war with Belgium because Germany did not originally declare war on Belgium. President Wilson's war only resulted in the sacrifice of a score of American lives and a hundred or two of the lives of Mexicans; it was entirely purposeless, has served no good object, has achieved nothing and has been abandoned by Mr. Wilson without obtaining the object because of which it was nominally entered into; it can therefore rightly be stigmatized as a peculiarly unwise, ignoble and inefficient war; but it was war nevertheless.

This has been bad enough. But the general course of the Administration toward Mexico has been worse and even more productive of wide and far-reaching harm. Here again, word-splitters may, if they desire, endeavor to show that the President did not "intervene" in Mexico; but if so they would be obliged to make a fine discrimination between intervention and officious and mischievous intermeddling. Whether it is said that President Wilson "intervened" in Mexican affairs, or that he merely intermeddled, so as to produce much evil and no good and to make us responsible for the actions of a peculiarly lawless, ignorant and blood-thirsty faction, is of small importance. The distinction is one merely of words. The simple fact is that thanks to President Wilson's action—and at times his inaction has been the most effective and vicious form of action—this country has become partially (and guiltily) responsible for some of the worst acts ever committed even in the civil wars of Mexico.

When Mr. Wilson became President of the United States, Huerta was President of Mexico. On any theory of non-interference with the affairs of our neighbors, on any theory of avoiding war and of refusing to take sides with or become responsible for the deeds of blood-stained contending factions, it was the clear duty of Mr. Wilson to accept Mr. Huerta as being President of Mexico. Unless Mr. Wilson was prepared actively to interfere in Mexico and to establish some sort of protectorate over it, he had no more business to pass judgment upon the methods of Mr. Huerta's selection (which had occurred prior to Mr. Wilson's advent to power) than Mexico would have had to refuse to recognize Mr. Hayes as President on the ground that it was not satisfied with his economic policy and moreover sympathized with Mr. Tilden's side of the controversy. And if Mr. Wilson made up his mind to interfere in Mexico—for of course the most trenchant type of interference was refusal to recognize the Mexican President—he should have notified Foreign Powers of his proposed action in order to prevent so far as possible Huerta's recognition by them. President Wilson interfered in such feeble fashion as to accomplish the maximum of evil to us and to other foreigners and the Mexicans, and the minimum of good to anybody. He hit; but he hit softly. Now, no one should ever hit if it can be avoided; but never should any one "hit soft."

When Mr. Wilson refused to recognize Huerta, he committed a definite act of interference of the most pronounced type. At the same time he and Mr. Bryan looked on with folded arms and without a protest of any kind while American citizens were murdered or robbed or shamefully maltreated in all parts of Mexico by the different sets of banditti who masqueraded as soldiers of the different factions. He maintained for a long time a friendly intercourse with one chief of political adventurers through irregularly appointed diplomatic agents, and he adopted an openly offensive attitude toward the chief of another set, although he was then the de facto head of whatever government Mexico had. Then he turned against this once-favored bandit in the interest of a third bandit. By his action in permitting the transmission of arms over the border President Wilson not only actively aided the insurrection but undoubtedly furnished it with the means essential to its triumph, while at the same time his active interference prevented Huerta from organizing an effective resistance. His defenders allege that he could not properly have forbidden the transmission of arms to the revolutionaries across the border. The answer is that he did forbid it at intervals. He thereby showed that he was taking an active interest in the arming of the revolutionaries, that he permitted it when he chose to do so and stopped it intermittently whenever he thought it best to stop it, and was therefore entirely responsible for it.

The nominal rights which the contending factions championed, and the actual and hideous wrongs done by all of them, were not our affair save in so far as Americans and other foreigners were maltreated. We may individually sympathize, as, for instance, I personally do, with the general purpose of the program for division of the lands among the Mexican cultivators, announced by Carranza, Villa and other revolutionary leaders; but this no more justified interference on our part than belief in the wisdom of the single tax for the United States by some foreign ruler would warrant his interference in the internal affairs of the United States. Moreover nothing in the career of Carranza and Villa or in the conduct of the Mexican people at present justifies us in any belief that this program will in any real sense be put into effect.

However, the interference took place. By the course President Wilson pursued toward Huerta and by the course he pursued toward Villa and Carranza, he actively interfered in the internal affairs of Mexico. He actively sided with the faction which ultimately triumphed—and which immediately split into other factions which are now no less actively engaged in fighting one another. Personally, I do not think that the Administration should have interfered in this manner. But one thing is certain. When the Administration did interfere, it was bound to accept the responsibility for its acts. It could not give any aid to the revolutionaries without accepting a corresponding share of responsibility for their deeds and misdeeds. It could not aid them because of their attitude on the land question without also assuming a corresponding share of responsibility for their attitude toward religion and toward the professors of religion. The United States would have had no responsibility whatever for what was done to the Church by any faction which did not owe its triumph to action by the United States. But when the United States takes part in civil war in Mexico, as Messrs. Wilson and Bryan forced our Government to take part, this country has thereby made itself responsible for the frightful wrong-doing, for the terrible outrages committed by the victorious revolutionists on hundreds of the religious people of both sexes.

To avoid the chance of anything but willful misrepresentation, let me emphasize my position. I hold that it was not our affair to interfere one way or the other in the purely internal affairs of Mexico, so far as they affected only Mexican citizens; because if the time came when such interference was absolutely required it could only be justified if it were thorough-going and effective. Moreover, I hold that it was our clear duty to have interfered promptly and effectively on behalf of American citizens who were wronged, instead of behaving as President Wilson and Secretary Bryan actually did behave. To our disgrace as a nation, they forced American citizens to claim and accept from British and German officials and officers the protection which our own government failed to give. When we did interfere in Mexican internal affairs to aid one faction, we thereby made ourselves responsible for the deeds of that faction, and we have no right to try to shirk that responsibility. Messrs. Wilson and Bryan declined to interfere to protect the rights of Americans or of other foreigners in Mexico. But they interfered as between the Mexicans themselves in the interest of one faction and with the result of placing that faction in power. They therefore bound themselves to accept responsibility for the deeds and misdeeds of that faction, and of the further factions into which it then split, in so far as Mr. Wilson sided with one of these as against the other.

Not long ago President Wilson, in a speech at Swarthmore, declared that "Nowhere in this hemisphere can any government endure which is stained by blood," and at Mobile that "we will never condone iniquity because it is most convenient to do so." At the very time he uttered those lofty words, the leaders and lieutenants of the faction which he was actively supporting were shooting their prisoners in cold blood by scores after each engagement, were torturing men reputed to be rich, were driving hundreds of peaceful people from their homes, were looting and defiling churches and treating ecclesiastics and religious women with every species of abominable infamy, from murder and rape down. In other words, at the very time that the President was stating that "nowhere on this hemisphere can any government endure which is stained by blood," he was actively engaged in helping install in power a government which was not only stained by blood but stained by much worse than blood. At the very time that he was announcing that he would "never condone iniquity because it was convenient to do so," he was not merely condoning but openly assisting iniquity and installing in power a set of men whose actions were those of ferocious barbarians.

Remember that I am not engaged in defending the factional opponents of these victorious wrong-doers. There is not evidence sufficient to decide which of the many factions behaved worst. But there is ample material to decide that they all behaved atrociously. Apparently the Administration took the ground that inasmuch as Mr. Huerta and his followers were bad men, it was our duty to condone the evil committed by their opponents. Father R. H. Tierney, of New York City, an entirely responsible man, informs me that when (in company with two other gentlemen whose names he gives me) he called upon Mr. Bryan to bring to his attention the abominable outrages committed on certain nuns by the followers of Carranza and Villa, Mr. Bryan informed Father Tierney that he had information that "the followers of Huerta had committed similar outrages on two American women from

Iowa!" (This sentence has been read to Father Tierney, who states that it describes the interview with exactness. The original of the affidavits herein quoted are in the possession of Father Tierney, 59 East Eighty-third street, New York City, and Father Kelly, and will be shown by them to any reputable person.) Apparently Mr. Bryan believed this disposed of the situation and relieved the revolutionaries of blame.

Surely, it ought not to be necessary to say that if the facts as thus stated to and by Mr. Bryan were true (and if there was any doubt immediate investigation as to their truth by the government was demanded), then the way to get justice was not by treating one infamy as wiping out the other but by exacting the sternest retribution for both and effectively providing against the repetition of either. Even assuming for the moment that the attitude of the Administration had not so committed the government that it was its duty to interfere on behalf of the nuns thus outraged, Mr. Bryan's statement to Father Tierney shows almost incredible callousness on his part to the most dreadful type of suffering, to acts far worse than the mere murder of any man. It seems literally impossible that any representative of the American government in high office could fail to be stirred to his depths by such wrong, or could have failed to insist on the immediate and condign punishment of the wrong-doers and on the amplest safeguarding against all possible repetition of the wrong. Apparently the only way in which it occurred to Mr. Bryan to take any action against the faction whose adherents had perpetrated these hideous wrongs on the two American women was by encouraging another faction which he must have known in advance and certainly did know after the event would commit and had committed wrongs equally hideous.

I have before me a copy of *El Heraldo de Toluca* of September 13th, 1914. It contains a manifesto on behalf of the victorious revolutionaries of the party of Messrs. Carranza and Villa, dealing with the "conditions under which the Roman Worship will have to be practiced." (I translate into English.) Among the preambles are the following: 1, that the ministers of the Catholic Worship circulate doctrines which are not in accordance with the principles of the true Christ; 2, that on account of the learning that these ministers have acquired they cannot in the minds of those who possess equal or greater learning (but who differ from them in opinion) pass as sincere believers in the doctrines they preach and that they thereby exploit the ignorance of the ignorant masses; 3, that inasmuch as this conduct harms people by frightening them with the fear of eternal punishment and thereby tends to make them subservient to the priesthood and that inasmuch as all kinds of people from workmen to capitalists give too much money to the churches and because of various other similar facts, the decree in question is promulgated.

This decree includes the forbidding "of any sermons which will encourage fanaticism;" the proscribing of any fasts or similar practices; the prohibition of any money being paid for christenings, marriages or other matters; the prohibition of the soliciting of contributions (that is, the passing of the plate); the prohibition of celebration of masses for the dead or the celebration of more than two masses a week; the prohibition of confession and with this object in view the closing of the churches excepting once a week at the hour of the masses; and, finally, the prohibition of more than one priest living in Toluca and the requirement that he, when he walks in the streets, shall be dressed absolutely as a civilian without anything in his costume revealing the fact that he is a minister. In order to be permitted to exercise the functions thus limited, the priest is required to affix his signature of acceptance to the foregoing regulations.

Now, in various South American countries there have been bitter contests between the Clericals and the anti-Clericals and again and again the extremists of each side have taken positions which in the eyes of sensible Americans of all religious creeds are intolerable. There are in our own country individuals who sincerely believe that the Masons or the Knights of Columbus, or the members of the Junior Order of American Mechanics, or the Catholic Church or the Methodist Church or the Ethical Culture Society, represent what is all wrong. There are sincere men in the United States who by argument desire to convince their fellows belonging to any one of the bodies above mentioned (and to any one of many others) that they are mistaken, either when they go to church or when they do not go to church, when they "preach sermons of a fanatical type" or inveigh against "sermons of a fanatical type," when they put money in the plate to help support a church or when they refuse to support a church, when they join secret societies or sit on the mourners' bench or practise confession. According to our ideas, all men have an absolute right to favor or oppose any of these practices. But, according to our ideas, no men have any right to endeavor to make the government either favor or oppose them. According to our ideas, we should emphatically disapprove of any action in any Spanish-American country which is designed to oppress either Catholics or Protestants, either Masons or anti-Masons, either Liberals or Clericals, or to interfere with religious liberty, whether by intolerance exercised for or against any religious creed, or by people who do or do not believe in any religious creed.

I hold that these should be our sympathies. But I emphatically hold that it is not the duty of this government to try to make other countries act *in accordance* with these sympathies, and, above all, not the duty of the government to help some other government which acts *against* these great principles with which we sympathize. Messrs. Wilson and Bryan by their actions have assumed a certain undoubted responsibility for the behavior of the victorious faction in Mexico which has just taken the kind of stand indicated in the proclamation above quoted; a stand, of course, hostile to every principle of real religious liberty, a stand which if applied logically would mean that no minister of any church could in public wear a high-cut waistcoat or perhaps even a black frock-coat, and which would put a stop even to such common-place actions as the passing of the plate in any church to encourage home missions.

But this attitude is only one of the offences committed. Catholic schools almost everywhere in Mexico have been closed, institutions of learning sacked and libraries and astronomical and other machinery destroyed, the priests and nuns expelled by hundreds and some of the priests killed and some of the nuns outraged. Archbishop Blenk of New Orleans, Father Tierney, editor of *America,* Father Kelly, president of the Catholic Church Extension Society, Mr. Petry, one of the directors of the Catholic Church Extension Society, and a Mexican bishop whose name I do not give because it might involve him in trouble, came to see me at my house; and in Chicago I saw other priests and refugees from Mexico, both priests, nuns and lay brothers. The statements and affidavits, submitted to me in the original and copies of which I have before me as I write, set forth conditions which are literally appalling and for which, be it remembered, the actions of Messrs. Wilson and Bryan have made this country partly responsible.

For example, Archbishop Blenk submitted to me an affidavit by the prioress of the Bare-footed Carmelite Nuns of the Convent of Queretaro. This sets forth from the personal knowledge of the prioress how the churches have been profaned by soldiers entering them on horseback, breaking statues, trampling on relics and scattering on the floor the Sacred Hosts and even throwing them into the horses' feed; how in some churches the revolutionaries have offered mock masses and have in other ways, some of them too repulsive and loathsome to mention, behaved precisely as the Red Terrorists of the French Revolution behaved in the churches of Paris; how, for example, St. Anthony's Church at Aguascalientes has been made into a legislative hall and the Church of St. Joseph at Queretaro and the great convent of the Carmelites and the lyceum of the Christian Brothers all have been confiscated; how the church property has been sequestered and the archives burned and the men and women in the cloistered communities expelled without being allowed to take even an extra suit of clothes or a book of prayer.

The prioress states that she has herself seen in Mexico City nuns who have been "victims of the passions of the revolutionary soldiers," and some whom she found in their own homes, others in hospitals and in maternity houses, who in consequence are about to be delivered of children. She deposes: "I have seen soldiers dressed up in chasubles, stoles, maniples and cinctures, with copes and altar linen, and their women dressed up in albs, surplices, and corporals used as handkerchiefs." She has seen the sacred vessels profaned in a thousand ways. She describes meeting seven nuns who had been outraged, whom she directed to a maternity house, and who had abandoned themselves to utter despair, saying "that they were already damned and abandoned by God and they cursed the hour of their religious profession." She describes how she escaped from Quaretaro with nuns who had been obliged to hide in private houses in order to escape being taken to the barracks by the soldiers. She describes how she had daily to beg the food necessary to sustain the twenty-four sisters with whom she escaped.

In Chicago I saw a French priest, Father Dominic Fournier, of the Congregation of the Passion, who had just escaped from Mexico with two young Spanish students for the priesthood. He had escaped from the City of Toluca with nothing whatever, not even a Rosary. He and the two novices described to me their experience in Toluca. The churches and religious houses were sacked and confiscated and the soldiers and their women indulged in orgies before and around the altars. One of the lay brothers named Mariano Gonzales tried to save some of the things from the church. The revolutionists seized him and accused him of robbing the state. He was shot by a file of soldiers on August 22nd, 1914, and his dead body was left all day long in the court in which Father Fournier and the other priests and the two novices who spoke to me and their associates were confined. They were kept in prison sixteen days and then allowed to go with nothing but what they had on.

I have seen the original of and have in my possession a translation of a letter written on October 24th by a young girl of Toluca to her pastor who had been exiled. She described how the bishop had been heavily fined and exiled. She describes how the clubs of boys and girls for whom she had been working had been broken up, but how some of the boys to whom they used to give breakfast on Sunday mornings still occasionally come to see them; and she asks advice how to keep these clubs of the poor together. But the dreadful and pathetic part of the letter is contained in the following sentence: "Now I will ask you a question. Suppose some one falls into the power of the Zapatistas. Would it be better for her to take her own life rather than allow them to do their will and what they are accustomed to do? As I never thought such a thing could happen, I did not ask you before about it, but now I see it is quite possible. If we had not our good God in whom we trust, I think we would give way to despair."

In other words, this girl who had been engaged in charitable work in connection with the church asks her pastor whether she is permitted to commit suicide in order to avoid the outrages to which so many hundreds of Mexican women, so many scores of nuns, have been exposed in the last few months. I cannot imagine any man of whatever creed—or of no creed—reading this letter without his blood tingling with horror and anger; and we Americans should bear in mind the fact that the actions of President Wilson and Secretary Bryan in supporting the Villistas (until President Wilson suddenly swapped bandits and supported the Carranzistas) have made us partly responsible for such outrages.

I have been given and shown letters from refugees in Galveston, in Corpus Christi, in San Antonio and Havana. These refugees include seven archbishops, six bishops, some hundreds of priests, and at least three hundred nuns. Most of these bishops and priests had been put in jail or in the penitentiary or otherwise confined and maltreated. Two-thirds of the institutions of higher learning in Mexico have been confiscated and more or less completely destroyed and a large part of the ordinary educational institutions have been treated in similar fashion.

Many of the affidavits before me recite tortures so dreadful that I am unwilling to put them in print. It would be tedious to recite all the facts set forth in these affidavits. For instance, there is one, by Daniel R. Loweree, a priest of the diocese of Guadalajara, the son of an American father, and librarian of the Seminary and professor of chemistry. He describes what took place in Guadalajara. On July 21st, about one hundred priests from the city and country round about were put in the jail, while the cathedral was used as a barracks. In the affidavit of Canon José Maria Vela, of the Cathedral of Zacatecas, he sets forth how the constitutionalists shot a priest named Velarde, how twenty-three priests were gathered together and under the orders of General Villa required to produce one million pesos within twenty-four hours, under penalty of being shot. A committee of the priests went out through the city begging from house to house and accepting even pennies from the children. A girl was forcibly violated by one of the soldiers in the room adjoining that in which these priests were kept. Finally, the citizens raised a couple of hundred thousand pesos and the priests were released and allowed to flee without any of their belongings. Seventeen of the fleeing priests are now in El Paso and their names are given in the document and those of some of them signed to an accompanying document.

In an affidavit by the Reverend Michael Kubicza, of the Society of Jesus, whose father was a Hungarian physician, he describes how he was tortured in order to make him give up money. A soldier nicknamed Baca, in the presence of Colonel Fierro, put a horsehair rope around his neck and choked him until he became unconscious. When he came to, Baca fired a revolver near his head and commanded him to give up and tell him where the Jesuit treasures were buried. On answering that there were none, he was again choked until he was unconscious, and this was repeated a third time. The affidavit describes at length some of the sufferings of the priests in fleeing.

All kinds of other affidavits have been submitted to me, dealing with torture and murder, as, for example, the killing of Father Alba, the parish priest of Cabra, the killing of the parish priest and vicar at Tula, the killing of the chaplain and rector and vice-president of the Christian Brothers' College, etc., etc.

The one feature in the events narrated to me and set forth in the affidavits to me which can give any American the least satisfaction is the statement of the kindness with which the unfortunate refugees had been treated in Vera Cruz by the officers and men of the Army and Navy, particular mention being made of General Funston.

What I have above stated is but a small part of the immense mass of facts available to the President (and Mr. Bryan) had they cared to examine them. They relate to outrages on Catholics. This is merely because the enormous majority of the religious people of Mexico are Catholics. I should set them forth just as minutely if they had been inflicted by Catholics on Freethinkers or Protestants or Masons—I am myself both a Protestant and a Mason and I claim and exercise the right of full liberty of thought. Even if we had no responsibility for them, I nevertheless fail to see how any American could read the account of them without a feeling of burning indignation. As things actually are, shame must be mingled with our indignation. The action of the President (and Mr. Bryan) has been such as to make this country partly responsible for the frightful wrongs that have been committed on the Mexicans themselves. For the wrongs committed on Americans, and neither prevented nor redressed, our Government is not merely partly, but wholly, responsible.

A year ago I was shown a letter from Naco, Arizona, written by a railway engineer on January 10, 1915. He mentions that five persons had been killed and forty-seven wounded on the American side of the boundary line by stray bullets shot by the Mexicans, and adds: "My wife was shot in the neck in our house, six hundred yards from the line, when she was reading. I would rather a thousand times be with Emperor Bill than an American citizen under such conditions." I have just been visited by a Boer gentleman, who has been resident in Mexico for a dozen years; after the Boer War he was exiled from Cape Colony and his property confiscated; but in Mexico he does not claim to be an American; he clings eagerly to his British citizenship; for England, like Germany and France, does try to protect her citizens, whereas bitter experience has taught the average American citizen in Mexico that in his case, robbery and murder will bring no protest from his home government.

At this moment the Administration is protesting about the seizure of cotton, copper and rubber in ships owned by American merchants and destined for one of the belligerent powers in Europe. It is standing strongly for the property right of the man who wishes to sell his goods to foreigners engaged in war. It at one time urged passage of a law to let it purchase the ships of one of the powers engaged in war, which ships had been interned in our waters; a purchase which would have been to the pecuniary advantage of certain banking and business firms, and to the pecuniary advantage of the power in question, but which might very well have embroiled us with the nations now at war with this power; so that the proposed law would have been very objectionable.

Yet while thus endeavoring to serve, sometimes properly and sometimes improperly, the interests of the business men which have been hurt by this war, the Administration pays not the smallest attention to the cases of the corresponding business men—certainly no less deserving—who have suffered so terribly in Mexico; and it pays no attention whatever to the cases of American citizens of humble position and small means, men, women and children, who have lost life or limb, or all their few worldly goods, during the past two years on the Mexican border and within Mexico itself.

The El Paso *Morning Times* of December 26, 1914, a Democratic paper supporting President Wilson, stated that in the firing by Mexican soldiers across the border "fully fifty persons, including American soldiers," were wounded. A former district-attorney of New Mexico writes me that the exact number was fifty-seven, some of whom were killed, and that the men shot included American soldiers walking their beats as sentries. This information was obtained from the coroner at Naco. From the same source I am informed that before President Wilson came into power, eighteen American citizens were killed and wounded in like manner at El Paso.

Perhaps the most extraordinary feature of the whole Naco affair is that at that point there is an open port of entry. The arms and ammunition used to kill American women and children, and American soldiers, were openly purchased in the United States and openly delivered through a port of entry to the warring factions in Mexico. An American army officer whose name, of course, I cannot give, who has been serving along the Mexican border, informs me that, among the enlisted men, man after man, when his enlistment ran out, refused to re-enlist because the orders of the Administration were that when fired at, on American soil, by Mexicans, he was not to return the fire. I speak of what I know personally when I say that this action by the Administration has not only deeply damaged us in the eyes of the Mexican people, but is a frightful source of demoralization among the American troops. It is literally incomprehensible to me that any American who knows the truth can be willing to tolerate such a condition of affairs.

Surely our people should ponder these facts. Here are American private citizens, men, women and children, and American soldiers, all on American soil, scores of whom have been killed or wounded by bullets shot across the line. Some of the killing has been done through sheer carelessness and contemptuous indifference for our rights; some has been done maliciously and of purpose; and yet President Wilson's Administration has failed to take any action. The culmination came in the month of January of the present year 1916, when sixteen Americans were taken from a train in the state of Chihuahua and murdered premeditatedly and in cold blood. Had Mr. Wilson had in him one faint spark of the courage of Andrew Jackson no Mexican would have dared even think of such action. The murder of these Americans was the direct result of President Wilson's recognition of Carranza's government for otherwise they would not have been in Mexico, and their murderers felt they could act with impunity because for three years President Wilson had shown again and again that American citizens could be murdered, and the American flag outraged, without hindrance from him. The record of the preceding Administration as regards Mexico was not a pleasant object of contemplation for Americans brought up to honor the flag; but the present Administration has made Americans in or near Mexico feel that they have no flag to honor.

Be it remembered also that there was not the slightest difficulty in stopping the particular kind of flagrant outrage that occurred along the border. There were difficulties connected with other features of possible policy in Mexico, but there never has been the slightest difficulty as regards this particular matter. At any moment since, some five years ago, the revolution began, this type of outrage could have been stopped within twenty-four hours. It can be stopped over night. All that is necessary is to notify the Mexican authorities that if there is any repetition of such action at any point, the American troops will promptly be sent over to the locality where the outrage occurs and will drive all the contestants to beyond extreme rifle range of the border, and will exact immediate punishment for any man or party violating the measures which the American officer in charge deems it necessary to take to protect our peaceable citizens within our own borders. It is literally incomprehensible that orders such as this should not have been issued years ago.

I speak of the cases of this type because they are so flagrant; because there can be no discussion about them and no defence of them which can puzzle any man of reasonable intelligence. But the wrongs thus committed constitute only the tiniest fraction of the innumerable wrongs committed upon Americans and upon foreigners of every nationality in the course of the five years of anarchy during which Mexico has been torn to pieces by various groups of banditti. The worst of these banditti have been more or less actively helped by the present Administration, and during the entire five years, but notably during the last three years, they have all of them been permitted to prey with impunity upon the persons and the property of Americans and of other foreigners in Mexico.

The Administration should be condemned for its policy in Mexico; but let us be frank with ourselves, we Americans, and say the condemnation should be visited upon us as a nation, for we have had the amplest knowledge of all that has happened. It has been put before us in detail officially. Yet we have declined to make our indignation felt by President Wilson, and by Mr. Bryan (when Mr. Bryan was in office). Messrs. Wilson and Bryan not merely sat supine, but actually encouraged the Mexican leaders who were responsible for the murder of American men and the outraging of American women. Since Mr. Bryan left office, President Wilson has continued the policy unchanged, and his is the sole responsibility for the innumerable murders and outrages that have since occurred; murders and outrages committed by Carranzistas and Villistas alike.

I wish that every American citizen would read the speech of Senator Albert B. Fall, of New Mexico, delivered in the Senate of the United States on March 9, 1914. Not only have Senator Fall's statements been left unanswered, but no adequate attempt has even been made to answer them. One or two Democratic Senators have striven to answer similar statements by the assertion that things as bad were permitted under the Administration of President Taft. But Senator Fall's speech was open to no such rejoinder, for he impartially cited outrages committed prior to the advent and subsequent to the advent of the present Administration to power.

The Senate partially performed its duty. On April 20, 1913, it sent to the President a formally worded request for information as to the number of Americans killed in Mexico, the number driven out of that country and as to what steps had been taken to obtain justice. No answer whatever was made to this request, and it was repeated in the following July. Then the President answered, declining to give the information on the ground that it was not compatible with the public interest. If the President had then had a well-thought-out policy which he intended forthwith to apply for remedying the conditions of affairs, such an answer might have been proper. But, as a matter of fact, events have shown that he had no policy whatever, save in so far as vacillating inability to do anything positive may be called a policy. Two years and a half have passed since this answer was returned to the Senate; murder and spoliation have continued unchecked; and still not one action has been taken by the present Administration to right the fearful wrongs that have been committed, and still the public has never been shown the material in possession of the State Department.

The following statements are contained in Senator Fall's speech. They form but a small proportion of the cases that have been brought to my own attention. But they are officially stated by Senator Fall. President Wilson and Secretary Bryan had it in their power, when these statements were made over two years ago, at once to find out whether or not they were well founded. It was their duty immediately to investigate every case thus specifically mentioned by Senator Fall and either to take action or to furnish to the Senate and the people refutation of the .charges. They did nothing whatsoever. They dared not do anything whatsoever.

Senator Fall recites extracts from the report of W. W. Suit, the chief of the Order of Railway Conductors in the republic of Mexico; the statement of Conductor T. J. O'Fallon; the affidavits of Conductor J. S. McCranie and Engineer J. D. Kennedy, of August 3, 1913; all reciting in detail the outrages committed in 1911, which resulted in 500 American railroad men being driven from Mexico. The chief of the Order of Railway Conductors remarks very pertinently, "Every American who has been in touch with the situation and every citizen of other civilized countries sees the necessity of adding the Big Stick to the Monroe Doctrine," which is merely a picturesquely idiomatic way of stating the common-

sense truth that unless resolute purpose and potential force are put back of every such doctrine
or declaration of foreign policy, our enunciation
of the doctrine or declaration excites mere derision.

These particular infamies complained of here,
like not a few to which Senator Fall calls attention, were committed prior to Mr. Wilson's coming to power; but Mr. Wilson has never sought
redress for them or for the outrages committed
since he has been in power. Senator Fall, for instance, asks, "What has been done to investigate
the death of Mrs. Anderson, which occurred in
Chihuahua on June 22, 1911? Not under this
Administration. This is no partisan question
and I think I will be acquitted of any attempt to
take any possible partisan or political advantage
in what I shall say as to the last Administration
and this Administration; but I should like to
know whether there has been any attempt whatsoever made to investigate the case to which I
have just referred."

He then recites the facts. Mrs. Anderson was
a poor woman, living with her little daughter of
thirteen and her little boy of seven in their house.
The soldiers of Madero's army entered the house
and demanded that she should cook for them.
She was shot, fell to the ground, compelled to rise
from the ground and continue to cook, although

bleeding to death; and at the same time her little daughter, thirteen years old, was outraged in her presence. The boy of a neighbor, running to their assistance, was shot at the door of the house and killed. The American colonists, not being at that time as intimidated as they have since been, procured the arrest of the men charged with this crime. They were convicted, were sent for six months to jail, and then were turned loose upon the community. The woman died.

A little American girl of twelve, Mabel Richardson, was assailed seventeen miles from where this first outrage occurred. Her assailants were never punished; and Senator Fall in his speech recited the fact that not one word, not one line of protest ever proceeded from our Government in the matter, although these were among the cases to which he referred in his speech in the Senate on July 22, 1912.

James W. Harvey was killed in the state of Chihuahua in May, 1912.

William Adams, a citizen of Senator Fall's own state, was murdered at about the same time, and not an effort was made by the Government to punish the perpetrator of the outrage.

In the case of A. J. Fountain, who was killed, the Government did act, and its action was worse than inaction. It notified the man responsible for the murder that American citizens must not be killed. This man, named Salazar, serving under Madero, disregarded the notice sent him, killed another American, and when Senator Fall made his speech he had fled from the Huertistas and was living under the protection of our Government at El Paso. Says Senator Fall: "He is eating three square meals a day on this side of the river at Fort Bliss, near El Paso, Texas, protected by American soldiers. Meals are being provided and paid for by the taxpayers of this Government for something over four thousand of the Mexicans who came across the river."

Joshua Stevens was killed near Colonia Pacheco, Mexico, on August 25, 1912, and his two little daughters assaulted. The case was brought to the attention of the State Department, but no protest was made.

Johnny Brooks was killed at Colonia, Chihuahua, in May, 1913. He, however, was a former Texas Ranger and, after being mortally wounded by five assailants, he killed their leader, a Mexican lieutenant, before he himself died. This man had been originally in the employ of Senator Fall himself. His life was taken without the slightest provocation, and nothing was ever done by our Government to demand reparation.

On July 26, 1913, near Tampico, Matthew Gourd, from the State of Iowa, and his daughter and niece were attacked by Mexicans. Gourd was tied to a tree and his daughter and niece outraged in his presence. Apparently the only action taken by President Wilson's Administration was to send word to the American Consul at Tampico that a Red Cross ship would be sent down there for a short while and that all Americans should be notified that if they desired they could go on board it and leave Mexico!

On June 18, 1913, Rogers Palmer, an English citizen, was killed, and Carl von Brandts and L. W. Elder, American citizens, were wounded in Tampico, while endeavoring to defend American women from the attack of certain of Villa's bandits.

About the same time H. W. Stepp, an American, was shot because of his refusal to pay five hundred pesos ransom.

Edmund Hayes and Robert Thomas were killed by Santa Caravo. Senator Fall personally called the attention of President Wilson and Secretary Bryan to the fact that the murderer was walking the streets of Juarez, five minutes' ride from El Paso. The Department demanded his arrest and punishment. He was arrested, but nothing more has been heard of the case; and Senator Fall could get no answer to his requests to know what the Government had done to back up its threats and to enforce the punishment of this man, a red-handed murderer of two men, among the best-known American pioneers in Mexico.

Benjamin Griffin, a ranchman, was murdered July 5, 1913. No reparation has been obtained.

John H. Williams, a mining engineer; Boris Gadow, a consulting engineer, and U. G. Wolf, a mining engineer, were all shot, but nothing was done about it. I quote verbatim from what Senator Fall says of the next case he mentions: "Frank Ward was shot in the back by bandits near Yago, Tepic Territory, April 9, 1913. I endeavored to obtain information, not by asking the State Department, but from other sources, as I have been compelled to obtain information in other cases. For a long while it was impossible for me to get the facts of the occurrence resulting in Ward's killing, because when American women are attacked and outraged, they themselves and their friends attempt to keep their names out of the press and avoid in every way possible publicity in matters of that kind. But I can say to you now, Mr. President, that an affidavit is on file in the American Embassy in the City of Mexico from Mrs. Ward herself stating that when her husband was shot, and writhing in his wounds on the floor, she was outraged by Mexican bandits, who then killed him. The affidavit is on file. Has any attempt been made to secure the punishment of those guilty of this crime?" No; President Wilson took no action whatever.

Senator Fall went on to enumerate scores of similar murders and outrages. It would be useless to recapitulate them. I call attention only to one or two cases. A United States Customs Inspector, John S. H. Howard, was assassinated near Eagle Pass, Texas. The United States Government did nothing, but in this particular case the State of Texas caught one of the assassins and dealt with him, says the Senator, "as Texas is prepared to deal, I am glad to say, with other assassins."

L. Bushnell, a mounted policeman, was killed in Naco, Arizona, by a bullet from over the line, March 24, 1913. R. H. Ferguson, a member of the troop F, Third United States Cavalry, was killed by a bullet fired over the border in similar manner.

Senator Fall states that it is probable that not as many Americans have been killed during the last two years as during the preceding three years, because the Americans have been driven out of Mexico by herds. On July 28, 1913, he notified the Secretary of State, Mr. Bryan, that he had in his possession a list of 284 men, 301 women and 1,266 children, all of them Americans, who had been driven out of Mexico for no fault of their own. They were people of small means;

their little cottages had been burned to the ground in most cases. Secretary of State Bryan acknowledged the receipt of the letter and did nothing whatever about it. President Wilson supported Mr. Bryan in the matter.

Senator Fall gave minutely and in detail case after case of unspeakable outrages. He showed that these cases were called specifically to the attention of the Administration and that the Administration deliberately declined to act on behalf of the unfortunate beings who had suffered such dreadful wrong. He recited, what has been told to me personally by other men who have seen Mr. Bryan, that Mr. Bryan declined to act in behalf of Americans who had lost their property, on the ground that he was not interested in "protecting American dollars." But the enormous majority of the men, women and children who have suffered in Mexico belong to the class of those persons of small means who support themselves by their own work. Undoubtedly the destruction of property has fallen upon the wealthy no less than upon the humble; but the American women who have been outraged, the American men who have been killed and the American children who have been deprived of their parents or of their homes, in the immense majority of cases, belong to the class whose means are small.

President Wilson and Secretary Bryan endeavored to "protect the dollars" of wealthy foreign corporations by purchasing from or through them the German ships interned in our ports, and they endeavored to "protect the dollars" of wealthy property owners who desired to make fortunes through the sale of contraband, but they made no effective protest, they took no action whatever, as regards the railway conductors, the brakemen, the small farmers and ranchmen, the mining engineers, our fellow citizens peacefully plying their trades in Mexico, whose property was taken from them, who themselves were sometimes killed and whose wives and daughters, American women, American girls, sometimes suffered outrages worse than death.

It is eminently right to "protect American dollars," so long as this can be done without interfering with the just rights of others. It is even more necessary to protect the persons and lives of American men and women. But what shall we say of the governmental representatives who do neither, and seek to cover their failure by prattle about despising "dollars"? Especially when on the high seas they treat "dollars" as of more importance than the lives of women and children?

Let me repeat that I quote Senator Fall only because he has spoken as a Senator, so that his remarks are contained in an official document, which should be circulated broadcast throughout the United States. I relate a few of the specific cases he quotes merely as instances, to show that our public officials have had multitudes of such cases specifically called to their attention. Any number of similar statements to those of Senator Fall have been made to me by private individuals. American after American has told me that our fellow-countrymen are eagerly seeking to obtain English or German citizenship, and American heads of corporations in Mexico have told me that they are employing only Germans or Englishmen, because, though Englishmen and Germans are not treated well in Mexico, they are infinitely better treated than Americans.

There is no government in the world for which the Mexican people now feel the profound contempt that they feel for the United States Government; and we owe this contempt to the way in which our governmental authorities have behaved during the last five years, but especially during the last three years. Well-meaning people praise President Wilson for having preserved "peace" with Mexico, and avoided the "hostility" of Mexico. As a matter of fact his action has steadily increased Mexican hostility, has not prevented the futile and infamous little "war" in which we first took and then abandoned Vera Cruz, and has been responsible for death, outrage and suffering which have befallen hundreds of Americans and hundreds of thousands of Mexicans during the carnival of crime and bloodshed with which this "peace" has prevented interference.

Senator Fall made it evident in his speech that he held no brief for either of the contending Mexican factions. He described Huerta in language of just severity, but he showed, what every man in his senses knows, that Villa has been a bandit and murderer by profession, and a murderer, robber and outrager of women since he has become a general in the revolution. Carranza and his party have stood precisely on the same level of bandit-murder. There was no reason whatever for any American to uphold Huerta; but to antagonize him on moral grounds, and then to endeavor to replace him by a polygamous bandit, was not compatible with any intelligent system of international ethics. Nor did any betterment follow from dropping this bandit, and putting the power of the United States Government behind another bandit. It may be entirely proper to take the view that we have no concern with the morality of any chief who is for the time being the ruler of Mexico. But to do as President Wilson has done and actively take sides against Huerta and for Villa, condemning the former for misdeeds, and ignoring the far worse misdeeds of the latter, and then to abandon Villa and support against him Carranza, who was responsible for exactly the same kind of hideous outrages against Americans, and insults to the American flag, is an affront to all who believe in straightforward sincerity in American public life.

Senator Fall gives in detail the circumstances of a few of Villa's crimes, some of them so shocking that any decent man's blood boils as he reads them. Villa's efficiency has unquestionably been great, but it has been efficiency of the type which in the reign of King Bomba gave certain Sicilian and Calabrian bandit chiefs international prominence. The statements of Senator Fall have never been successfully questioned. Villa can, of course, be defended, but only in the sense that it is possible to defend Geronimo or some other Apache chief of Geronimo's type; to defend Villa as representing freedom and justice and democracy in the sense that the words are used in speaking of civilized nations is literally like defending an old-time Apache chief on the same grounds. The sincerity of such a defence can escape question only if the defender is admitted to be entirely ignorant of all concerning which he speaks.

It is not possible to give all the facts in full. For this the responsibility lies entirely with the President, for he has consistently carried out a policy of secrecy as regards the outrages on our citizens in Mexico. He has persistently refused to let the facts be known. He has worked in the darkness and behind cover. He has followed the policy of preventing all publicity. He has concealed the truth and furtively evaded telling the truth. But nevertheless we do know the facts in a very large number of cases. From the information available, it appears that over two hundred American lives have been lost in Mexico; that as regards none of them has redress been secured, and that as regards most of them it has not even been demanded.

Apparently many hundreds of millions of dollars of American capital was invested in Mexico, and of this almost all is gone. As before stated, when remonstrated with on this subject, Mr. Bryan, speaking for President Wilson, repeatedly informed callers that he was not "interested in American dollars"; that Americans who invested in property in foreign countries could not look to this Government to protect them. Yet at that very time another member of the Cabinet who sat at the same council board with Mr. Bryan was making an earnest appeal that Americans should invest their property—"dollars"—in enterprises in South America; and at that very time Mr. Bryan, in accordance with the orders of Mr. Wilson, was making protests about the in-

terference with American property—"dollars"—
on the high seas.

Of course what Messrs. Wilson and Bryan
say about "American dollars" is a mere rhetor-
ical flourish in any event. If we have no right
under any circumstances to jeopardize life to protect property in international matters, then we
have no right to jeopardize it to protect property
in municipal matters. If the Wilson-Bryan doctrine is true, then no policeman should arrest any
violent offender for a crime less than murder or
rape, and no householder should defend himself
against a burglar or highwayman, for in such
case he is undoubtedly jeopardizing the life either
of his assailant or himself in order to "protect
dollars."

However, President Wilson's practice is a little
worse even than his theory. His theory has been
that he would not protect American property in
Mexico. His practice has been that he would not
protect American men from murder and American women from rape in Mexico. And at the
same time President Wilson, in striving to
secure and protect certain kinds of property—that is, in dealing with matters of contraband and of the purchase of the interned ships
of one of the powers now at war—has been following in feeble and irresolute fashion a policy
which it is quite conceivable would, if successful,

let us drift into war in peculiarly ignoble fashion.

The Hague conventions bound us to protest against the dreadful wrong done to the men, women and children of Belgium. President Wilson declined to make any protest on behalf of human life, lest to do so might embroil us with some powerful outside nation; but he protests heartily against any interference with our selling copper to be used in the warlike operations against these same Belgians; thereby showing that in practice he puts property rights above those highest of human rights which concern the lives of the helpless.

A year ago President Wilson spoke on the subject of Mexico in a speech at Indianapolis. At the beginning of his speech he said, "I got very tired staying in Washington and saying sweet things. I wanted to come out and get in touch with you once more and say what I really thought." Disregarding the implication as to his own past sincerity contained in this statement, we have a right to take the speech as expressing his deliberate conviction and purpose. He said that he possessed "a reckless enthusiasm for human liberty," and then spoke of his own policy of "watchful waiting in Mexico." Apparently, in his mind "watchful waiting" is a species of "reckless enthusiasm." He asserted that the people of Mexico have a right to do anything they please about their business, saying, "It is none of my business; it is none of your business how long they take in determining it. It is none of my business and it is none of yours how they go about the business. Haven't the European nations taken as long as they wanted and spilled as much blood as they pleased in settling their affairs? Shall we deny that to Mexico because she is weak?"

This is the kind of language that can be used about Mexico with sincerity only if it is also to be applied to Dahomey and to outrages like those of the French Commune. It cannot in the long run be accepted by any great state which is both strong and civilized nor by any statesman with a serious purpose to better mankind. In point of public morality it is fundamentally as evil a declaration as has ever been put forth by an American President in treating of foreign affairs; and there is to it the added touch of inefficiency.

Moreover, President Wilson's words, bad though they are, have not been borne out by his deeds. He has actively interfered in Mexico on behalf of some of those spillers of blood whose right to "spill" blood he exuberantly champions. He has not interfered to punish the bandits and murderers who have killed American men and outraged American women. He has not interfered to protect the honor and the interest of the United States. He has not interfered to protect the lives and the property of our citizens or of the citizens of any other country. But he has interfered to help put into power the very worst among the leaders of the various murderous and thieving groups and factions, and then to replace him with the next worst.

President Wilson refused to run the risk of shedding the blood of any American soldiers to protect American citizens and put a stop to anarchy and murder and prevent further bloodspilling or to try to bring peace to the distracted land of Mexico. He refused to run the risk of shedding the blood of any American soldier in order to prevent the killing of American soldiers and American private citizens on our own territory by Mexicans who shot at or toward them from the other side of the border line. The rape of women, the murder of men and the cruel treatment of little children left his tepid soul unstirred. Insult to the American flag, nameless infamies on American women, caused him not one single pulse of emotion. But he wantonly and without the smallest excuse and without the smallest benefit to this country shed the blood of several scores of American soldiers and sailors in order to help put one blood-stained bandit in the place of another blood-stained bandit. And he now, without any reason of morality or sound public policy, is helping a third blood-stained bandit against his former ally and protégé, the second bandit.

Murder and torture; rape and robbery; the death of women by outrage and children by starvation; the shooting of men by the thousand in cold blood—Mr. Wilson takes note of these facts only to defend the right of vicious and disorderly Mexicans to "spill" as much as they please of the blood of their peaceful fellow-citizens and of law-abiding foreigners. But when the chance came for him to use the Army and Navy of the United States in favor of the worst offender among all the rival bandit chiefs, he eagerly clutched at it.

Senator Lodge, in his speech of January 6, 1915, discussed at length what President Wilson has done in this matter, and no successful attempt has been made or can be made to answer what he then said. His speech, together with the speech of Senator Fall and the speech of Senator Borah, should be circulated among all honest citizens who wish to know what the facts really are.

The country should clearly understand the awful misery that has been brought upon Mexico by President Wilson's policy. It is extraordinary that we do not realize that, thanks to our own selfishness and heedlessness, thanks to the dishonorable timidity of the Administration, the conditions of life in Mexico are worse at this moment than the conditions of life in the regions over which the contending armies in Europe have fought. In 1914 we sent Christmas ships abroad to the war-stricken countries of Europe. This was well; but why did we neglect Mexico, where our own responsibility is so heavy?

At that very time a pathetic appeal had been issued by a company of Mexicans near the international boundary line addressed "To the American People and their Exalted Authorities." It was a plea for work for the men and bread for the women and children. They asked for work, for justice, for bread. Conditions like those which in Europe have shocked the civilized world have existed here right against our own borders, for four years, unconsidered by us.

As the wife of one of our consuls-general has said: "Mexico is peopled with widows and orphans, and famine is in the land. One sees it daily, in emaciated forms, shrunken cheeks, tightly drawn skin and burning eyes. It is in the faces of women, old men and little children. Many have died on American soil during the past year, ostensibly from obscure disease, but actually from starvation, and there are hundreds of children who have never had sufficient food in their pitiful little lives. That is the heartbreaking tragedy in it all—the unsmiling little children who sit silently by the doors of the huts through the long hours of long days. The sound of laughter and of playing children has been stilled in Mexico. From these people comes a cry of bread for the starving. The United States has claimed the exclusive right to intervene in Mexican affairs. Will we demand the right and repudiate the obligation?"

This is the state of affairs to which Mexico has been brought by the practical application of Mr. Bryan's doctrine as to not caring for "American dollars" (it is American dollars that buy food for the starving, Mr. Bryan!) and of President Wilson's doctrine that we must not interfere or let any one else interfere to stop "spilling blood" in Mexico. President Wilson's position meets the enthusiastic approval of the bandits who spill the blood. It meets and it merits the enthusiastic support of the blood-smeared leaders to whom his inaction has given the chance to murder men and outrage women and to let little children starve.

But the laughter of little children has been stilled in Mexico. It has been stilled because President Wilson in his handling of the Mexican problem, as in his handling of every other branch of our foreign affairs, has placed this country in the position of shirking its plain duty, of seeking its own ignoble ease beyond everything else, and of declining to protect its own citizens or to fulfill its international obligations or to interfere for the weak and helpless, when rapine and murder stalk in insolent mastery over the land.

Our course as regards Mexico has been a terrible thing for Mexico. It has been a shameful thing for the United States. But if this policy is permanently continued, there will be yet further shame in store for the United States. Sooner or later the war in Europe will come to an end; and then the great armed nations, after a more or less brief interval, will certainly turn their attention to us and to Mexico. We cannot forbid interference with Mexico in the name of the Monroe Doctrine and yet fail to fulfill the obligation imposed on us by common humanity if we maintain that doctrine.

Spaniards, Germans, Englishmen, Italians, Frenchmen, have been wronged in Mexico, only less than our own citizens have been wronged— only less than decent and well-behaved Mexicans have been wronged—by the inhuman bandits to whom our Government has furnished arms and aid for the perpetration of their crimes. President Wilson in his messages has confusedly advocated, first that we stay unprepared and helpless in the face of military nations, and next that we go into a policy of half-way preparation; and in actual fact he has not made even the smallest advance towards preparedness. He also advocates that in Mexico we pursue the policy of letting the violent and disorderly elements of the population slowly destroy all the leading men, all the reputable people, and bring destruction by fire and steel, by disease and famine, on the humble men and women and little children, and also on the strangers within their gates.

The self-respecting and powerful nations of the world will not permanently permit such a course of action. We will not permanently be permitted to render ourselves impotent in the face of possible aggression and at the same time try to forbid other nations from righting wrongs which we are too weak, too timid or too short-sighted ourselves to right. In the end foreign nations will assuredly take issue with the Wilson-Bryan theory, which is that America can adopt as her permanent policy the shirking of national duty by this country, combined with a protest against any other country doing the duty which we have shirked. Either we shall have to abandon the Monroe Doctrine and let other nations restore order in Mexico, and then deprive us of any right to speak in behalf of any people of the Western Hemisphere, or else we must in good faith ourselves undertake the task and bring peace and order and prosperity to Mexico, as by our wise intervention it was brought to Cuba.

In the last five years the suffering in Mexico has in the aggregate far surpassed the suffering in Belgium during the last eighteen months. Dark deeds have been done in Belgium, but they have not been as dark as the fiendish atrocities perpetrated in Mexico. For these Mexican atrocities the United States Government must shoulder a very heavy load of responsibility, thanks chiefly to President Wilson's Administration.

The other day a friend of mine, a German diplomat, wrote to me taking exception to my condemnation of Germany because of its acts toward Belgium, and his letter ran partly as follows: "You do not refer to the present Mexican question, at which I am not astonished. Don't you believe it would have been rather queer to get a protest about Belgium from a government which had created the most extraordinary breach of international-law-impossibilities (please excuse this queer expression) by at first not recognizing a President of a neighboring country, with whom it seemed on good terms, then allowing arms to be sent to the revolutionaries in that country, not to recognize them as belligerents though; then to forbid this export of arms, then to allow it again; to occupy by force a port, to leave it again, and to wind up by leaving the country in question—which was supposed to benefit by all this, at least that was what we outsiders were told—with, I think, five Presidents fighting one another and ruining the country completely. I think the results for Mexico have been worse than our invasion of Belgium."

There was no adequate answer that I could make to my German friend; and in the wrongs done to Belgium by Germany, Germany has at least shown strength and fearlessness and efficiency, whereas the course of the Administration in regard to Mexico has branded our country with the brand of feebleness, timidity and vacillation. A weakling who fears to stand up manfully for the right may work as much mischief as any strong-armed wrongdoer. For two years President Wilson has decreed that Mexican malefactors shall be allowed at will to spill the blood of the innocent, and because of this attitude of President Wilson, American men have been wantonly murdered and American women outraged, while the famine-stricken women of Mexico mourn, and among their starving children there is no laughter.

CHAPTER IX

WHEN IS AN AMERICAN NOT AN AMERICAN?

THE following two letters show an attitude on the part of the National Administration which challenges the careful consideration of every American. The letters, which were sent me by Mr. John M. Parker, of New Orleans, explain themselves:

Hon. William Jennings Bryan, Secretary of State, Washington, D. C.
Your Excellency:

My father, P. A. Lelong, was a native of France and came to New Orleans when he was about twenty years of age; lived here about forty years. He died here about two years ago, but about five years before his death took out naturalization papers.

I was born in New Orleans, June 18, 1880. I have never been out of the United States and have regularly voted as an American citizen since I reached the age of twenty-one years, and if war had ever occurred between France and the United States, I most certainly would have fought for the United States. I have held the office of Township Commissioner in Henderson County, North Carolina; have held several court appointments, both Federal and State, and am a member of the State and Federal bar, and have considered myself as much an American citizen as President Wilson or any of the members of the Cabinet.

I wish to visit France on business in the near future, and am informed by Mr. Ferrand and the French Consul here that if I go to France I could be either impressed into the French service or punished for not having reported for military duty, and also for having served in the State Militia of Louisiana without permission from the French Government.

I contend that if the French Government had any right to claim me as a citizen under their laws, in times of peace they should have called on me to serve my three years in their military service.

Wishing to know whether my constitutional privileges as an American citizen follow me wherever I go, with its constitutional guarantees, or whether the United States Government will allow the French Government to act in the manner as stated by Mr. Ferrand, the French Consul,

I respectfully request an answer at as early a date as possible.

> Respectfully yours,
> (Signed)   P. A. LELONG, JR.

To this the following answer was returned:

DEPARTMENT OF STATE,
> WASHINGTON, April 2, 1915.

Mr. P. A. Lelong, Junior, 832 Union Street,
New Orleans, Louisiana.

Sir:

The Department has received your letter of March 27, 1915, stating that you expect to go to France on business in the near future and inquiring whether you would be molested by the French military authorities. You say that you were born in New Orleans, June 18, 1880, and that your father, a native of France, resided in this country about forty years and obtained naturalization as a citizen of the United States shortly before his death, which occurred about two years ago.

Under the provision of the Fourteenth Amendment to the Constitution, all persons born in the United States and subject to the jurisdiction thereof are citizens of the United States. Section one, Article VII of the French Civil Code, states that the following are Frenchmen: "Every person born of a Frenchman in France or abroad."

It thus appears that you were born with a dual nationality, and the Department cannot therefore give you any assurance that you would not be held liable for the performance of military service in France should you voluntarily place yourself within French jurisdiction.

> I am, sir,
>> Your obedient servant,
>>> For the Secretary of State,
>>>> (Signed) ROBERT LANSING,
>>>>> Counselor.

One effect of this decision, on an American citizen who actually went abroad, reached me in a letter I received, dated November 6th, 1915, from Camp House, Short Hills, New Jersey. The writer is an Italian woman, Elizabeth Parness. Her husband, Vito Parness, is not only a naturalized citizen, but has served in the Eleventh Cavalry, United States Army, for three years, being discharged a non-commissioned officer. In November, 1914, he went to Italy to see his old father and mother and has not been allowed to return. His wife writes me that she is in dire poverty, having no means of support; that the State Department has been notified, but that nothing has been done. But it is, perhaps, natural that when native-born Americans are murdered and their wives raped with impunity in Mexico, naturalized Americans, even although ex-United States soldiers, receive no protection in Europe.

I hold that it is the clear duty of the American people immediately to repudiate the doctrine thus laid down by the Wilson Administration. According to this doctrine there are in our country very many citizens—and, as a matter of fact, this ruling would apply to millions of citizens—who are "born with a dual nationality." Two or three years ago it was announced that Germany had passed a law by which she provided for her citizens, who became naturalized in the United States or elsewhere, the means of also retaining their German citizenship, so that these men would preserve a dual citizenship, what the Department of State in this letter of April 2nd last calls "a dual nationality." I hold that it was the business of our Government as soon as this statement was published to investigate the facts, to require would-be citizens to repudiate this law, and to notify the German Government that we protested against and would refuse to recognize its action; that we declined to recognize or acquiesce in the principle of such a dual citizenship or a dual nationality; that we would hold naturalized citizens to the full performance of the duties

288

of American citizenship, which were necessarily exclusive of and inconsistent with the profession of citizenship in or allegiance to any other nation, and that in return we would extend the same protection to these citizens that is extended to native-born citizens. Such action was not taken. It is a reproach to us as a nation that it was not taken. We should not for a moment tolerate the assumption by Germany or by any other foreign power that foreign-born citizens of the United States can retain any citizenship in or allegiance to the country from which they came.

But the present case is even worse. It seems incredible that the Department of State can promulgate the doctrine of dual nationality promulgated in its letter above quoted. Yet it has been asserted and reasserted, both before and since Mr. Bryan left office. It is dangerously close to treason to the United States to hold that men born here of foreign parentage, men who have served in the militia in this country, who vote and hold office and exercize all the other rights of citizenship, and who in good faith are and always have been Americans, should, nevertheless, be blandly informed by the State Department that if they visit the countries in which their parents were born they can be seized, punished for evasion of military duty, or made to serve in the army.

Let me point out a few of the possible applications of the doctrines thus laid down by the Department of State. If Colonel Goethals went to Holland he would be liable to be shipped out for military service in Sumatra. If Admirals Osterhaus and Schroeder had gone to Germany they could have been forced to serve under Admiral von Tirpitz in the German navy. If General Barry should visit England he could be seized and sent to the trenches in France. If my neighbors Messrs. Peter Dunne and Mark Sullivan, and my friends Judge O'Brien and James Conolly and Charles Conolly, went to England they could be impressed into the British army for service in Flanders or Ireland. If the sons of Jacob Riis went to Denmark they could be retained in the Danish forces. If the son of the great war correspondent McGahan, whose mother was a Russian lady, went to Russia, he could be sent to serve in the Carpathians. President Andrew Jackson on this theory could have been impressed for military service in the English army against which he fought at New Orleans, if he had ever happened to visit England; and President Arthur would have been in the same plight.

Such incidents seem like the phantasmagoria of an unpleasant dream. Until I saw this letter of April 2nd last, I had not supposed that it would be possible for any human being in our country to uphold such a proposition. Yet in point of rights, Mr. Lelong stands exactly level with the men whom I have thus instanced. Surely it ought not to be necessary to say that the rights of every citizen in this land are as great and as sacred as those of any other citizen. The United States cannot with self-respect permit its organic and fundamental law to be overridden by the laws of a foreign country. It cannot acknowledge any such theory as this of "a dual nationality"—which, incidentally, is a self-evident absurdity.

Mr. Lelong was born in this country; when he became of age he elected to exercise his birthright granted to him by the Constitution of the United States; he took an oath to support that Constitution, and he has held military office under its authority, and under the authority of two states of the American Union. He is eligible to the Presidency of the United States. He is a citizen of the United States, standing on an exact equality of right with all other citizens, and he is entitled to the full protection of the United States both in and out of any foreign country, free and exempt from any provision of the law of that country as to citizenship. There should not be a moment's delay in asserting this doctrine, not only as regards Mr. Lelong and France, but as regards Germany in connection with her law providing for a dual citizenship so far as it concerns immigrants from Germany who become citizens of the United States.

We should assert in the face of all the nations of the world, of France and England, of Russia, Austria and Germany, the principle that we ourselves determine for ourselves the rights of citizenship of our citizens, that we champion them in the full exercise of these rights as against any foreign power that interferes with them, and that in return we hold them to a full accountability for the exercise of these rights in the sole interest of the United States as against any foreign power which claims any allegiance whatsoever from them.

CHAPTER X

JAPAN is indeed a wonderful land. Nothing in history has quite paralleled her rise during the last fifty years. Her progress has been remarkable alike in war, in industry, in statesmanship, in science. Her admirals and generals, her statesmen and administrators, have accomplished feats with which only the greatest feats of the picked men of corresponding position in Europe and the two Americas during the same time can be compared—and in order to match in the aggregate these great men of a single island nation, more than one of the countries of the Occident must be drawn on.

Among the Japanese administrators of high note is Count Terauchi, and among Japan's many feats of consequence is her administration of Korea. Count Terauchi is the Governor-General of Korea—Chosen, as the Japanese term it—and he has just compiled and published at Seoul (Keijo) a report on the "Reform and Progress in Chosen" for the years 1912-1913. It is in English; and no book of the kind recently issued is better worth the study of statesmen and of scholars interested in every kind of social reform. Moreover, its study is of capital consequence from the standpoint of those who recognize the importance of bringing home to our people the knowledge of the admirable and masterly achievements of the Japanese in the difficult task of colonial administration.

In its essence the work that has been done in Korea under Count Terauchi is like that done under similar conditions by the chief colonial administrators of the United States, England, France and Germany. Korea as an independent nation could not keep order at home and was powerless to strike an effective blow on her own behalf when assailed from abroad. She had been dominated by Russia, so that all obligations of foreign powers to help her keep her independence had lapsed long before the outbreak of the Russo-Japanese war; and under the circumstances her subsequent domination, and, in 1910, her final annexation by Japan was inevitable. The Japanese have restored and enforced order, built roads and railways, carried out great engineering works, introduced modern sanitation, introduced a modern school system and doubled the commerce and the agricultural output, substantially as the most advanced nations of Europe and America have done under like conditions.

All of these matters and many others—such as the administration of justice, the founding of industrial and agricultural banks, the establishment of government experiment farms, the revenues, the government monopoly in ginseng and salt manufacture, the charitable institutions—are treated in full in the volume before me, and in addition to the letter-press there are numerous first-rate photographs.

One of the interesting touches in the book is that describing the way tourist parties of Koreans are formed to visit Japan and study its advanced systems of agriculture, industry and education. The visits are generally timed so as to see a national or some local industrial exhibition. Tourist parties of Korean countrymen often visit the capital, Keijo, with a similar educational purpose. The Japanese are endeavoring to introduce their language, culture and industry into the country, and are taking very practical steps to introduce the Koreans to the high modern civilization of the new rulers of the land.

One of the great works done by the Japanese in Korea has been in reforesting the country. This has been carried on in the most scientific manner—a manner, I regret to say, smacking more of German efficiency than of any large-scale forestry process in our own country. Over five million trees have been planted, the best

European models serving as examples. Arbor Day has been instituted, and is celebrated just as in various states of the American Union, the school children being especially interested. But, with their usual wisdom and far-sighted, practical good sense, the Japanese officials not only adopt anything foreign that may be useful, but also develop anything native that can be made more useful. The provincial governments have devoted much energy to the revival of an ancient Korean guild, the Songkei, which had for its object the promoting of interest in pine forests. All kinds of interesting contrasts between the very old and the very new are brought out incidentally; as, for example, the trouble of the health authorities with the Korean "grave geomancers," and their efforts to substitute the hygienic practice of cremation for burial.

An excellent instance of the kind of foresight which ought to be imitated in the United States is the action taken in protecting whales. Whaling on the east coast of Korea is very lucrative; but the whales have been over-fished; and the government has now established a close season, has prohibited all whaling outside certain areas, has limited the number of vessels that can be employed, and has forbidden the capture of mother whales accompanied by their young.

All this of which I speak is only to indicate

what the volume tells of Japanese administration
in Korea. To describe it fully, and to comment
on it with knowledge, would need an expert. I
am writing as the merest layman. My purpose
is simply to call attention to the matter. It is to
be wished that the Japanese society would repub-
lish the volume and make it generally accessible.

But the chief lesson it teaches is one which by
rights our people ought already to know well.
Japan is as advanced and civilized a power as the
United States or any power in Europe. She has
as much to teach us as we have to teach her.
In true patriotism—for there is no such thing as
true patriotism that does not include eager and
foresighted desire to make one's country able to
defend herself against foreign attack—Japan is
far ahead of us. There is no nation in the world
more worthy of admiration and respect. There
is no nation in the world with which it is more
important that the United States should be on
terms of cordial friendship and absolutely equal
mutuality of respect.

Japan's whole sea-front, and her entire home
maritime interest, bear on the Pacific; and of the
other great nations of the earth the United
States has the greatest proportion of her sea-
front on, and the greatest proportion of her interest in, the Pacific. But there is not the slightest real or necessary conflict of interests between

Japan and the United States in the Pacific. When compared with each other, the interest of Japan is overwhelmingly Asiatic, that of the United States overwhelmingly American. Relatively to each other, one is dominant in Asia, the other in North America. Neither has any desire, nor any excuse for desiring, to acquire territory on the other's continent. With the exception of the Philippines, which the present Administration has definitely committed the United States to abandon in the near future, the insular possessions of each clearly appertain to their respective continents; Hawaii is almost as much American as Formosa is Asiatic. Neither has any interest in the Pacific Ocean itself except to keep it as a broad highway open to all. Each is a good customer of the other. Each has something to learn from and something to teach the other. Each has every interest in preserving the friendship of the other. For either to incur the hostility of the other would in the end turn out to be a folly, a calamity unrelieved by the slightest benefit. It may almost be said that the farsightedness and intelligence of any citizen of either country can largely be measured by the friendly respect he feels and shows for the other country. Neither territorially, nor in commercial interest, nor in international rivalry, is there any excuse for clashing. The two nations should for all time work hand in hand.

The Japanese statesmen and leaders of thought are doing all they can to keep on the best possible footing with the United States. Although Japan was engaged in war she did everything in her power to make the California-Panama Exposition a success. Her exhibit was of peculiar importance, because the exhibits of most of the other great powers were greatly interfered with by the war.

Every consideration, permanent and temporary, makes the continuance of a good understanding between the two nations of capital importance. It is a grave offence against the United States for any man, by word or deed, to jeopardize this good understanding. To do so by the act of a state legislature is even graver. Any action by a state legislature touching on the rights of foreigners of any other nation should be taken with extreme caution, or it may cause serious mischief. Such action cannot possibly have good effect on the only matter that can ever cause trouble between Japan and the United States—the settlement in mass by individuals of either nation within the limits of the other nation. Such immigration is the only thing that can ever cause trouble between these two peoples; and if permitted it is absolutely certain that the trouble will be caused. It can be dealt with only by the two national governments themselves.

All true friends of international good-will between the two countries, all men who recognize that good-will for the other should be a prime feature of the foreign policy of each, will face this fact and deal with it. The treatment of it should be on an absolutely reciprocal basis. Exactly the same types and classes should be admitted and excluded, in one country as in the other. Students, travelers, men engaged in international business, sojourners for scholarship, health or pleasure, of either country ought to be welcomed in the other; and not thus to welcome them indicates defective civilization in the should-be hosts. But it is essentially to the interest of both that neither should admit the workers—industrial or agricultural or engaged in small trade—from the other, for neither country is yet ready to admit such settlement in mass, and nothing but grave harm can come from permitting it.

Instead of ignoring this fact, it would be better frankly to acknowledge and recognize it. It does not in any way imply any inferiority in either nation to the other; it merely connotes the acceptance of the truth that in international as in private affairs, it is well not to hurry matters that if unhurried will in the end come out all right. The astounding thing, the thing unprecedented in all history, is that two civilized peoples whose civilizations had developed for thousands of years on almost wholly independent lines, should within half a century grow so close together. Fifty years ago there was no intellectual or social community at all between the two nations. Nowadays, the man of broad cultivation, whether in statesmanship, science, art or philosophy, who dwells in one country, is as much at home in the other as is a Russian in England, or a Spaniard in the United States, or an Italian in Sweden; the men of this type, whether Japanese or Europeans, or North or South Americans, are knit together in a kind of freemasonry of social and intellectual taste.

It is quite impossible that a movement like this shall be as rapid throughout all the classes of society as among the selected few. It has taken many centuries for Europeans to achieve a common standard such as to permit of the free immigration of the workers of one nation into another nation, and there is small cause for wonder in the fact that a few decades have been insufficient to bring it about between Japan and the American and Australian commonwealths. Japan would not, and could not, at this time afford to admit into competition with her own people masses of immigrants, industrial or agricultural workers, or miners or small tradesmen, from the United States. It would be equally unwise for the United States to admit similar groups from Japan. This does not mean that either side is inferior; it means that they are different.

Three or four centuries ago exactly the same thing was true as between and among the European countries from which the ancestors of the mixed people of the United States came. At that time English mobs killed and drove out Flemish and French workingmen; Scotchmen would not tolerate the presence of Englishmen even in time of peace; Germans and Scandinavians met on terms of intimacy only when they fought one another; and Russians as immigrants in western Europe were quite as unthinkable as Tartars. Normally, no one of these nations would then have tolerated any immigration of the people of any other. Yet they were all of practically the same racial blood, and in essentials of the same ancestral culture, that of Græco-Roman Christianity. And their descendants not only now live side by side in the United States, but have merged into one people. What would have been ruinous even to attempt four centuries ago now seems entirely natural because it has gone on so slowly. To try to force the process with unnatural speed would have insured disaster, even af-

ter the upper classes of the countries concerned
had already begun to mingle on a footing of
equality.

Surely these obvious historical facts have their
lesson for Japanese and American statesmen to-
day. Three centuries ago the students, the
writers, the educated and cultivated men in England and France (countries of equal, and practically the same, civilization) associated less in-
timately than the like men of America and Japan
do to-day, and any attempt at immigration of
the workers of one country into the other would
have been met by immediate rioting. Time, and
time alone, rendered possible the constantly
closer association of the peoples. Time must be
given the same chance now, in order to secure a
lasting and firmly based friendship between the
Japanese and the English-speaking peoples of
America and Australia.

The volume which has served as a text for this
article is only one additional proof of the way
in which Japan has modernized and brought
abreast of all modern needs her high and ancient
civilization. She is already playing a very great
part in the civilized world. She will play a still
greater part in the future. It may well be that
she will prove the regenerator of all eastern
Asia. She and the United States have great interests on and in the Pacific. These interests in

no way conflict. They can be served to best purpose for each nation by the heartiest and most friendly coöperation between them on a footing of absolute equality. There is but one real chance of friction. This should be eliminated, not by pretending to ignore facts, but by facing them with good-natured and courteous wisdom—for, as Emerson somewhere says, "in the long run the most unpleasant truth is a safer traveling companion than the most agreeable falsehood." Each country should receive exactly the rights which it grants. Travelers, scholars, men engaged in international business, all sojourners for health, pleasure and study, should be heartily welcomed in both countries. From neither country should there be any emigration of workers of any kind to, or any settlement in mass in, the other country.

CHAPTER XI

IN 1903 a shameless and sordid attempt was made by the then dictator of Colombia and his subordinate fellow-politicians at Bogotá to force the United States by scandalously improper tactics to pay a vastly larger sum for the privilege of building the Panama Canal than had been agreed upon in a solemn treaty. As President of the United States I resisted this attempt, and prevented the United States from being blackmailed. Had I not successfully resisted the attempt, the Panama Canal would not now be built, and would probably never have been built. The attempt was blackmail then; and to yield to it now is to yield to blackmail.

Yet the present Administration now proposes to pay Colombia twenty-five million dollars, and to make what is practically an apology for our conduct in acquiring the right to build the canal. Apparently this is done on the theory of soothing the would-be blackmailers and making them forget the mortification caused them by the failure of their initial attempt to hold up the United States.

In brief, the facts in the case were as follows:

A private French company had attempted to build a canal across the Isthmus of Panama, and had failed after making only a beginning of the work. Various propositions for a trans-Isthmian canal to be undertaken by the United States Government had been made. One of these was to cross the Isthmus at Darien. Another was a proposition to go through Nicaragua. Different companies had been organized in the United States to back these different propositions. One of these companies had ex-Senator Warner Miller at its head. The then Senator Platt of New York was much interested in another company. Congress only considered seriously, however, the Panama and Nicaragua routes, and was in much doubt between them. A commission of experts appointed by the President for that purpose had reported that if we could buy the rights of the French canal company for $40,000,000 we ought to take the Panama route, but that otherwise we should take the Nicaragua route. It was at that time well and widely known that the sum of $10,000,000 (aside from a small yearly payment to be made on different grounds) was all that we would pay or would be asked to pay Colombia, and Colombia herself had advertised this fact.

The recommendation, therefore, was in effect that we should go by Panama if we could acquire our rights by paying $40,000,000 to the French and $10,000,000 to the Colombians.

The French had real rights. They had spent hundreds of millions of dollars, and although much of this had been wasted, yet we received at least $40,000,000 worth of property and of accomplished work for the $40,000,000 we agreed to pay them. Colombia had no rights that were not of the most shadowy and unsubstantial kind; and even these shadowy rights existed only because of the action of the United States. She had done nothing whatever except to misgovern the Isthmus for fifty years. During these fifty years her possession of the Isthmus as against foreign powers had been maintained solely by the guarantee and the potential strength of the United States. The only effective policing of the Isthmus during those fifty years had been done by the United States on the frequent occasions when it was forced to land marines and sailors for that purpose. Ten million dollars represented the very outside limit which generosity could fix as a payment to Colombia for rights which she was impotent to maintain save by our assistance and protection, and for an opportunity which she was utterly unable herself to develop. Nobody of any consequence in the United States, within or without Congress, would at that time for one moment have considered agreeing to pay $25,000,000 or any sum remotely approaching it.

If Colombia had at that time announced any such demand, unquestionably the Congress of the United States would have directed the Executive to take the Nicaragua route. The exact language of Congress in its Act providing for the construction of the canal, approved June 28, 1902, was that if "the President be unable to obtain for the United States a satisfactory title to the property of the New Panama Canal Company and the control of the necessary territory of the Republic of Colombia within a reasonable time and upon reasonable terms, then the President" should endeavor to provide for a canal by the Nicaragua route.

This language defined with exactness and precision what was to be done, and what as a matter of fact I actually did. I was directed to take the Nicaragua route, but only if within a reasonable time I could not obtain control of the necessary territory of the Republic of Colombia upon reasonable terms; the direction being explicit that if I could not thus get the control within a reasonable time and upon reasonable terms I must go to Nicaragua. Colombia showed by its actions that it was thoroughly acquainted with this fact, and eagerly demanded and entered into a treaty with the United States, the Hay-Herran treaty, under which $10,000,000 was the price stipulated to be paid in exchange for our acquiring the right to the zone on which to build the canal.

Let it be remembered that this $10,000,000 was the price stipulated by Colombia herself as payment to those in possession of the Isthmus, and it was the price we actually did pay to those who actually were in possession of the Isthmus. The only difference was that, thanks to the most just and proper revolution which freed Panama from the intolerable oppression and wrongdoing of Colombia, we were able to give this $10,000,-000 to the men who themselves dwelt on the Isthmus, instead of to alien taskmasters and oppressors of theirs.

The proposal now is that after having paid $10,000,000 to the rightful owners of the Isthmus we shall in addition pay $25,000,000 to their former taskmasters and oppressors; a sum two and a half times what these tricky oppressors originally asked, a sum which is to be paid to them merely because they failed in carrying to successful completion what must truthfully be characterized as a bit of international villainy as wicked as it was preposterous. In point of good sense and sound morality, the proposal is exactly on a par with paying a discomfited burglar a heavy sum for the damage done his feelings by detecting him and expelling him from the house.

Our people should also remember that what we were paying for was the right to expend our own money and our own labor to do a piece of work which if left undone would render the Isthmus of Panama utterly valueless. If we had gone to Nicaragua, or had undertaken to build a canal anywhere else across the Isthmus, then the right which Colombia was so eager to sell for $10,000,000 would not have been worth ten cents. The whole value was created by our prospective action; and this action was to be taken wholly at our own expense and without making Colombia or any one else pay a dollar, and this although no power would benefit more by the canal than Colombia, as it would give her waterway communication by a short and almost direct route between her Caribbean and Pacific ports.

The people of the United States should remember that the United States paid $50,000,000 to Panama and the French company for every real right of every sort or description which existed on the Isthmus. There would have been no value even to these rights unless for the action that the United States then intended to take, and has since actually taken. The property of the French company would not have been worth any more than any other scrap heap save for our subsequent action, and the right to cross the Isthmus of Panama would have been valueless to Colombia or to any other nation or body of men if we had failed to build a canal across it and had built one somewhere else. The whole value then and now of any right upon that Isthmus depended upon the fact that we then intended to spend and now have spent in building the canal some $375,-000,000.

The proposal of Mr. Wilson's Administration is that, having given to the Isthmus of Panama its whole present value by the expenditure of $375,000,000, we shall now pay $25,000,000 additional to the power that did its best to prevent the Isthmus from having any value by treacherously depriving us of the right to build the canal at all, or to spend a dollar on the Isthmus. If Colombia's action had been successful, the Isthmus would now be worthless; and yet the present Administration actually proposes to pay her $25,000,000 so as to atone to her for our not having permitted her to follow a course of conduct which would have prevented the Isthmus from being worth twenty-five cents.

Most people, when we began the building of the canal, believed that we would fail. There were plenty of such skeptics in this country, and a much larger number abroad. If the American engineers had not been successful, if the American people had not backed them with money, and if the Government had not started the work on a basis of absolutely non-partisan efficiency, there would exist nothing for which to pay any sum at the present moment. This proposed treaty is a proposal to pay blackmail to that Government which sought in vain to forbid us to use our national efficiency in the interest of the world at large.

I cannot too strongly emphasize the fact that Panama represented to Colombia an asset of no value whatsoever save such as might accrue from the action which we were ready to undertake at great expense. She enjoyed this asset at all only because of our guaranteeing her against having it taken away from her by any foreign power. We had never guaranteed her against a movement for independence on the Isthmus, or against action on our own part if she misbehaved herself. Presidents and secretaries of state had repeatedly given the true interpretation of the obligations to New Granada (the South American republic which then included the present Republic of Colombia) by the treaty of 1846. In 1856 Secretary Cass officially stated the position of the Government as follows:

Sovereignty has its duties as well as its rights, and none of these local governments (on the Isthmus) would be permitted in a spirit of Eastern isolation to close the gates of intercourse on the great highways of the world, and justify the act by the pretension that these avenues of trade and travel belong to them and that they choose to shut them, or what is almost equivalent, to encumber them with such unjust relations as would prevent their general use.

Seven years later Secretary Seward in different communications explicitly stated that the United States had not undertaken any duty in connection with "any question of internal revolution in the state of Panama" but merely "to protect the transit trade across the Isthmus against invasion of either domestic or foreign disturbers;" and that the United States had not "become bound to take sides in the domestic broils of New Granada" but merely to protect New Granada "as against other and foreign governments." In the final portion of my message to Congress of December 7, 1903, and in my special message to Congress of January 4, 1904, I enumerated a partial list of revolutions, insurrections, disturbances and other outbreaks that had occurred on the Isthmus of Panama during the fifty-three years preceding the negotiation of our treaty with the Republic of Panama itself. These revolutions, unsuccessful rebellions and other outbreaks numbered just fifty-three during these fifty-three years.

313

In detail they are as follows:

May 22, 1850.—Outbreak; two Americans killed. War vessel demanded to quell outbreak.

October, 1850.—Revolutionary plot to bring about independence of the Isthmus.

July 22, 1851.—Revolution in four southern provinces.

November 14, 1851.—Outbreak at Chagres. Man-of-war requested for Chagres.

June 27, 1853.—Insurrection at Bogotá and consequent disturbance on Isthmus. War vessel demanded.

May 23, 1854.—Political disturbances. War vessel requested.

June 28, 1854.—Attempted revolution.

October 24, 1854.—Independence of Isthmus demanded by provincial legislature.

April, 1856.—Riot and massacre of Americans.

May 4, 1856.—Riot.

May 18, 1856.—Riot.

June 3, 1856.—Riot.

October 2, 1856.—Conflict between two native parties. United States forces landed.

December 18, 1858.—Attempted secession of Panama.

April, 1859.—Riots.

September, 1860.—Outbreaks.

October 4, 1860.—Landing of United States forces in consequence.

May 23, 1861.—Intervention of the United States forces required by intendente.

October 2, 1861.—Insurrection and civil war.

April 4, 1862.—Measures to prevent rebels crossing Isthmus.

June 13, 1862.—Mosquera's troops refused admittance to Panama.

March, 1865.—Revolution, and United States troops landed.

August, 1865.—Riots; unsuccessful attempt to invade Panama.

March, 1866.—Unsuccessful revolution.

April, 1867.—Attempt to overthrow Government.

August, 1867.—Attempt at revolution.

July 5, 1868.—Revolution; provisional government inaugurated.

August 29, 1868.—Revolution; provisional government overthrown.

April, 1871.—Revolution; followed apparently by counter revolution.

April, 1873.—Revolution and civil war which lasted to October, 1875.

August, 1876.—Civil war which lasted until April, 1877.

July, 1878.—Rebellion.

December, 1878.—Revolt.

April, 1879.—Revolution.

June, 1879.—Revolution.

March, 1883.—Riot.

May, 1883.—Riot.

June, 1884.—Revolutionary attempt.

December, 1884.—Revolutionary attempt.

January, 1885.—Revolutionary disturbances.

March, 1885.—Revolution.

April, 1887.—Disturbance on Panama Railroad.

November, 1887.—Disturbance on line of canal.

January, 1889.—Riot.

January, 1895.—Revolution which lasted until April.

March, 1895.—Incendiary attempt.

October, 1899.—Revolution.

February, 1900, to July, 1900.—Revolution.

January, 1901.—Revolution.

July, 1901.—Revolutionary disturbances.

September, 1901.—City of Colon taken by rebels.

March, 1902.—Revolutionary disturbances.

July, 1902.—Revolution.

Colombia had shown herself utterly incapable of keeping order on the Isthmus. Only the active interference of the United States had enabled her to preserve so much as a semblance of sovereignty. In 1856, in 1860, and in 1873, in

1885, in 1901, and in 1902, sailors and marines from United States warships were forced to land in order to protect life and property and to see that the transit across the Isthmus was kept open. In 1861, in 1862, in 1885, and in 1900, the Colombia Government asked for the landing of troops by the United States Government to protect its interests and to maintain order on the Isthmus. Immediately after the revolution by which Panama obtained its independence in 1903, the Colombian Government made another request to land troops to preserve Colombian sovereignty.

This request was made through General Reyes, afterward President of the republic. President Marroquin in making the request offered if we would grant it, to "approve by decree" the ratification of the Hay-Herran canal treaty as signed, acting thus "by virtue of vested constitutional authority," or if the Government of the United States preferred, to call an extra session of Congress "with new and friendly members" to approve the treaty.

This dispatch has an especial interest. In the first place, it requested the United States to restore order and secure Colombia supremacy on the very Isthmus from which the Colombian Government had just decided to bar us by preventing the construction of the canal. In the second place, by the offer made it showed that the constitutional objections which had been urged against ratifying the treaty were obviously not made in good faith, and that the Government which made the treaty really had absolute control over its ratification, but chose to exercise that control adversely to us. As a matter of fact, whatever duty we had in the peninsula was to the Panamanians and not to the Colombians at all. As John Hay put it, "the covenant ran with the land." Our original treaty was with the United States of New Granada. This body suffered various changes, various portions splitting off and sometimes rejoining, and finally the Republic of Colombia succeeded to most of it. We, however, recognized whatever power was in lawful possession of the Isthmus, as the successor of the one with which we had made the treaty.

In the constitutions of 1858 and 1861, Panama explicitly reserved the right to secede from the confederation and to nullify any act inconsistent with its own "autonomy." Colombia later published a new constitution by Executive Decree, reducing Panama to the condition of a crown colony; but Panama never accepted this action as proper, and when in 1903 it set up an independent government by unanimous action of her citizens, they were merely reasserting the constitutional and legal rights which they had never relinquished.

318

As Secretary Root wrote the Colombian Minister in 1906, our action in recognizing the independence of Panama was merely "a recognition of the just rights of the people of Panama." On technical grounds Panama's case was clear, Colombia had no case whatever, and the United States was bound to act as she did act. Morally, of course, there is no question whatever that Panama's action was imperatively demanded and that the United States would have been guilty of culpable misconduct toward an oppressed people if she had failed to support Panama.

I wish to emphasize the nature of the Colombian Government at the time when Panama declared her independence. It was a pure dictatorship. This was no concern of ours; for I hold it is not our affair to say to another nation what kind of government it shall have save in so far as the rights of our own citizens or of our own Government are concerned. The then President, Mr. Marroquin, had been elected as vicepresident. Soon after his inauguration by a *coup d'état* he unseated the President and put him in prison. He then announced that under the Constitution, in the absence of the President, the vice-president wielded all the executive powers. Accordingly he exercised them.

In a few months the absence of the President became permanent, for he opportunely died in prison, and Mr. Marroquin continued to act as President. He declined to call Congress together for a period in the neighborhood of five years, and announced that under the Constitution in the absence of Congress he possessed all the legislative functions. Accordingly he exercised these also. He was careful to explain that his course was entirely "constitutional" and that it was in accordance with the mandate of the Constitution that he who had been elected vice-president exercised all the functions both of President and of Congress. As a matter of fact, while he did not permit any elections to take place for a number of years, yet his power was so absolute that he elected whomever he wished as soon as the election did take place; as already related, he notified me, when it became to his interest to do so, that he would elect a Congress with a guarantee that it would perform what he desired in case I would be satisfied therewith.

Having this absolute power not only to initiate but to ratify and carry out any treaty, he, through Mr. Herran, negotiated with Mr. Hay a treaty with the United States Government which conceded us the right to take the Panama Canal zone and build the canal for the sum of $10,000,000. (I disregard the minor details of the treaty.) He was exceedingly anxious to negotiate this treaty because it was a matter vital to Panama, and therefore of concern to the absentee owners of Panama; for if the treaty were not negotiated it was certain that the United States would go to Nicaragua. Having this treaty, and having received from the French company the assurance that they would sell us that property for $40,000,000, we selected the Panama route. As soon as we had done this Mr. Marroquin and his associates concluded that we were hopelessly committed, and that it was safe for him to repudiate his promise and try to extort more money. Under its original contract the time during which the French company had to complete the canal lapsed the following year. Colombia had granted an extension of some years; but Mr. Marroquin and his associates now announced that this extension of time, which they had themselves given, was unconstitutional.

Again I wish to call attention to the solemn farce, the contemptible farce, of these men appealing to the Constitution as a make-believe fetish, when the entire governmental power of the nation was vested at the moment in an irresponsible dictator who had never been elected to the office of President at all, who refused to summon Congress, and who yet exercised all its powers in the absence of Congress. It was dishonest on their part thus to talk of the Constitution, and it is an act of unspeakable silliness for any of our people to take that talk seriously.

Accordingly Marroquin summoned a Congress, the only one that had been held under his Administration. It was an absolutely obsequious body. It did not attempt to pass a law, or do anything but repudiate the proposed treaty. Its committee, in the report which the Congress adopted, announced the real object of their action when it said that the following year the rights of the French company would lapse and Colombia would take possession of the French company's belongings, and then would be in a "more advantageous" position to negotiate with the United States. In other words, they expected to combine piracy with blackmail, and to take possession of the French company's belongings and get from us the $40,000,000 we were to pay the French. Of course France would never have allowed this, and if I had acted with the pliant submission to Colombia's demand which the present Administration is at this moment showing, we would have had on the Isthmus France instead of Colombia, and the difficulty and danger of the whole problem would have been infinitely increased.

The Congress as well as the Dictator had ample warning of all the dangers they by their action were inviting. Representatives from Panama warned the Colombian Administration that Panama would revolt if the treaty was rejected; and our Department of State in the gravest manner called their attention to the serious situation their conduct would create.

Our Minister, Mr. Beaupré, an admirable public servant, who—unlike his successor who negotiated the preposterous treaty now before the Senate—conceived himself under obligation faithfully to represent the interests of the American people, encountered great difficulties while endeavoring to perform his duties at this time. The State Department's messages to him were intercepted, and in several cases not delivered, as shown in his cable to Hay of August 6, 1903; and he was directed by the Department of State to protest against such interference with his official communications. Mr. Beaupré showed conclusively in his correspondence that the delay in dealing with the Panama Canal treaty by Colombia was for the purpose of wringing money from either the French company or the United States, or both.

For example, in his message of June 10, 1903, he stated that the local agent of the Panama Canal Company had informed him that he had received an official note from the Colombian Government stating that the treaty would be rejected unless the French company paid Colombia

$10,000,000. This shows that the Colombian Government then expected only twenty millions all told—ten legitimately from us and ten as an extorted bribe from the unfortunate French company. President Wilson now proposes to give five millions extra, apparently to soothe the feelings of those who failed to extort a smaller sum by scandalously improper methods.

In his message of July 21, Minister Beaupré reported that the Colombian Government had sounded both Germany and England to see if they could not be persuaded to construct, or aid in the construction of, the canal in place of the United States. The Government of Colombia, therefore, not only sought to blackmail us and to blackmail the French company, but endeavored to put one of the great Old World powers on the Isthmus in possession of the canal. And because the then Administration refused to submit to such infamy on the part of Colombia, the present Administration actually proposes to pay the wrongdoer $25,000,000 of blackmail.

There are in every great country a few men whose mental or moral make-up is such that they always try to smirch their own people, and sometimes go to the length of moral treason in the effort to discredit their own national government. A campaign of mendacity was started against this treaty from the outset by certain public men and certain newspapers. One of the favorite assertions of these men and newspapers was that the United States Government had in some way or other instigated, and through its agents been privy to, the revolutionary movement on the Isthmus. The statement is a deliberate falsehood, and every man who makes it knows that it is a falsehood. Mr. H. A. Gudger, late Chief Judge of the Department of Panama, was consul in Panama at the time, and had been consul for six years previously. It was impossible for any such encouragement or aid by the United States Government of the revolutionary movement to have occurred without his knowledge, and he has explicitly stated that he did not know of any such encouragement.

Mr. Hay, on behalf of the State Department, made an exactly similar statement to me at the same time. I repeated the statement in my message to Congress. The simple truth, as everybody with any knowledge knew at the time, was that the Isthmus was seething with revolution, and that a revolution was certain to occur if the treaty were rejected. Minister Beaupré notified us that the Panama delegates in the Congress during the debates about the treaty, had informed the Congress explicitly that such would be the case. The newspapers of the United States repeatedly published news from Panama stating that such revolutions were impending. Quotations from the daily papers could be multiplied to prove this. It is only necessary to refer to the Washington *Post* of August 31 and of September 1, the New York *Herald* of September 10, the New York *Times* of September 13, the New York *Herald* of October 26, the Washington *Post* of October 29, the New York *Herald* of October 30 and of November 2; all of the year 1903.

In my special message to Congress of January 4, 1904, I described the report made to me at the request of Lieutenant-General Young by Captain Humphrey and Lieutenant Murphy of the Army, who in the course of a visit which on their own initiative (and without my knowledge) they had made to Panama, had discovered that various revolutionary movements were being inaugurated, and that a revolution would certainly occur, possibly immediately after the closing of the Colombian Congress at the end of October, but probably not before early November. This definitely localized the probability of the revolution taking place somewhere during the last ten days of October, or the first week in November. This was known on the Isthmus. It was known to the American newspapers. It was also known at Bogotá, where measures were taken to meet the situation. If it had not been known to the President and to the Secretary of

State, they would have shown themselves culpably unfit for their positions.

After my interview with the army officers named, on October 16 I directed the Navy Department to issue instructions to send ships to the Isthmus so as to protect American interests and the lives of American citizens if a revolutionary outbreak should occur. Most fortunately the United States steamer *Nashville,* under Commander Hubbard, in consequence of these orders, reached the Isthmus just in time to prevent a bloody massacre of American men, women and children. Troops from Bogotá had already been landed in Colon on November 3, when the revolution broke out on the same day. On November 4, as Commander Hubbard officially reported, his marines were landed, in view of the fact that the American Consul had been notified by the officer commanding the Colombia troops that he intended to open fire on the town of Colon at 2 p. m. and kill every United States citizen in the place. Accordingly various men, women and children took refuge first in the shed of the Panama Railway Company, and then on a German steamer and a Panama Railway steamer which were at the dock. Commander Hubbard showed himself loyal to the best traditions of the American Navy. He brought the *Nashville* close up to the water-front, landed some of his men to garrison the shed of the Panama Railway Company, and although the Colombians outnumbered him ten to one, succeeded in protecting the lives of the American citizens who were menaced. Thanks to the firmness of himself and his men, he so impressed the Colombian commander that next day the latter reëmbarked and withdrew with his troops to Colombia.

So far from there having been too much foresight about the revolution on the part of the American Government, this plain official account by a naval officer of what occurred on November 4 showed that the American Government had, if anything, delayed too long its orders for the movement of American warships to Panama, and that it was only the coolness and gallantry of forty-two marines and sailors in the face of ten times their number of armed foes that prevented the carrying out of the atrocious threat of the Colombian commander. In accordance with our settled principles of conduct we refused to allow the transportation of troops across the Isthmus by either the Colombians or the Panamanians, so as to prevent bloodshed and interference with traffic.

No one connected with this Government had any part in preparing, inciting or encouraging the revolution on the Isthmus of Panama. Save from the reports of our military and naval officers given in full in the message of the President to the Senate, and from the official reports in the Department of State, no one connected with the Government had any previous knowledge of the revolution except such as was accessible to any person of ordinary intelligence who read the newspapers and kept up a current acquaintance with public affairs.

Secretary of State John Hay stated officially at the time:

> The action of the President in the Panama matter is not only in the strictest accordance with the best precedents of our public policy, but it was the only course he could have taken in compliance with our treaty rights and obligations.

I saw at the time very many men, Americans, natives of Panama, and Europeans, all of whom told me that they believed a revolution was impending, and most of whom asked me to take sides one way or the other. The most noted of these men whom I now recollect seeing was Mr. Bunau-Varilla. He, however, did not ask me to take sides one way or the other. To no one of these men did I give any private assurance of any kind one way or the other, referring them simply to my published declarations and acts.

For some reason certain newspapers have repeatedly stated that Mr. Nelson Cromwell was responsible for the revolution. I do not remember whether Mr. Nelson Cromwell was or was not among my callers during the months immediately preceding the revolution. But if he was I certainly did not discuss with him anything connected with the revolution. I do not remember his ever speaking to me about the revolution until after it occurred, and my understanding was, and is, that he had nothing whatever to do with the revolutionary movement which actually took place.

There were, as I have said, various revolutionary movements on foot in the Isthmus, and it was my understanding that there was considerable jealousy among the instigators of these movements as to which one would come off first and would be effective. On information received after the event, I believed then, and believe now, that the revolutionary movement which actually succeeded was the one with which Mr. Bunau-Varilla was connected. He was sent by the Government of Panama as Minister to this country as soon as Panama became an independent state, and he then made no secret of the fact that he had been one of those who had organized the successful revolution; precisely as was the case with the President and other officials of the new republic. Neither did Mr. Bunau-Varilla make any secret of the fact that in acting as he did he was influenced both by his indignation as a resident of Panama at the Colombian treatment of Panama, and also by his indignation as a Frenchman at the Colombian proposal to blackmail the company, and if it would not submit to blackmail, then to confiscate its possessions.

In view of this double attitude of the Colombian Government, an attitude of tyranny toward Panama and of robbery toward the French company, Mr. Bunau-Varilla conceived it to be his duty to do all he could to aid the natives of Panama in throwing off the yoke of Colombia. I believe his attitude was entirely proper, alike from the standpoint of his duty as a resident of Panama, from the standpoint of his duty as a Frenchman to the investors and property holders of the French company, and from the standpoint of his duty as a citizen of the world. But until after the event I had no knowledge of his activities save the knowledge possessed by all intelligent men who had studied the affairs of the Isthmus. I gave him no aid or encouragement. My attitude was open to the knowledge of all; it was set forth with minute accuracy in my message to Congress.

No one connected with the American Government instigated the revolution. I thought that a revolution might very probably occur, but so far from fomenting it I was at the time, as has repeatedly been made public since, preparing my message on the basis that it would be necessary for us openly to take possession of the Isthmus in view of the scandalous conduct of Colombia. However, the fact that the revolution occurred and that the independent republic of Panama was actually seated on the Isthmus, rendered it unnecessary for me to send in this original draft of my message.

Even had I desired to foment a revolution—which I did not—it would have been wholly unnecessary for me to do so. The Isthmus was seething with revolution. Any interference from me would have had to take the shape of preventing a revolution, not of creating one. All the people residing on the Isthmus ardently desired the revolution. The citizens of Panama desired it. Every municipal council, every governmental body the citizens themselves could elect or control, demanded and supported it. When the revolution had occurred, and was successful, and Panama was an independent republic, I certainly did prevent Colombia from carrying on a bloody war on the Isthmus in the effort to overthrow the revolutionists. I certainly did refuse to do what Colombia requested, that is, to use the Army and Navy of the United States against our friends in the interests of the foes who had just been trying to blackmail us. We were solemnly pledged to keep transit across the Isthmus open. Again and again we had landed forces in time of revolutionary disturbance to secure this object. If Colombia had attempted the reconquest of the Isthmus, there would have been a far more bloody contest than ever before on the Isthmus, and the only way by which that contest could have been carried on would have been by using the railroad line and interrupting transit across the Isthmus.

It is therefore perfectly true that I prevented any attempt by Colombia to land troops on the Isthmus and plunge the Isthmus into a long drawn-out and bloody war. What I did then was as plainly my duty as it would be the duty of the President to act in a similar manner now. Panama was an independent republic *de facto* then just as she is now. Colombia had not a particle more right to land troops and conquer her then than she has now. If I was wrong in preventing Colombia from making an effort by a long drawn-out and bloody war to reconquer the Isthmus in 1903, then it would be a wrong to prevent her from making a similar effort at reconquest now.

If Mr. Wilson is sincere in his criticism of me for preventing such a war of reconquest in 1903, it is his duty to permit Colombia unhampered to make the reconquest at this moment; and

to advocate one course of action is not one whit
more immoral than to advocate the other.
This Administration pretends to be for "peace."
My course has brought twelve years of absolute peace to the Isthmus, for the first time
in its history, and any other course would have
plunged it into bloodshed. The Administration
stands for a make-believe peace of cowardice. I
stand for what I then secured: the real and lasting peace of honor and justice.

Among the provisions in the present proposed
treaty with Colombia is the following phrase:

> The Republic of Colombia shall be at lib-
> erty at all times to transport through the
> interoceanic canal its troops, materials of
> war, and ships of war, even in case of war
> between Colombia and another country,
> without paying any charges to the United
> States.

To grant such a right to both Colombia and
Panama was permissible so long as we also insisted on exercising it ourselves, on the grounds
set forth by the then Secretary of State, Mr. Root,
in his note to the British Government of January
16, 1909. In this note Secretary Root took the
ground that the United States had the right to
except from "coming within any schedule of tolls
which might thereafter be established" the ships

of the powers entering into the agreement necessary in order to give title to the land through which the canal was to be built, and to authorize its construction and the necessary jurisdiction or control over it when built. These nations were Panama, Colombia and the United States. Since then the present Administration has surrendered the right so far as the United States is concerned; and yet it proposes to give to the most envenomed opponent of the building of the canal rights to its use which are denied to the power giving the rights. In other words, the Administration says that our people, who built the canal, can give to others rights which they dare not themselves exercise. Such a position is a wicked absurdity.

Moreover, the proposed treaty may be construed under certain conditions to give Colombia the right to use the canal in a war against Panama, and we could only prevent such an outrage by breaking faith. We have already guaranteed the independence of Panama against Colombia by a solemn treaty. The Administration now proposes to guarantee to Colombia the right to use the canal against Panama. The two conflicting guarantees could not both be observed. Doubtless in the event of such conflict the United States would refuse to allow Colombia the rights which the proposed treaty would grant her; and in that case another and far greater grievance would be committed against Colombia; and then some future Administration, if it possessed the present Administration's nervous amiability toward all nations hostile to America, might agree to pay a hundred millions, with a suitable apology, as atonement for the conduct of its predecessor.

It may seem as if I am discussing the future possible actions of American Administrations ironically. I am really discussing them quite seriously. If the proposed treaty is ratified, it will render it quite impossible to consider any treaty as beyond the realm of probability. It had never entered my head that President Wilson could do what he proposes to do in connection with the proposed treaty with Colombia. If we pay $25,000,000 to Colombia now, then there is no reason why we should not at some future time pay her another $100,000,000; or pay Mexico ten times that sum for having taken Texas and California, Arizona and New Mexico; or pay a hundred times that sum to Great Britain because our ancestors deprived her of the thirteen colonies.

The Administration has succeeded in getting Congress to take the position that the United States has no special rights in its own canal. It now proposes by treaty to get Congress to give to the one nation which conspicuously wronged us in connection with that canal special rights which it would deny to ourselves and to all other countries. President Wilson denies that we have the right to exempt our own vessels engaged in peaceful coast commerce from tolls, and yet he now proposes to exempt from tolls the war vessels and transports of Colombia. Three years ago I should have deemed it impossible that two such propositions could have been entertained by the same Administration. Furthermore, the President, through the Secretary of State, has recently stated that "if cordial relations are to be restored to Colombia, they must be restored on a basis that is satisfactory to Colombia." On the contrary, I take the position that the basis should be one of justice and right, and therefore one satisfactory to the honor and dignity of the United States Government and of the American people. The Administration's attitude is precisely as if when a householder has a disagreement with a burglar the effort should be to restore "peace" upon a basis satisfactory to the burglar instead of to the householder. Any burglar will welcome the "peace" which comes if the householder tenders him a large sum of money to atone for the heartlessness of a former occupant of the house in preventing him from getting away with the loose silver.

Mr. Bryan has also stated that Colombia suffered a loss financially, which we ought to make up, when she lost Panama. This represents the doctrine that when one country holds another in subjection and by misgovernment drives it to revolt, the moral and equitable rights are on the side of the tyrant country and not on the country that has declared its independence. If Mr. Bryan is right in his theory, France owes Great Britain an enormous sum of money for its misconduct in assisting the revolted colonies to become the United States of America. Yet the misgovernment of the colonies by Great Britain against which the colonies revolted did not even remotely approach the misgovernment against which Panama revolted; and it would not be more absurd for President Wilson to take the position that France owes Great Britain an enormous sum of money for her conduct in the Revolutionary War than to take the position which is now taken in reference to the payment of this $25,000,000 of sheer blackmail to Colombia.

We have at different times paid sums of money to various nations for the acquisition of territory from them. We have paid money to Russia and to France. We have paid money to Spain. But we have never paid to any nation, not to the most powerful European nation, nor to any American nation, a sum of money equal to the sum which it is now proposed to pay to Colombia in tendering her an apology for having refused to permit her to reconquer a little people whom she had shamelessly oppressed, and for having acquired the right which she sought to deny us, the right to spend hundreds of millions of our own money in constructing a canal in our own interest, in her interest, and in the interest of all the civilized powers of the world.

As Mr. Bonaparte, late Attorney-General, has said:

> By the treaty we promise to pay Colombia, as a compensation for an alleged injury, a much larger sum of money than we paid France for Louisiana, or Mexico for California, or Spain for the Philippines, or Panama for the Canal Zone, or than Great Britain paid us in settlement of the Alabama claims; if we acknowledge that we have so wronged her as as to make it proper for us to buy her forgiveness, it is consistent and appropriate to add to this acknowledgment of wrong an apology, or, in other words, an expression of sorrow; if we have nothing to apologize for, because we have done her no wrong, then it is utterly unworthy of a great nation and a forfeiture of our right to self-respect for us to pay her a red cent.

The proposed treaty is a crime against the United States. It is an attack upon the honor of the United States which if justified would convict the United States of infamy. It is a menace to the future well-being of our people. Either there is or there is not warrant for paying this enormous sum and for making the apology. If there is no warrant for it—and of course not the slightest vestige of warrant exists—then the payment is simply the payment of belated blackmail. If there is warrant for it, then we have no business to be on the Isthmus at all. The payment can only be justified upon the ground that this nation has played the part of a thief, or of a receiver of stolen goods. In such a case it would be a crime to remain on the Isthmus, and it is much worse than an absurdity for the President, who wishes to pay the $25,000,000, to take part in opening the canal; for if the President and the Secretary of State are justified in paying the $25,000,000, it is proof positive that in opening the canal they are in their own opinion engaged in the dedication of stolen goods.

To recapitulate:

1. The land could not have been acquired and the canal could not have been built save by taking precisely and exactly the action which was taken. Unless the nation is prepared heartily to indorse and stand by this action, it has no right to take any pride in anything that has been done on the Isthmus and it has no right to remain on the Isthmus. If there is a moral justification for paying Colombia $25,000,000, then there is no

moral justification for our staying on the Isthmus at all and we should promptly get off. If President Wilson is right in his position, then he has no business to take part in any ceremony connected with opening the canal; on his theory he would be engaged in the dedication of stolen goods.

2. In the words of John Hay, "the covenant ran with the land." Our agreement was with the power which owned the Isthmus of Panama, whether this was New Granada or Colombia or Panama itself. This agreement guaranteed the state that was in control of the Isthmus against interference by foreign powers, but it imposed no responsibility upon us as regards internecine troubles. This was explicitly set forth in statements by Secretaries Cass and Seward, one a Democrat and one a Republican.

As a matter of fact, every action we took was not only open and straightforward, but was rendered absolutely necessary by the misconduct of Colombia. Every action we took was in accordance with the highest principles of national, international, and private morality. The honor of the United States, and the interest not only of the United States but of the world, demanded the building of the canal. The canal could not have been built, it would not now have been begun, had our Government not acted precisely as it did act in 1903. No action ever taken by the Government, in dealing with any foreign power since the days of the Revolution, was more vitally necessary to the well-being of our people, and no action we ever took was taken with a higher regard for the standards of honor, of courage, and of efficiency which should distinguish the attitude of the United States in all its dealings with the rest of the world.

CHAPTER XII

FEAR God and take your own part! This is another way of saying that a nation must have power and will for self-sacrifice and also power and will for self-protection. There must be both unselfishness and self-expression, each to supplement the other, neither wholly good without the other. The nation must be willing to stand disinterestedly for a lofty ideal and yet it must also be able to insist that its own rights be heeded by others. Evil will come if it does not possess the will and the power for unselfish action on behalf of non-utilitarian ideals and also the will and the power for self-mastery, self-control, self-discipline. It must possess those high and stern qualities of soul which will enable it to conquer softness and weakness and timidity and train itself to subordinate momentary pleasure, momentary profit, momentary safety to the larger future.

There is not the slightest use of saying any of this unless we are willing and able to translate our speech into action. National unselfishness

343

and self-sacrifice must be an affair of deeds. To utter lofty sentiments on the subject, to indulge in oratory about it, to write notes about it, and then when the occasion arises not to act in accordance with these sentiments, means moral degradation for the nation. Oratorical insincerity of this kind is nauseating to all honest men. Prolonged indulgence in this kind of emotional insincerity eats into the moral fiber of the people like a corrosive acid.

In the spring of 1910 at Christiania before the Nobel Prize Committee, in acknowledging the receipt of the Nobel Peace Prize, I outlined the plan for securing international peace by means of an international league pledged to put force back of it, the plan which I elaborated in the volume published over a year ago called "America and the World War." But it is a sham and a mockery to advocate such a plan until and unless we in the first place make it evident that when we give a promise we mean to keep it, and in the next place make it evident that we are willing to show the courage, the resolution, the forethought in training and preparation that will enable us to put strength behind our promise. I believe in nationalism as the absolute pre-requisite to internationalism. I believe in patriotism as the absolute pre-requisite to the larger Americanism. I believe in Americanism because unless our people are good Americans first, America can accomplish little or nothing worth accomplishing for the good of the world as a whole.

But none of these objects can be attained by merely talking about them. National unselfishness and self-sacrifice, national self-mastery, and the development of national power, can never be achieved by words alone. National unselfishness —which is another way of saying service rendered to internationalism—can become effective only if the nation is willing to sacrifice something, is willing to face risk and effort and endure hardship in order to render service. The towering idealism of Lincoln's Gettysburg speech and second inaugural counted only because it represented the labor and effort and willingness to face death and eager pride in fighting for ideals, which marked a mighty people led by a mighty leader.

We of America, thanks to the failure of President Wilson's Administration to do its duty, have ourselves failed to serve the cause of internationalism as it was our bounden duty to serve it by standing efficiently for heroic Belgium when, under the lead of their heroic King and Queen, the Belgian people chose to tread the hard path of national suffering and honor rather than the easy path which led through fields of safety and disgrace. The Belgians have walked through

the valley of the shadow rather than prove false
to their ideals. We, rich, prosperous, at ease,
and potentially powerful, have not lifted a finger
to right their wrongs, lest our own safety and
comfort might be jeopardized. This represents
on our part neither readiness for national self-
sacrifice, nor appreciation of true internationalism. It represents the gross selfishness which
puts material well-being above fealty to a high
ideal.

This national selfishness, manifested under the
lead of President Wilson and Secretary Bryan,
was doubly offensive because it was loudly trumpeted as a virtue. One of our besetting sins as a
nation has been to encourage in our public servants, in our speech-making leaders of all kinds,
the preaching of impossible ideals; and then to
treat this as offsetting the fact that in practice
these representatives did not live up to any ideals
whatever. The vital need is that we as a nation
shall say what we mean and shall make our public
servants say what they mean; say it to other nations and say it to us, ourselves. Let us demand
that we and they preach realizable ideals and that
we and they live up to the ideals thus preached.
Let there be no impassable gulf between exuber-
ance of impossible promise and pitiful insuffi-
ciency in quality of possible performance.

Belgium is the test of just how much our public servants and our professional humanitarians mean when they speak in favor of high ideals and lofty international morality. If we clamor for peace without saying that Belgium's wrongs are to be righted before peace can properly come, we are false to every true standard of international morality. If we are not willing to encounter hazard and the risk of loss and the need of effort in order to help Belgium, then we show ourselves unfit to talk about internationalism.

But this is not all. It is odious hypocrisy to do as this Administration has done and refuse to stand for the rights of neutrals when, as in the case of Belgium, these rights were most flagrantly trodden under foot, but when we had no pecuniary interest involved; and yet promptly to clamor on behalf of the rights of neutrals when the exercise of these rights would redound to our own pecuniary advantage. This is to put the body above the soul, the dollar above the man. Moreover, when we thus, in the first and greatest case of the violation of neutral rights, flinched from our duty, we rendered it impossible with effect or indeed with propriety to protest about subsequent and lesser violations of neutral rights. With colossal effrontery Germany, the first and infinitely the greatest offender against humanity and the rights of neutrals, has clamored that we should take steps to "secure neutral rights on the seas," to "establish the freedom of the seas," "to secure the neutralization of the ocean." The pro-Germans on this side of the water have repeated these words with parrot-like fidelity of phrase. In the first place, all offences against the freedom of the seas that have been perpetrated in this war are unimportant compared with the infamy committed on Belgium—save only those offences committed by the German and Austrian submarines, which resulted in the murder of over two thousand non-combatants. In the next place, until the civilized world which is at peace, and more especially the United States, in some way takes effective action to rebuke the violation by Germany of the neutralized territory of Belgium, it is utterly useless to talk about the neutralization of the seas. If the United States had promptly and effectively interfered on behalf of Belgium, it would have been its clear duty to interfere against all the nations who on sea or on shore have subsequently been guilty of violations of international law and of the rules laid down in The Hague Conventions, the Geneva Convention and other similar conventions. But until the first duty has been efficiently performed and the major offender dealt with, it is a proof of cowardice and of bad faith to deal with minor offences.

Let us be true to our democratic ideal, not by the utterance of cheap platitudes, not by windy oratory, but by living our lives in such manner as to show that democracy can be efficient in promoting the public welfare during periods of peace and efficient in securing national freedom in time of war. If a free government cannot organize and maintain armies and navies which can and will fight as well as those of an autocracy or a despotism, it will not survive. We must have a first-class navy and a first-class professional army. We must also secure universal and obligatory military training for all our young men. Our democracy must prove itself effective in making the people healthy, strong and industrially productive, in securing justice, in inspiring intense patriotism and in making every man and woman within our borders realize that if they are not willing at time of need to serve the nation against all comers in war, they are not fit to be citizens of the nation in time of peace. The democratic ideal must be that of subordinating chaos to order, of subordinating the individual to the community, of subordinating individual selfishness to collective self-sacrifice for a lofty ideal, of training every man to realize that no one is entitled to citizenship in a great free commonwealth unless he does his full duty to his neighbor, his full duty in his family life, and his full duty to the nation; and unless he is prepared to do this duty not only in time of peace but also in time of war. It is by no means necessary that a great nation should always stand at the heroic level. But no nation has the root of greatness in it unless in time of need it can rise to the heroic mood.

APPENDIX A

MURDER ON THE HIGH SEAS

On the ninth of May, 1915, two days after the *Lusitania* was torpedoed without warning by a German submarine, I made the following statement in the press:—

THE German submarines have established no effective blockade of the British and French coast lines. They have endeavored to prevent the access of French, British *and neutral* ships to Britain and France by attacks upon them which defy every principle of international law as laid down in innumerable existing treaties, including The Hague Conventions. Many of these attacks have represented pure piracy; and not a few of them have been accompanied by murder on an extended scale. In the case of the *Lusitania* the scale was so vast that the murder became wholesale.

A number of American ships had already been torpedoed in similar fashion. In two cases American lives were lost. When the *Lusitania* sank some twelve hundred non-combatants, men, women and children, were drowned, and more than a hundred of these were Americans. Centuries have passed since any war vessel of a civilized power has shown such ruthless brutality toward non-combatants, and especially toward women and children. The Moslem pirates of the Barbary Coast behaved at times in similar fashion, until the civilized nations joined in suppressing them; and the other pirates who were outcasts from among these civilized nations also at one time perpetrated similar deeds, until they were sunk or hung. But none of these old-time pirates committed murder on so vast a scale as in the case of the *Lusitania*.

The day after the tragedy the newspapers reported in one column that in Queenstown there lay by the score the bodies of women and children, some of the dead women still clasping the bodies of the little children they held in their arms when death overwhelmed them. In another column they reported the glee expressed by the Berlin journals at this "great victory of German naval policy." It was a victory over the defenceless and the unoffending, and its signs and trophies were the bodies of the murdered women and children.

Our treaties with Prussia in 1785, 1799, and 1828, still in force in this regard, provide that if one of the contracting parties should be at war with any other power the free intercourse and commerce of the subjects or citizens of the party remaining neutral with the belligerent powers shall not be interrupted. Germany has treated this treaty as she has treated other scraps of paper.

But the offence goes far deeper than this. The action of the German submarines in the cases cited can be justified only by a plea which would likewise justify the wholesale poisoning of wells in the path of a hostile army, or the shipping of infected rags into the cities of a hostile country; a plea which would justify the torture of prisoners and the reduction of captured women to the slavery of concubinage. Those who advance such a plea will accept but one counter plea—strength, the strength and courage of the just man armed.

When those who guide the military policy of a state hold up to the soldiers of their army the Huns, and the terror once caused by the Huns, for their imitation, they thereby render themselves responsible for any Hunnish deed which may follow. The destruction of cities like Louvain and Dinant, the scientific vivisection of Belgium as a warning to other nations, the hideous wrongdoing to civilians, men, women and children in Belgium and northern France, in order thereby to terrorize the civilian population—all these deeds, and those like them, done on the land, have now been paralleled by what has happened on the sea.

In the teeth of these things, we earn as a nation measureless scorn and contempt if we follow the lead of those who exalt peace above righteousness, if we heed the voices of those feeble folk who bleat to high heaven that there is peace when there is no peace. For many months our government has preserved between right and wrong a neutrality which would have excited the emulous admiration of Pontius Pilate—the arch-typical neutral of all time. We have urged as a justification for failing to do our duty in Mexico that to do so would benefit American dollars. Are we now to change faces and advance the supreme interest of American dollars as a justification for continuance in the refusal to do the duty imposed on us in connection with the world war?

Unless we act with immediate decision and vigor we shall have failed in the duty demanded by humanity at large, and demanded even more clearly by the self-respect of the American Republic."

We did not act with immediate decision and vigor. We did not act at all. The President immediately after the sinking made a speech in which occurred his sentence about our "being too proud to fight." This was accepted, very properly, by foreign nations as the statement of our official head that we ranked in point of national spirit and power with China. I then published the following interview:

"I think that China is entitled to draw all the comfort she can from this statement, and it would be well for the United States to ponder seriously what the effect upon China has been of managing her foreign affairs during the last fifteen years on the theory thus enunciated.

"If the United States is satisfied with occupying some time in the future the precise international position that China now occupies, then the United States can afford to act on this theory. But it cannot so act if it desires to regain the position won for it under Washington and by the men who in the days of Abraham Lincoln wore the blue under Grant and the gray under Lee.

"I very earnestly hope that the President will act promptly. The proper time for deliberation was prior to sending his message that our Government would hold Germany to a 'strict accountability' if it did the things which it has now actually done.

"The 150 babies drowned on the *Lusitania,* the hundreds of women drowned with them—scores of these women and children being Americans— and the American ship, the *Gulflight,* which was torpedoed, offer an eloquent commentary on the actual working of the theory that it is not necessary to assert rights and that a policy of blood

354

and iron can safely be met by a policy of milk and water.

"I see it stated in the dispatches from Washington that Germany now offers to stop the practice of murder on the high seas, committed in violation of the neutral rights she is pledged to preserve, if we will now abandon further neutral rights, which by her treaty she has solemnly pledged herself to see that we exercise without molestation.

"Such a proposal is not even entitled to an answer. The manufacture and shipments of arms and ammunition to any belligerent is moral or immoral, according to the use to which the arms and munitions are to be put. If they are to be used to prevent the redress of hideous wrongs inflicted on Belgium then it is immoral to ship them. If they are to be used for the redress of those wrongs and the restoration of Belgium to her deeply-wronged and unoffending people, then it is eminently moral to send them.

"Without 24 hours' delay this country should and could take effective action. It should take possession of all the interned German ships, including the German warships, and hold them as a guarantee that ample satisfaction shall be given us. Furthermore it should declare that in view of Germany's murderous offences against the rights of neutrals all commerce with Germany shall be forthwith forbidden and all commerce of every kind permitted and encouraged with France, England, Russia, and the rest of the civilized world.

"I do not believe that the firm assertion of our rights means war, but, in any event, it is well to remember there are things worse than war.

FEAR GOD AND TAKE YOUR OWN PART

"Let us as a nation understand that peace is worth
having only when it is the hand-maiden of international righteousness and of national self-respect."

APPENDIX B

Address delivered before the Knights of Columbus, Carnegie Hall, New York, Oct. 12, 1915

FOUR centuries and a quarter have gone by since Columbus by discovering America opened the greatest era in world history. Four centuries have passed since the Spaniards began that colonization on the main land which has resulted in the growth of the nations of Latin-America. Three centuries have passed since, with the settlements on the coasts of Virginia and Massachusetts, the real history of what is now the United States began. All this we ultimately owe to the action of an Italian seaman in the service of a Spanish King and a Spanish Queen. It is eminently fitting that one of the largest and most influential social organizations of this great Republic,—a Republic in which the tongue is English, and the blood derived from many sources—should, in its name, commemorate the great Italian. It is eminently fitting to make an address on Americanism before this society.

We of the United States need above all things to remember that, while we are by blood and culture kin to each of the nations of Europe, we are also separate from each of them. We are a new and distinct nationality. We are developing our own distinctive culture and civilization, and the worth of this civilization will largely depend upon our determination to keep it distinctively our

357

own. Our sons and daughters should be educated here and not abroad. We should freely take from every other nation whatever we can make of use, but we should adopt and develop to our own peculiar needs what we thus take, and never be content merely to copy.

Our nation was founded to perpetuate democratic principles. These principles are that each man is to be treated on his worth as a man without regard to the land from which his forefathers came and without regard to the creed which he professes. If the United States proves false to these principles of civil and religious liberty, it will have inflicted the greatest blow on the system of free popular government that has ever been inflicted. Here we have had a virgin continent on which to try the experiment of making out of divers race stocks a new nation and of treating all the citizens of that nation in such a fashion as to preserve them equality of opportunity in industrial, civil and political life. Our duty is to secure each man against any injustice by his fellows.

One of the most important things to secure for him is the right to hold and to express the religious views that best meet his own soul needs. Any political movement directed against any body of our fellow citizens because of their religious creed is a grave offense against American principles and American institutions. It is a wicked thing either to support or to oppose a man because of the creed he professes. This applies to Jew and Gentile, to Catholic and Protestant, and to the man who would be regarded as unorthodox by all of them alike. Political movements directed against certain men because of their religious belief, and intended to prevent men of that creed from holding office, have never accomplished anything but harm. This was true in the days of the "Know-Nothing" and Native-American parties in the middle of the last century; and it is just as true to-day. Such a movement directly contravenes the spirit of the Constitution itself. Washington and his associates believed that it was essential to the existence of this Republic that there should never be any union of Church and State; and such union is partially accomplished wherever a given creed is aided by the State or when any public servant is elected or defeated because of his creed. The Constitution explicitly forbids the requiring of any religious test as a qualification for holding office. To impose such a test by popular vote is as bad as to impose it by law. To vote either for or against a man because of his creed is to impose upon him a religious test and is a clear violation of the spirit of the Constitution.

Moreover, it is well to remember that these movements never achieve the end they nominally have in view. They do nothing whatsoever except to increase among the men of the various churches the spirit of sectarian intolerance which is base and unlovely in any civilization but which is utterly revolting among a free people that profess the principles we profess. No such movement can ever permanently succeed here. All that it does is for a decade or so greatly to increase the spirit of theological animosity, both among the people to whom it appeals and among the people whom it assails. Furthermore, it has in the past invariably resulted, in so far as it was successful at all, in putting unworthy men into office; for there is nothing that a man of loose principles and of evil practices in public life so desires as the chance to distract attention from his own shortcomings and misdeeds by exciting and inflaming theological and sectarian prejudice.

We must recognize that it is a cardinal sin against democracy to support a man for public office because he belongs to a given creed or to oppose him because he belongs to a given creed. It is just as evil as to draw the line between class and class, between occupation and occupation in political life. No man who tries to draw either line is a good American. True Americanism demands that we judge each man on his conduct, that we so judge him in private life and that we so judge him in public life. The line of cleavage drawn on principle and conduct in public affairs is never in any healthy community identical with the line of cleavage between creed and creed or between class and class. On the contrary, where the community life is healthy, these lines of cleavage almost always run nearly at right angles to one another. It is eminently necessary to all of us that we should have able and honest public officials in the nation, in the city, in the state. If we make a serious and resolute effort to get such officials of the right kind, men who shall not only be honest but shall be able and shall take the right view of public questions, we will find as a matter of fact that the men we thus choose will be drawn from the professors of every creed and from among men who do not adhere to any creed.

For thirty-five years I have been more or less actively engaged in public life, in the performance of my political duties, now in a public position, now in a private position. I have fought with all the fervor I possessed for the various causes in which with all my heart I believed; and in every fight I thus made I have had with me and against me Catholics, Protestants and Jews. There have been times when I have had to make the fight for or against some man of each creed on grounds of plain public morality, unconnected with questions of public policy. There were other times when I have made such a fight for or against a given man, not on grounds of public morality, for he may have been morally a good man, but on account of his attitude on questions of public policy, of governmental principle. In both cases, I have always found myself fighting beside, and fighting against, men of every creed. The one sure way to have secured the defeat of every good principle worth fighting for would have been to have permitted the fight to be changed into one along sectarian lines and inspired by the spirit of sectarian bitterness, either for the purpose of putting into public life or of keeping out of public life the believers in any given creed. Such conduct represents an assault upon Americanism. The man guilty of it is not a good American.

I hold that in this country there must be complete severance of Church and State; that public moneys shall not be used for the purpose of advancing any particular creed; and therefore that the public schools shall be nonsectarian and no public moneys appropriated for sectarian schools. As a necessary corollary to this, not only the pupils but the members of the teaching force and the school officials of all kinds must be treated exactly on a par, no matter what their creed; and there must be no more discrimination against Jew or Catholic or Protestant than discrimination in favor of Jew, Catholic or Protestant. Whoever makes such discrimination is an enemy of the public schools.

What is true of creed is no less true of nationality. There is no room in this country for hyphenated Americanism. When I refer to hyphenated Americans, I do not refer to naturalized Americans. Some of the very best Americans I have ever known were naturalized Americans, Americans born abroad. But a hyphenated American is not an American at all. This is just as true of the man who puts "native" before the hyphen as of the man who puts German or Irish or English or French before the hyphen. Americanism is a matter of the spirit and of the soul. Our allegiance must be purely to the United States. We must unsparingly condemn any man who holds any other allegiance. But if he is heartily and singly loyal to this Republic, then no matter where he was born, he is just as good an American as any one else.

The one absolutely certain way of bringing this nation to ruin, of preventing all possibility of its continuing to be a nation at all, would be to permit it to become a tangle of squabbling nationalities, an intricate knot of German-Americans, Irish-Americans, English-Americans, French-Americans, Scandinavian-Americans or Italian-Americans, each preserving its separate nationality, each at heart feeling more sympathy with Europeans of that nationality than with the other citizens of the American Republic. The men who do not become Americans and nothing else are hyphenated Americans; and there ought to be no room for them in this country. The man who calls himself an American citizen and who yet shows by his actions that he is primarily the citizen of a foreign land, plays a thoroughly mischievous part in the life of our body politic. He has no place here; and the sooner he returns to the land to which he feels his real heart-allegiance, the better it will be for every good American. There is no such thing as a hyphenated American who is a good American. The only man who is a good American is the man who is an American and nothing else.

I appeal to history. Among the generals of Washington in the Revolutionary War were Greene, Putnam and Lee, who were of English descent; Wayne and Sullivan, who were of Irish descent; Marion, who was of French descent; Schuyler, who was of Dutch descent, and Muhlenberg and Herkimer, who were of German descent. But they were all of them Americans and nothing else, just as much as Washington. Carroll of Carrollton was a Catholic; Hancock a Protestant; Jefferson was heterodox from the standpoint of any orthodox creed; but these and all the other signers of the Declaration of Independence stood on an equality of duty and right and liberty, as Americans and nothing else.

So it was in the Civil War. Farragut's father was born in Spain and Sheridan's father in Ireland; Sherman and Thomas were of English and Custer of German descent; and Grant came of a long line of American ancestors whose original home had been Scotland. But the Admiral was not a Spanish-American; and the Generals were not Scotch-Americans or Irish-Americans or English-Americans or German-Americans. They were all Americans and nothing else. This was just as true of Lee and of Stonewall Jackson and of Beauregard.

When in 1909 our battlefleet returned from its voyage around the world, Admirals Wainwright and Schroeder represented the best traditions and the most efficient action in our navy; one was of old American blood and of English descent; the other was the son of German immigrants. But one was not a native-American and the other a German-American. Each was an American pure and simple. Each bore allegiance only to the flag of the United States. Each would have been incapable of considering the interests of Germany or of England or of any other country except the United States.

To take charge of the most important work under my administration, the building of the Panama Canal, I chose General Goethals. Both of his parents were born in Holland. But he was just plain United States. He wasn't a Dutch-American; if he had been I wouldn't have appointed him. So it was with such men, among those who served under me, as Admiral Osterhaus and General Barry. The father of one was born in Germany, the father of the other in Ireland. But they were both Americans, pure and simple, and first rate fighting men in addition.

In my Cabinet at the time there were men of English and French, German, Irish and Dutch blood, men born on this side and men born in Germany and Scotland; but they were all Americans and nothing else; and every one of them was incapable of thinking of himself or of his fellow-countrymen, excepting in terms of American citizenship. If any one of them had anything in the nature of a dual or divided allegiance in his soul, he never would have been appointed to serve under me, and he would have been instantly removed when the discovery was made. There wasn't one of them who was capable of desiring that the policy of the United States should be shaped with reference to the interests of any foreign country or with consideration for anything, outside of the general welfare of humanity, save the honor and interest of the United States, and each was incapable of making any discrimination whatsoever among the citizens of the country he served, of our common country, save discrimination based on conduct and on conduct alone.

For an American citizen to vote as a German-American, an Irish-American or an English-American is to be a traitor to American institutions; and those hyphenated Americans who terrorize American politicians by threats of the foreign vote are engaged in treason to the American Republic.

Now this is a declaration of principles. How are we in practical fashion to secure the making of these principles part of the very fiber of our national life? First and foremost let us all resolve that in this country hereafter we shall place far less emphasis upon the question of right and much greater emphasis upon the matter of duty. A republic can't succeed and won't succeed in the tremendous international stress of the modern world unless its citizens possess that form of high-minded patriotism which consists in putting devotion to duty before the question of individual rights. This must be done in our family relations or the family will go to pieces; and no better tract for family life in this country can be imagined than the little story called "Mother," written by an American woman, Kathleen Norris, who happens to be a member of your own church.

What is true of the family, the foundation stone of our national life, is not less true of the entire super-structure. I am, as you know, a most ardent believer in national preparedness against war as a means of securing that honorable and self-respecting peace which is the only peace desired by all high-spirited people. But it is an absolute impossibility to secure such preparedness in full and proper form if it is an isolated feature of our policy. The lamentable fate of Belgium has shown that no justice in legislation or success in business will be of the slightest avail if the nation has not prepared in advance the strength to protect its rights. But it is equally true that there cannot be this preparation in advance for military strength unless there is a solid basis of civil and social life behind it. There must be social, economic and military preparedness all alike, all harmoniously developed; and above all there must be spiritual and mental preparedness.

There must be not merely preparedness in things material; there must be preparedness in soul and mind. To prepare a great army and navy without preparing a proper national spirit would avail nothing. And if there is not only a proper national spirit but proper national intelligence, we shall realize that even from the standpoint of the army and navy some civil preparedness is indispensable. For example, a plan for national defence which does not include the most far-reaching use and co-operation of our railroads must prove largely futile. These railroads are organized in time of peace. But we must have the most carefully thought out organization from the national and centralized standpoint in order to use them in time of war. This means first that those in charge of them from the highest to the lowest must understand their duty in time of war, must be permeated with the spirit of genuine patriotism; and second, that they and we shall understand that efficiency is as essential as patriotism; one is useless without the other.

Again: every citizen should be trained sedulously by every activity at our command to realize his duty to the nation. In France at this moment the workingmen who are not at the front are spending all their energies with the single thought of helping their brethren at the front by what they do in the munition plants, on the railroads, in the factories. It is a shocking, a lamentable thing that many of the trade unions of England have taken a directly opposite view. It is doubtless true that many of their employers have made excessive profits out of war conditions; and the Government should have drastically controlled and minimized such profit-making. Such wealthy men should be dealt with in radical fashion; but their misconduct doesn't excuse the misconduct of those labor men who are trying to make gains at the cost of their brethren who fight in the trenches. The thing for us Americans to realize is that we must do our best to prevent similar conditions from growing up here. Business men, professional men, and wage workers alike must understand that there should be no question of their enjoying any rights whatsoever unless in the fullest way they recognize and live up to the duties that go with those rights. This is just as true of the corporation as of the trade union, and if either corporation or trade union fails heartily to acknowledge this truth, then its activities are necessarily anti-social and detrimental to the welfare of the body politic as a whole. In war time, when the welfare of the nation is at stake, it should be accepted as axiomatic that the employer is to make no profit out of the war save that which is necessary to the efficient running of the business and to the living expenses of himself and family, and that the wage worker is to treat his wage from exactly the same standpoint and is to see to it that the labor organization to which he belongs is, in all its activities, subordinated to the service of the nation.

Now there must be some application of this spirit in times of peace or we cannot suddenly develop it in time of war. The strike situation in the United States at this time is a scandal to the country as a whole and discreditable alike to employer and employee. Any employer who fails to recognize that human rights come first and that the friendly relationship between himself and those working for him should be one of partnership and comradeship in mutual help no less than self-help is recreant to his duty as an American citizen and it is to his interest, having in view the enormous destruction of life in the present war, to conserve, and to train to higher efficiency alike for his benefit and for its, the labor supply. In return any employee who acts along the lines publicly advocated by the men who profess to speak for the I. W. W. is not merely an open enemy of business but of this entire country and is out of place in our government.

You, Knights of Columbus, are particularly fitted to play a great part in the movement for national solidarity, without which there can be no real efficiency in either peace or war. During the last year and a quarter it has been brought home to us in startling fashion that many of the elements of our nation are not yet properly fused. It ought to be a literally appalling fact that members of two of the foreign embassies in this country have been discovered to be implicated in inciting their fellow-countrymen, whether naturalized American citizens or not, to the destruction of property and the crippling of American industries that are operating in accordance with internal law and international agreement. The malign activity of one of these embassies, the Austrian, has been brought home directly to the ambassador in such shape that his recall has been forced. The activities of the other, the German, have been set forth in detail by the publication in the press of its letters in such fashion as to make it perfectly clear that they were of the same general character. Of course, the two embassies were merely carrying out the instructions of their home governments.

Nor is it only the Germans and Austrians who take the view that as a matter of right they can treat their countrymen resident in America, even if naturalized citizens of the United States, as their allies and subjects to be used in keeping alive separate national groups profoundly anti-American in sentiment if the contest comes between American interests and those of foreign lands in question. It has recently been announced that the Russian government is to rent a house in New York as a national center to be Russian in faith and patriotism, to foster the Russian language and keep alive the national feeling in immigrants who come hither. All of this is utterly antagonistic to proper American sentiment, whether perpetrated in the name of Germany, of Austria, of Russia, of England, or France or any other country.

AMERICANISM

We should meet this situation by on the one hand seeing that these immigrants get all their rights as American citizens, and on the other hand insisting that they live up to their duties as American citizens. Any discrimination against aliens is a wrong, for it tends to put the immigrant at a disadvantage and to cause him to feel bitterness and resentment during the very years when he should be preparing himself for American citizenship. If an immigrant is not fit to become a citizen, he should not be allowed to come here. If he is fit, he should be given all the rights to earn his own livelihood, and to better himself, that any man can have. Take such a matter as the illiteracy test; I entirely agree with those who feel that many very excellent possible citizens would be barred improperly by an illiteracy test. But why do you not admit aliens under a bond to learn to read and write English within a certain time? It would then be a duty to see that they were given ample opportunity to learn to read and write and that they were deported if they failed to take advantage of the opportunity. No man can be a good citizen if he is not at least in process of learning to speak the language of his fellow-citizens. And an alien who remains here without learning to speak English for more than a certain number of years should at the end of that time be treated as having refused to take the preliminary steps necessary to complete Americanization and should be deported. But there should be no denial or limitation of the alien's opportunity to work, to own property and to take advantage of civic opportunities. Special legislation should deal with the aliens who do not come here to be made citizens. But the alien who comes here intending to become a citizen should be helped in every way to advance himself, should be removed from every possible disadvantage and in return should be required under penalty of being sent back to the country from which he came, to prove that he is in good faith fitting himself to be an American citizen. We should set a high standard, and insist on men reaching it; but if they do reach it we should treat them as on a full equality with ourselves.

Therefore, we should devote ourselves as a preparative to preparedness, alike in peace and war, to secure the three elemental things; one, a common language, the English language; two, the increase in our social loyalty—citizenship absolutely undivided, a citizenship which acknowledges no flag except the flag of the United States and which emphatically repudiates all duality of national loyalty; and third, an intelligent and resolute effort for the removal of industrial and social unrest, an effort which shall aim equally to secure every man his rights and to make every man understand that unless he in good faith performs his duties he is not entitled to any rights at all.

The American people should itself do these things for the immigrants. If we leave the immigrant to be helped by representatives of foreign governments, by foreign societies, by a press and institutions conducted in a foreign language and in the interest of foreign governments, and if we permit the immigrants to exist as alien groups, each group sundered from the rest of the citizens of the country, we shall store up for ourselves bitter trouble in the future.

I am certain that the only permanently safe attitude for this country as regards national preparedness for self-defense is along the lines of obligatory universal service on the Swiss model. Switzerland is the most democratic of nations. Its army is the most democratic army in the world. There isn't a touch of militarism or aggressiveness about Switzerland. It has been found as a matter of actual practical experience in Switzerland that the universal military training has made a very marked increase in social efficiency and in the ability of the man thus trained to do well for himself in industry. The man who has received the training is a better citizen, is more self-respecting, more orderly, better able to hold his own, and more willing to respect the rights of others, and at the same time he is a more valuable and better paid man in his business. We need that the navy and the army should be greatly increased and that their efficiency as units and in the aggregate should be increased to an even greater degree than their numbers. An adequate regular reserve should be established. Economy should be insisted on, and first of all in the abolition of useless army posts and navy yards. The National Guard should be supervised and controlled by the Federal War Department. Training camps such as at Plattsburg should be provided on a nation-wide basis and the government should pay the expenses. Foreign-born as well as native-born citizens should be brought together in those camps; and each man at the camp should take the oath of allegiance as unreservedly and unqualifiedly as the men of the regular army and navy now take it. Not only should battleships, battle cruisers, submarines, aircraft, ample coast and field artillery be provided and a greater ammunition supply system, but there should be a utilization of those engaged in such professions as the ownership and management of motor cars, aviation, and the profession of engineering. Map-making and road improvement should be attended to, and, as I have already said, the railroads brought into intimate touch with the War Department. Moreover, the government should deal with conservation of all necessary war supplies such as mine products, potash, oil lands and the like. Further-more, all munition plants should be carefully surveyed with special reference to their geographic distribution. Provision should be made for munition and supply factories west of the Alleghenies. Finally, remember that the men must be sedulously trained in peace to use this material or we shall merely prepare our ships, guns and products as gifts to the enemy. All of these things should be done in any event. But let us never forget that the most important of all things is to introduce universal military service.

Let me repeat that this preparedness against war must be based upon efficiency and justice in the handling of ourselves in time of peace. If belligerent governments, while we are not hostile to them but merely neutral, strive nevertheless to make of this nation many nations, each hostile to the others and none of them loyal to the central government, then it may be accepted as certain that they would do far worse to us in time of war. If Germany and Austria encourage strikes and sabotage in our munition plants while we are neutral it may be accepted as axiomatic that they would do far worse to us if we were hostile. It is our duty from the standpoint of self-defence to secure the complete Americanization of our people; to make of the many peoples of this country a united nation, one in speech and feeling and all, so far as possible, sharers in the best that each has brought to our shores.

The foreign-born population of this country must be an Americanized population—no other kind can fight the battles of America either in war or peace. It must talk the language of its native-born fellow citizens, it must possess American citizenship and American ideals—and therefore we native born citizens must ourselves practice a high and fine idealism, and shun as we would the plague the sordid materialism which treats pecuniary profit and gross bodily comfort as the only evidences of success. It must stand firm by its oath of allegiance in word and deed and must show that in very fact it has renounced allegiance to every prince, potentate or foreign government. It must be maintained on an American standard of living so as to prevent labor disturbances in important plants and at critical times. None of these objects can be secured as long as we have immigrant colonies, ghettos, and immigrant sections, and above all they cannot be assured so long as we consider the immigrant only as an industrial asset. The immigrant must not be allowed to drift or to be put at the mercy of the exploiter. Our object is not to imitate one of the older racial types, but to maintain a new American type and then to secure loyalty to this type. We cannot secure such loyalty unless we make this a country where men shall feel that they have justice and also where they shall feel that they are required to perform the duties imposed upon them. The policy of "Let alone" which we have hitherto pursued is thoroughly vicious from two standpoints. By this policy we have permitted the immigrants, and too often the native-born laborers as well, to suffer injustice. Moreover, by this policy we have failed to impress upon the immigrant and upon the native-born as well that they are expected to do justice as well as to receive justice, that they are expected to be heartily and actively and single-mindedly loyal to the flag no less than to benefit by living under it.

We cannot afford to continue to use hundreds of thousands of immigrants merely as industrial assets while they remain social outcasts and menaces any more than fifty years ago we could afford to keep the black man merely as an industrial asset and not as a human being. We cannot afford to build a big industrial plant and herd men and women about it without care for their welfare. We cannot afford to permit squalid overcrowding or the kind of living system which makes impossible the decencies and necessities of life. We cannot afford the low wage rates and the merely seasonal industries which mean the sacrifice of both individual and family life and morals to the industrial machinery. We cannot afford to leave American mines, munitions plants and general resources in the hands of alien workmen, alien to America and even likely to be made hostile to America by machinations such as have recently been provided in the case of the above-named foreign embassies in Washington. We cannot afford to run the risk of having in time of war men working on our railways or working in our munition plants who would in the name of duty to their own foreign countries bring destruction to us. Recent events have shown us that incitements to sabotage and strikes are in the view of at least two of the great foreign powers of Europe within their definition of neutral practices. What would be done to us in the name of war if these things are done to us in the name of neutrality?

Justice Dowling in his speech has described the excellent fourth degree of your order, of how in it you dwell upon duties rather than rights, upon the great duties of patriotism and of national spirit. It is a fine thing to have a society that holds up such a standard of duty. I ask you to make a special effort to deal with Americanization, the fusing into one nation, a nation necessarily different from all other nations, of all who come to our shores. Pay heed to the three principal essentials: (1) The need of a common language, English, with a minimum amount of illiteracy; (2) the need of a common civil standard, similar ideals, beliefs and customs symbolized by the oath of allegiance to America; and (3) the need of a high standard of living, of reasonable equality of opportunity and of social and industrial justice. In every great crisis in our history, in the Revolution and in the Civil War, and in the lesser crises, like the Spanish War, all factions and races have been forgotten in the common spirit of Americanism. Protestant and Catholic, men of English or of French, of Irish or of German descent, have joined with a single-minded purpose to secure for the country what only can be achieved by the resultant union of all patriotic citizens. You of this organization have done a great service by your insistence that citizens should pay heed first of all to their duties. Hitherto undue prominence has been given to the question of rights. Your organization is a splendid engine for giving to the stranger within our gates a high conception of American citizenship. Strive for unity. We suffer at present from a lack of leadership in these matters.

Even in the matter of national defence there is such a labyrinth of committees and counsels and advisers that there is a tendency on the part of the average citizen to become confused and do nothing. I ask you to help strike the note that shall unite our people. As a people we must be united. If we are not united we shall slip into the gulf of measureless disaster. We must be strong in purpose for our own defence and bent on securing justice within our borders. If as a nation we are split into warring camps, if we teach our citizens not to look upon one another as brothers but as enemies divided by the hatred of creed for creed or of those of one race against those of another race, surely we shall fail and our great democratic experiment on this continent will go down in crushing overthrow. I ask you here to-night and those like you to take a foremost part in the movement—a young men's movement—for a greater and better America in the future.

All of us, no matter from what land our parents came, no matter in what way we may severally worship our Creator, must stand shoulder to shoulder in a united America for the elimination of race and religious prejudice. We must stand for a reign of equal justice to both big and small. We must insist on the maintenance of the American standard of living. We must stand for an adequate national control which shall secure a better training of our young men in time of peace, both for the work of peace and for the work of war. We must direct every national resource, material and spiritual, to the task not of shirking difficulties, but of training our people to overcome difficulties. Our aim must be, not to make life easy and soft, not to soften soul and body, but to fit us in virile fashion to do a great work for all mankind. This great work can only be done by a mighty democracy, with those qualities of soul, guided by those qualities of mind, which will both make it refuse to do injustice to any other nation, and also enable it to hold its own against aggression by any other nation. In our relations with the outside world, we must abhor wrongdoing, and disdain to commit it, and we must no less disdain the baseness of spirit which tamely submits to wrongdoing. Finally and most important of all, we must strive for the establishment within our own borders of that stern and lofty standard of personal and public morality which shall guarantee to each man his rights, and which shall insist in return upon the full performance by each man of his duties both to his neighbor and to the great nation whose flag must symbolize in the future as it has symbolized in the past the highest hopes of all mankind.

APPENDIX C

November 24, 1915.

My dear Mr. Dutton:

Even to nerves dulled and jaded by the heaped-up horrors of the past year and a half, the news of the terrible fate that has befallen the Armenians must give a fresh shock of sympathy and indignation. Let me emphatically point out that the sympathy is useless unless it is accompanied with indignation, and that the indignation is useless if it exhausts itself in words instead of taking shape in deeds.

If this people through its government had not shirked its duty in Mexico for the last five years, and if this people through its government had not shirked its duty in connection with the world war for the last sixteen months, we would now be able to take effective action on behalf of Armenia. Mass meetings on behalf of the Armenians amount to nothing whatever if they are mere methods of giving a sentimental but ineffective and safe outlet to the emotion of those engaged in them. Indeed they amount to less than nothing. The habit of giving emotional expression to feelings without following the expression by action is in the end thoroughly detrimental both to the will power and to the morality of the persons concerned. As long as this government proceeds, whether as regards Mexico or as regards Germany, whether as regards the European War, or as regards Belgium, on the principles of the peace-at-any-price men, of the professional pacifists, just so long

377

it will be as absolutely ineffective for international righteousness as China itself. The men who act on the motto
of "safety first" are acting on a motto which could be
appropriately used by the men on a sinking steamer who
jump into the boats ahead of the women and children
—and who at least do not commemorate this fact by
wearing buttons with "safety first" on them as a device.
Until we put honor and duty first, and are willing to
risk something in order to achieve righteousness both
for ourselves and for others, we shall accomplish nothing; and we shall earn and deserve the contempt of
the strong nations of mankind.

One reason why I do not wish to take part in a mass
meeting only for the denunciation of the atrocities committed on the Armenians is because there are ignoble
souls who have preached professional pacifism as a
creed, or who have refused to attend similar meetings
on behalf of the Belgians, who yet do not fear to take
such action on behalf of the Armenians—for the simple
reason that there is in America no Turkish vote, and
because Turkey is not our neighbor as Mexico is, and
not a formidable aggressive power like Germany, and so
it is safe both politically and materially to denounce
her. The American professional pacifists, the American men and women of the peace-at-any-price type, who
join in meetings to "denounce war" or with empty words
"protest" on behalf of the Armenians or other tortured
and ruined peoples carry precisely the weight that an
equal number of Chinese pacifists would carry if at
a similar meeting they went through similar antics in
Peking. They do not wear pigtails; but it is to be regretted that they do not carry some similar outward and
visible sign of their inward and spiritual disgrace. They
accomplish nothing for peace; and they do accomplish

something against justice. They do harm instead of good; and they deeply discredit the nation to which they belong. It was announced the other day, by certain politicians interested in securing votes, that at the end of the war this Government would "insist" on Russia and Roumania doing justice to all Jews. The conduct of this Government during the present war, and its utter refusal to back words with deeds, has made it utterly unable to "insist" on anything of the kind, whether as regards Russia or Roumania or any other power. A nation too timid to protect its own men, women and children from murder and outrage and too timid even to speak on behalf of Belgium, will not carry much weight by "protest" or "insistence" on behalf of the suffering Jews and Armenians. Foreign powers will attribute such "protests" or "insistence," coupled with our failure to act in cases of other nationalities, merely to the fact that there is in this country neither a Russian nor a Turkish vote—and will despise us accordingly.

All of the terrible iniquities of the past year and a half, including this crowning iniquity of the wholesale slaughter of the Armenians, can be traced directly to the initial wrong committed on Belgium by her invasion and subjugation; and the criminal responsibility of Germany must be shared by the neutral powers, headed by the United States, for their failure to protest when this initial wrong was committed. In the case of the United States additional responsibility rests upon it because its lack of influence for justice and peace during the last sixteen months has been largely due to the course of timid and unworthy abandonment of duty which it has followed for nearly five years as regards Mexico. Scores of our soldiers have been killed and

379

wounded, hundreds of our civilians, both men and women, have been murdered or outraged in person or property, by the Mexicans; and we have not only taken no action but have permitted arms to be exported to the bandits who were cutting one another's throats in Mexico and who used these arms to kill Americans; and although we have refused to help our own citizens against any of the chiefs of these bandits, we have now and then improperly helped one chief against another. The failure to do our duty in Mexico created the contempt which made Germany rightfully think it safe to go into the wholesale murder that accompanied the sinking of the *Lusitania;* and the failure to do our duty in the case of the *Lusitania* made Germany, acting through Austria, rightfully think it safe to go into the wholesale murder that marked the sinking of the *Ancona.*

The invasion of Belgium was followed by a policy of terrorism toward the Belgian population, the shooting of men, women and children, the destruction of Dinant and Louvain and many other places; the bombardment of unfortified places, not only by ships and by land forces but by air-craft, resulting in the killing of many hundreds of civilians, men, women and children, in England, France, Belgium and Italy; in the destruction of mighty temples and great monuments of art, in Rheims, in Venice, in Verona. The devastation of Poland and of Serbia has been awful beyond description and has been associated with infamies surpassing those of the dreadful religious and racial wars of seventeenth-century Europe. Such deeds as have been done by the nominally Christian powers in Europe, from the invasion of Belgium by Germany to the killing of Miss Cavell by the German Government, things done wholesale, things done retail, have been such as we had hoped would never again occur in civilized warfare. They are far worse than anything that has occurred in such warfare since the close of the Napoleonic contests a century ago. Such a deed as the execution of Miss Cavell, for instance, would have been utterly impossible in the days of the worst excitement during our Civil War. For all of this, the pacifists who dare not speak for righteousness, and who possess such an unpleasant and evil prominence in the United States, must share the responsibility with the most brutal type of militarists. The weak and timid milk-and-water policy of the professional pacifists is just as responsible as the blood-and-iron policy of the ruthless and unscrupulous militarist for the terrible recrudescence of evil on a gigantic scale in the civilized world.

The crowning outrage has been committed by the Turks on the Armenians. They have suffered atrocities so hideous that it is difficult to name them, atrocities such as those inflicted upon conquered nations by the followers of Attila and of Genghis Khan. It is dreadful to think that these things can be done and that this nation nevertheless remains "neutral not only in deed but in thought," between right and the most hideous wrong, neutral between despairing and hunted people, people whose little children are murdered and their women raped, and the victorious and evil wrongdoers.

There are many sincere and wise men in China who are now endeavoring to lift China from the old conditions. These old conditions made her the greatest example of a pacifistic, peace-at-any-price, non-militaristic people. Because of their cult of pacifism, the

Chinese, like the Koreans, and utterly unlike the Japanese, became absolutely powerless to defend themselves, or to win or retain the respect of other nations. They were also of course utterly helpless to work for the good of others. The professional pacifists of the United States are seeking to make the United States follow in the footsteps of China. They represent what has been on the whole the most evil influence at work in the United States for the last fifty years; and for five years they have in international affairs shaped our governmental policy. These men, whether politicians, publicists, college presidents, capitalists, labor leaders, or self-styled philanthropists, have done everything they could to relax the fiber of the American character and weaken the strength of the American will. They teach our people to seek that debasing security which is to be found in love of ease, in fear of risk, in the craven effort to avoid any duty that is hard or hazardous—a security which purchases peace in the present not only at the cost of humiliation in the present but at the cost of disaster in the future. They are seeking to Chinafy this country. In so doing they not only make us work for our own undoing, and for the ultimate ruin of the great democratic experiment for which our great American republic stands; but they also render us utterly powerless to work for others. We have refused to do our duty by Belgium; we refuse to do our duty by Armenia; because we have deified peace at any price, because we have preached and practised that evil pacifism which is the complement to and the encouragement of alien militarism. Such pacifism puts peace above righteousness, and safety in the present above both duty in the present and safety in the future.

I trust that all Americans worthy of the name feel

their deepest indignation and keenest sympathy aroused by the dreadful Armenian atrocities. I trust that they feel in the same way about the ruin of Belgium's nationality, and realize that a peace obtained without restoring Belgium to its own people and righting the wrongs of the Armenians would be worse than any war. I trust they realize that unless America prepares to defend itself she can perform no duty to others; and under such circumstances she earns only derision if she prattles about forming a league for world peace, or about arbitration treaties and disarmament proposals, and commission-investigation treaties such as the unspeakably foolish ones negotiated a year or two ago at Washington and promptly disregarded by the very Administration that negotiated them.

Let us realize that the words of the weakling and the coward, of the pacifist and the poltroon, are worthless to stop wrongdoing. Wrongdoing will only be stopped by men who are brave as well as just, who put honor above safety, who are true to a lofty ideal of duty, who prepare in advance to make their strength effective, and who shrink from no hazard, not even the final hazard of war, if necessary in order to serve the great cause of righteousness. When our people take this stand, we shall also be able effectively to take a stand in international matters which shall prevent such cataclysms of wrong as have been witnessed in Belgium and on an even greater scale in Armenia.

Sincerely yours,

THEODORE ROOSEVELT.

SAMUEL T. DUTTON, ESQ.,
70 Fifth Ave.,
New York City.
Chairman of the Committee on the Armenian Outrages.

APPENDIX D

[Speech of Senator Miles Poindexter; reprinted from the *Congressional Record* of January 12, 1916.]

Col. Roosevelt's Record on Preparedness—The Truth of History for the Information of Secretary Garrison—An Incessant and Earnest Advocate of Preparedness for More Than 30 Years —President Wilson's Policy Outlined and Condemned 18 Years in Advance—Preparedness Urged in Every Message to Congress While President —A Big, Efficient Navy and an Efficient Army Demanded as the Surest Guaranty of Peace— The Swiss System of Military Service Held Up as a Model to Congress in 1906—Hyphenated Americans Condemned as Undesirable Citizens in 1894—Arbitration Treaties Declared Useless When Unbacked by Force.

IN a carefully prepared statement issued recently at Washington (Dec. 21, 1915) the Secretary of War, Mr. Garrison, representing President Wilson, and speaking in the unruffled serenity of that state of bliss in which 'tis said 'tis folly to be wise, made the following engaging observations:

"Mr. Roosevelt is welcomed as a convert on the issue of preparedness, but the front pew is already filled before the conversion, and he must now rely on the strength of his voice for recognition.

"'Preparedness' was with him an acquired taste.

384

Others brought it forward and urged it upon the attention of the people, and it was only after he found that it suited their taste that he became vocal in its behalf."

THE PLAIN TALE OF HISTORY

"Mark now, how plain a tale shall put you down," Mr. Secretary.

Theodore Roosevelt began to advocate preparedness 33 years ago, and has advocated it unceasingly and unwaveringly from that time to the present moment. He has been during all those years at every opportunity not merely "vocal" on the subject but vociferously vocal.

Shortly after his graduation from Harvard in 1882 he wrote in the preface to his history of the War of 1812 these passages:

CRIMINAL FOLLY OF JEFFERSON AND MADISON

"The operations of this war on land teach nothing new; it is the old, old lesson that miserly economy in preparation may in the end involve a lavish outlay of men and money which, after all, comes too late to more than partially offset the evils produced by the original shortsighted parsimony. It was criminal folly for Jefferson and his follower, Madison, to neglect to give us a force either of Regulars or of well-trained Volunteers during the 12 years they had in which to prepare for the struggle that any one might see was inevitable.

"The necessity for an efficient Navy is so evident that only our almost incredible shortsightedness prevents our at once preparing one."

Fifteen years later, writing a condensed history of the same war for an English publication, Col. Roosevelt reiterated his earlier views:

TWENTY SHIPS OF THE LINE WOULD HAVE PREVENTED THE WAR

(From "The War with the United States, 1812-15,"

written for the English History of the Royal Navy in 1897.)

"Had America possessed (in 1812) a fleet of 20 ships of the line her sailors could have plied their trade unmolested, and the three years of war with its loss in blood and money would have been avoided. From the merely monetary standpoint such a navy would have been the cheapest kind of insurance, and morally its advantages would have been incalculable, for every American worth the name would have lifted his head higher because of its existence."

JEFFERSON'S PASSION FOR PEACE

"But unfortunately the Nation lacked the wisdom to see this, and it chose and rechose for the Presidency Thomas Jefferson, who avowed that his 'passion was peace,' and whose timidity surpassed even his philanthropy."

EVIL CAUSED BY JEFFERSON AND MADISON

"There never was a better example of the ultimate evil caused by a timid effort to secure peace and the refusal to make preparations for war than that afforded by the American people under the Presidencies of Jefferson and Madison."

These citations disclose the original inventor of President Wilson's "too-proud-to-fight" policy. Jefferson's "passion was peace." In his recent address to Congress, President Wilson said of the American people that "their passion is for peace."

Instead of being a "convert" to any phase of President Wilson's policy, 18 years before that policy was put into operation Theodore Roosevelt was outlining it with singular accuracy and denouncing it as leading to national humiliation and dishonor, as the following citations abundantly testify:

RECORD ON PREPAREDNESS

PRESIDENT WILSON'S FOREIGN POLICY DENOUNCED 18 YEARS IN ADVANCE—NO PEACE AT THE PRICE OF NATIONAL HONOR

(Address, as Assistant Secretary of the Navy, before the Naval War College, June, 1897.)

"A really great people, proud and high-spirited, would face all the disasters of war rather than purchase that base prosperity which is bought at the price of national honor."

WORDS WITHOUT DEEDS CAUSE OF HUMILIATION

"Unreadiness for war is merely rendered more disastrous by readiness to bluster; to talk defiance and advocate a vigorous policy in words, while refusing to back up these words by deeds, is cause for humiliation.

No material loss can begin to compensate for the loss of national self-respect.

No nation should ever wage war wantonly, but no nation should ever avoid it at the cost of national honor."

DIPLOMACY WITHOUT FORCE USELESS

"Diplomacy is utterly useless unless there is force behind it; the diplomat is the servant, not the master, of the soldier."

SAY WHAT IS NECESSARY AND STAND BY IT

(Speech at Chicago, April 2, 1903.)

"This is in substance what my theory of what our foreign policy should be: Let us not boast, not insult any one, but make up our minds coolly what is necessary to say, and then stand by it whatever the consequences may be."

A COWARD'S PEACE CONTEMPTIBLE

(Speech at Clark University, Worcester, Mass., June 21, 1905.)

"Peace of a valuable type comes not to the man who

craves it because he is afraid, but to the man who demands it because it is right.

The peace granted contemptuously to the weakling and the coward is but a poor boon after it has been granted."

A GREAT NATION SHOULD NOT BLUFF

(Address at Williams College, Williamstown, Mass., June 22, 1905.)

"I demand that the Nation do its duty and accept the responsibility that must go with greatness.

I ask that the Nation dare to be great, and that in daring to be great it show that it knows how to do justice to the weak no less than to exact justice from the strong.

In order to take such a position of being a great nation the one thing that we must not do is to bluff.

The unpardonable thing is to say that we will act as a big nation and then decline to take the necessary steps to make the words good.

Keep on building and maintaining at the highest point of efficiency the United States Navy or quit trying to be a big nation. Do one or the other."

RIGHTEOUSNESS BEFORE PEACE

(Address at Harvard University, June 28, 1905.)

"Of course I am for peace. Of course every President who is fit to be President must be for peace. But I am for one thing before peace; I am for righteousness first and then peace."

(Address at Richmond, Va., October 18, 1905.)

"Our mission in the world should be one of peace, but not the peace of cravens, the peace granted contemptuously to those who purchase it by surrendering the right.

No! Our voice must be effective for peace because

it is raised for righteousness first and for peace only as the handmaiden of righteousness."

(Annual message to Congress, December 3, 1906.)

"It must ever be kept in mind that war is not merely justifiable, but imperative upon honorable men, upon an honorable nation, where peace can only be obtained by the sacrifice of conscientious conviction or of national welfare.

Peace is normally a great good, and normally it coincides with righteousness; but it is righteousness and not peace which should bind the conscience of a nation, as it should bind the conscience of an individual; and neither a nation nor an individual can surrender conscience to another's keeping.

A just war is in the long run far better for a nation's soul than the most prosperous peace obtained by acquiescence in wrong or injustice."

CRIMINAL NOT TO PREPARE FOR WAR

"Moreover, though it is criminal for a nation not to prepare for war, so that it may escape the dreadful consequences of being defeated in war, yet it must always be remembered that even to be defeated in war may be far better than not to have fought at all.

As has been well and finely said, a beaten nation is not necessarily a disgraced nation; but the nation or man is disgraced if the obligation to defend the right is shirked."

A NATION NOT AFRAID

(Address to the graduating class of the Naval Academy, Annapolis, June 23, 1905.)

"What we desire is to have it evident that this Nation seeks peace, not because it is afraid, but because it believes in the eternal laws of justice and right living."

CONSCIENCELESS WAR A CRIME AGAINST ALL HUMANITY

(Annual message to Congress, December 5, 1905.)

"A wanton or useless war, or a war of mere aggression—in short, any war begun or carried on in a conscienceless spirit—is to be condemned as a peculiarly atrocious crime against all humanity.

Our aim is righteousness. Peace is normally the handmaiden of righteousness; but when peace and righteousness conflict, then a great and upright people can never for a moment hesitate to follow the path which leads toward righteousness, even though that path also leads to war."

NO CHOICE LEFT TO ROOSEVELT

When President Wilson put into operation the precise policy thus condemned in advance, what choice had Col. Roosevelt but to denounce him? Could he, on the plea that all must "stand by the President," abandon the convictions and utterances of a lifetime and defend a policy of national dishonor?

"I would have thrown up my hat for Wilson," the Colonel said recently, "if only he had given me the chance by acting in the Presidency as a sound American of rugged strength and patriotism. When he trailed the honor of the United States in the dust, I, as a good American, had no alternative but to oppose him."

So long ago as 1905, as the first quotation cited above shows, the Colonel specified the kind of war that Germany is waging as a "particularly atrocious crime against all humanity," and defined the course which, in his opinion, the Nation should not for a moment hesitate to follow in regard to it.

SAMPLES OF ROOSEVELT'S METHOD

Not in words alone but in acts does Col. Roosevelt's record show flat disagreement with the Wilson policy in international controversies. What stronger contrast could there be to President Wilson's methods in dealing with Germany than is afforded in the following incident, which is described in a recently published "Life of John Hay"?

GERMANY BROUGHT TO BOOK IN 1902

(From the "Life of John Hay," by William Roscoe Thayer, Vol. II, pp. 284, 285, 286.)

"In 1902 one of the periodic outbreaks to which Venezuela was addicted gave him (Hay) an excuse for putting to the test whether or not the United States would defend the Monroe Doctrine by force of arms. The Venezuelans owed the Germans, the English, and the Italians large amounts, which they had put off paying until their creditors began to suspect that they never intended to pay at all. The Kaiser apparently counted on the resistance of the Venezuelans to furnish him a pretext for occupying one or more of their seaboard towns.

In order to disguise the fact that this was a German undertaking, he looked about for accomplices who would give to it an international semblance. It happened just at that time that Germany found herself isolated, as France and Russia had renewed their bond of friendship. England, too, always suspicious of Russia, and recently irritated by France, seemed to be looking for a friend.

By offers which cannot yet be made public, Germany persuaded the Tory government to draw closer to her. The immediate result of this adventure in international coquetry was the joint demand of Germany and England on Venezuela to pay them their due. Venezuela procrastinated.

The allies then sent warships and established what they called a 'pacific blockade' on the Venezuelan ports (December 8, 1901). During the following year Secretary Hay tried to persuade the blockaders of the unwisdom of their action. He persistently called their attention to the fact that a 'pacific blockade' was a contradiction in terms and that its enforcement against the rights of neutral nations could not be tolerated. He also urged arbitration.

Germany deemed that her opportunity had now come, and on December 8, 1902, she and Great Britain severed diplomatic relations with Venezuela, making it plain that the next steps would be the bombardment of Venezuelan towns and the occupation of Venezuelan territory.

Here came the test of the Monroe Doctrine. If the United States permitted foreign nations, under the pretense of supporting their creditors' claims, to invade a weak debtor State by naval or military expedition, and to take possession of its territory, what would become of the doctrine?

ROOSEVELT IN PERSONAL CHARGE

At this point the direction of the American policy passed from Secretary Hay to President Roosevelt.

England and Italy were willing to come to an understanding. Germany refused. She stated that if she took possession of territory such possession would only be 'temporary'; but such possessions easily become permanent; and, besides, it is difficult to trust the guaranties which may be treated as 'scraps of paper.'

President Roosevelt did not shirk the test. Although his action has never been officially described, there is no reason now for not describing it.

One day, when the crisis was at its height, he summoned to the White House Dr. Holleben, the German ambassador, and told him that unless Germany consented to arbitrate, the American squadron under Admiral

Dewey would be given orders by noon 10 days later to proceed to the Venezuelan coast and prevent any taking possession of Venezuelan territory.

Dr. Holleben began to protest that his imperial master, having once refused to arbitrate, could not change his mind. The President said that he was not arguing the question, because arguments had already been gone over until no useful purpose would be served by repeating them; he was simply giving information which the ambassador might think it important to transmit to Berlin.

GERMANY NOT ALLOWED TO DODGE

A week passed in silence. Then Dr. Holleben again called on the President, but said nothing of the Venezuelan matter. When he rose to go, the President asked him about it, and when he stated that he had received nothing from his Government, the President informed him in substance that in view of this fact Admiral Dewey would be instructed to sail a day earlier than the day he, the President, had originally mentioned.

Much perturbed, the ambassador protested; the President informed him that not a stroke of a pen had been put on paper; that if the Emperor would agree to arbitrate, he, the President, would heartily praise him for such action and would treat it as taken on German initiative; but that within 48 hours there must be an offer to arbitrate or Dewey would sail with orders indicated.

Within 36 hours Dr. Holleben returned to the White House and announced to President Roosevelt that a dispatch had just come from Berlin, saying that the Kaiser would arbitrate.

Neither Admiral Dewey (who with an American fleet was then maneuvering in the West Indies) nor any one else knew of the step that was to be taken; the naval authorities were merely required to be in readiness, but were not told what for.

On the announcement that Germany had consented to arbitrate, the President publicly complimented the Kaiser on being so staunch an advocate of arbitration.

The humor of this was probably relished more in the White House than in the palace at Berlin."

In this wise the German Kaiser learned that the Monroe Doctrine was a fact.

There was no note, sharp or otherwise, no bluff or bluster. Simply verbal information to Germany that the step contemplated by her would not be tolerated—that if she did not abandon it the American fleet would sail for the scene of action.

AMERICAN LIFE PROTECTED IN MOROCCO

Two years later, on a much smaller scale, another international controversy arose. This raised the simple question of whether or not the United States Government could be depended upon to protect its citizens abroad as well as at home. This case is recorded also by Mr. Thayer.

"PERDICARIS ALIVE OR RAIZULI DEAD"

"In June, 1904, an American citizen, Ion H. Perdicaris, was seized by Raizuli, a Moroccan bandit, and held for ransom. After much shilly-shallying, and threats by Raizuli that he would kill his prisoner unless the money was speedily paid, Hay cabled to Gummeré, American consul at Tangier, on June 22:

'We want Perdicaris alive or Raizuli dead,' adding that Gummeré was 'not to commit us about landing marines or seizing customhouse.'

In his diary Hay made the following entries:

'June 23. My telegram to Gummeré had an uncalled-for success. It is curious how a concise impropriety hits the public.'

'June 24. Gummeré telegraphs that he expects Perdicaris to-night.'

'June 27. Perdicaris wires his thanks.'"

"So speedily," comments William Roscoe Thayer, in his "Life of John Hay," "did even a brigand, apparently safe in the depths of Morocco, recognize the note of command in the voice from over seas."

AMERICAN OPINIONS AT THE TIME

The news of the cable message was published on June 22. The Republican national convention, which on the following day nominated Roosevelt for President, was in session at the time in Chicago. The correspondent of the New York *Tribune* wrote about it as follows:

"'Perdicaris alive or Raizuli dead' went through the convention like an electric thrill, and it was more talked about at night than any feature of the day's work. The prevailing impression was that if Secretary Hay had sent the telegram it was after consultation with the President, and that there must have been ample justification. Delegates from all sections of the country discussed it in all its potential phases, and in almost every instance warmly commended it.

"'It is pithy, pungent, and peremptory. I like it, and so do the people,' said Senator McComas, of Maryland.

"'It is the kind of a telegram,' said Senator Spooner, of Wisconsin, 'that would provoke rapturous applause in any political convention. It touches a popular chord. This Government is bound to protect its citizens abroad as well as at home.'

"'The American people will not back down on a message of that kind,' said Representative Grosvenor, of Ohio. 'The people admire a declaration of that kind when the justification is sufficient. It may not be couched exactly in diplomatic words, but its meaning is unmistakable. The people are quick to respond when their patriotism is appealed to. The Morocco bandit will find that there is a vigorous and united sentiment supporting the President and Secretary Hay in the stand they have taken.'

" 'It was good, hot stuff, and echoed my sentiments,' said Congressman Dwight, of New York. 'The people want an administration that will stand by its citizens, even if it takes a fleet to do it.'

" 'It was magnificent—magnificent!' said Senator Depew. 'Every right-minded American will heartily indorse Mr. Hay's strong stand.'

" 'Do I like it?' exclaimed W. A. Elstun, of Kansas, one of the delegates. 'Bet your bottom dollar I like it. Roosevelt is behind that cable message to that fine old body snatcher, Raisuli. Out in Kansas we believe in keeping the peace but in fighting against the wrong. Roosevelt and Hay know what they are doing. Our people like courage. We'll stand for anything those two men do.' "

Commenting on the message a few days later, after Perdicaris had been released, the *Tribune* said:

"It is easy to sneer at it. A dog may bay at the moon. But every rational man knows that a nation that does not protect its own citizens is unworthy of the name of Government, and that, moreover, the only way to make citizenship respected and secure is to make outrage upon it perilous."

THE TRUE AMERICAN POLICY

The quoted comments by American statesmen reflect accurately the old-time American view of what the duty of a national administration is in cases affecting the lives of American citizens abroad. It accords with the view of that duty which Theodore Roosevelt holds and expounds to-day, as he has always held and expounded it. It is diametrically opposed to the policy pursued by the Wilson administration. In both the instances above referred to the outcome was not war, but peace with honor.

TWENTY YEARS' ADVOCACY OF PREPAREDNESS

From the moment he became Assistant Secretary of the Navy in 1897, down to the time when he retired from the Presidency in 1909, in all his public addresses, in all his annual messages to Congress, Col. Roosevelt advocated with tireless energy preparedness for war as the surest guaranty for peace. For the information of Secretary Garrison a partial collection of these utterances, beginning with those of his annual messages, is appended:

PREPAREDNESS URGED IN MESSAGES TO CONGRESS

(First annual message to Congress Dec. 7, 1901.)

"The work of upbuilding the Navy must be steadily continued. No one point of our policy, foreign or domestic, is more important than this to the honor and material welfare, and above all, to the peace of our Nation in the future."

PREPARATION LED TO VICTORY IN 1898

"It was forethought and preparation which secured us the overwhelming triumph in 1898. If we fail to show forethought and preparation now there may come a time when disaster will befall us instead of triumph."

(Second annual message to Congress, Dec. 2, 1902.)

"There should be no halt in the work of building up the Navy, providing every year additional fighting craft."

A GOOD NAVY THE SUREST GUARANTY OF PEACE

"A good Navy is not a provocation to war. It is the surest guaranty of peace.

The refusal to maintain such a Navy would invite trouble, and if trouble came would insure disaster.

Fatuous self-complacency or vanity, or shortsightedness in refusing to prepare for danger, is both foolish and wicked in such a Nation as ours, and past experience has shown that such fatuity in refusing to recognize or prepare for any crisis in advance is usually succeeded by a mad panic of hysterical fear once the crisis has actually arrived."

HIGHEST POINT OF EFFICIENCY NECESSARY

"The Army has been reduced to the minimum allowed by law. It is very small for the size of the Nation, and most certainly should be kept at the highest point of efficiency."

GENERAL STAFF FOR THE ARMY URGED

"I urgently call your attention to the need of passing a bill providing for a general staff and for the reorganization of the supply department on the lines of the bill proposed by the Secretary of War last year."

TO STAND STILL MEANS TO GO BACK

(Third annual message to Congress, Dec. 7, 1903.)

"I heartily congratulate the Congress upon the steady progress in building up the American Navy. We can not afford a let-up in this great work. To stand still means to go back."

GENERAL STAFF SECURED

"The effect of the law providing a general staff for the Army and for the more effective use of the National Guard has been excellent. Great improvement has been made in the efficiency of our Army in recent years.

We should not rest satisfied with what has been done."

(Fourth annual message to Congress, Dec. 4, 1904.)

"I most earnestly recommend that there be no halt in the work of upbuilding the American Navy."

RECORD ON PREPAREDNESS

"Our voice is now potent for peace, and is so potent because we are not afraid of war. But our protestations upon behalf of peace would neither receive nor deserve the slightest attention if we were impotent to make them good.

It is very important that the officers of the Army should be accustomed to handle their men in masses, as it is also important that the National Guard of the several States should be accustomed to actual field maneuvering, especially in connection with the regulars."

EFFICIENCY ALWAYS EFFICIENCY

(Fifth annual message to Congress, Dec. 5, 1905.)

"We have most wisely continued for a number of years to build up our Navy, and it has now reached a fairly high standard of efficiency. This standard of efficiency must not only be maintained, but increased.

We now have a very small Army—indeed, one well-nigh infinitesimal when compared with the army of any other large nation.

I do not believe that any army in the world has a better average of enlisted men or a better type of junior officer, but the Army should be trained to act effectively in mass."

(Sixth annual message to Congress, Dec. 3, 1906.)

"The United States Navy is the surest guarantee of peace which this country possesses.

I do not ask that we increase our Navy. I ask merely that it be maintained at its present strength, and this can be done only if we replace the obsolete outworn ships by new and good ones, the equals of any afloat in any navy.

In both the Army and Navy there is urgent need that everything possible should be done to maintain the highest standard for the personnel, alike as regards the officers and the enlisted men."

SWISS SYSTEM A MODEL

"The little Republic of Switzerland offers us an excellent example in all matters connected with building up an efficient citizen soldiery."

FOUR BATTLESHIPS A YEAR URGED

(Seventh annual message to Congress, Dec. 3, 1907.)

"To build one battleship of the best and most advanced type a year would hardly keep our fleet up to its present force. This is not enough. In my judgment we should this year provide for four battleships.

Again and again in the past our little Regular Army has rendered service literally vital to the country and it may at any time have to do so in the future.

Its standard of efficiency and instruction is higher now than ever in the past. But it is too small. There are not enough officers, and it is impossible to secure enough enlisted men."

EXTRA OFFICERS FOR THE ARMY NEEDED

"We should maintain in peace a fairly complete skeleton of a large army.

In particular it is essential that we should possess a number of extra officers trained in peace to perform efficiently the duties urgently required upon the breaking out of war."

From public utterances made by Col. Roosevelt at various points throughout the country during the same period, the following instructive citations are taken, my desire being to have Secretary Garrison's information thorough and complete:

TOO LATE TO PREPARE AFTER WAR BEGINS

(Address as Assistant Secretary of the Navy before the Naval War College, June, 1897.)

RECORD ON PREPAREDNESS

"We must make up our minds once for all to the fact that it is too late to make ready for war when the fight is once begun.

There must be adequate preparation for conflict, if conflict is not to mean disaster. Furthermore, this preparation must take the shape of an efficient fighting navy."

A BOLD FRONT MAKES FOR PEACE

"In public as in private life, a bold front tends to insure peace and not strife.

If we possess a formidable navy, small is the chance, indeed, that we shall ever be dragged into a war to uphold the Monroe Doctrine. If we do not possess such a navy, war may be forced on us at any time."

NOT IN THE INTEREST OF WAR BUT OF PEACE

"We ask that the work of upbuilding the Navy and of putting the United States where it should be put among the maritime powers go forward without a break. We ask this not in the interest of war, but in the interest of peace."

PREPAREDNESS NEVER A MENACE TO PEACE

"In all our history there has never been a time when preparedness for war was any menace to peace.

On the contrary, again and again we have owed peace to the fact that we were prepared for war."

IF THE NAVY FAILS, DEFEAT FOLLOWS

(Address to the graduating class, Naval Academy, Annapolis, May 2, 1902.)

"We all of us earnestly hope that the occasion for war may never arise, but if it has to come, then this Nation must win; and in winning the prime factor must of necessity be the United States Navy. If the Navy fails us, then we are doomed to defeat."

ONLY THE SHOTS THAT HIT COUNT

"In battle the only shots that count are those that hit,

and marksmanship is a matter of long practice and intelligent reasoning."

EFFICIENCY DEPENDS UPON PREPARATION

"A navy's efficiency in a war depends mainly upon its preparedness at the outset of that war. We are not to be excused as a nation if there is not such preparedness of our Navy."

PREPAREDNESS ALONE COMMANDS RESPECT

(Speech at Chamber of Commerce banquet, New York, Nov. 11, 1902.)

"We need to keep in a condition of preparedness, especially as regards our Navy, not because we want war, but because we desire to stand with those whose plea for peace is listened to with respectful attention."

PREPARATION WON AT MANILA

(Speech at San Francisco, May 14, 1903.)

"Remember that after the war has begun it is too late to improvise a navy. A naval war is two-thirds settled in advance, at least two-thirds, because it is mainly settled by the preparation which has gone on for years preceding its outbreak. We won at Manila because the shipbuilders of the country, under the wise provisions of Congress, had for 15 years before been preparing the Navy."

(Speech in Brooklyn, May 30, 1905.)

"If our Navy is good enough, we have a long career of peace before us. The only likelihood of trouble ever coming to us as a Nation will arise if we let our Navy become too small or inefficient."

AN INEFFICIENT WARSHIP A MENACE TO THE NATIONAL HONOR

"Every warship which is not first class in efficiency becomes in battle not a help to the Nation, but a menace to the national honor."

RECORD ON PREPAREDNESS

NAVY'S PRIME USE TO AVERT WAR

(Speech at the banquet of the National Convention for the Extension of the Foreign Commerce of the United States, Washington, Jan. 16, 1907.)

"Remember, gentlemen, that the prime use of the United States Navy is to avert war. The United States Navy is the cheapest insurance Uncle Sam has. It is the surest guaranty against our ever being drawn into war; and the guaranty is effective in proportion as the Navy is efficient."

A MAKESHIFT NAVY IMPOSSIBLE

(Speech at Cairo, Ill., Oct. 3, 1907.)

"It is utterly impossible to improvise a makeshift navy under conditions of modern warfare."

NAVY MUST BE BUILT IN TIME OF PEACE

"The Navy must be built and all its training given in time of peace. When once war has broken out it is too late to do anything."

NO FINER MATERIAL FOR VOLUNTEER SOLDIERY ANYWHERE

(Speech at Fargo, N. Dak., Apr. 7, 1903.)

"I believe that no other great country has such fine natural material for volunteer soldiers as we have, and it is the obvious duty of the Nation and of the States to make such provision as will enable the volunteer soldiery to be organized with all possible rapidity and efficiency in time of war; and, furthermore, to help in every way the National Guard in time of peace."

It is quite plain from these various utterances in messages and addresses that Col. Roosevelt has been advocating for nearly 20 years the same kind of efficient army and navy as he is advocating to-day.

"What I ask for," he said recently, "is a big efficient navy, and a small efficient army of a quarter of a million men, and back of the Army a nation of freemen trained to the use of arms."

So also with the danger of militarism and other arguments of the peace-at-any-price advocates. His opinions of these to-day are the same that he has always held, as a few citations will show:

NO NATION MORE FREE FROM MILITARISM THAN OURS

(Annual message to Congress, Dec. 3, 1907.)

"Not only there is not now, but there never has been, any other nation in the world so wholly free from the evils of militarism as is ours."

FOOLISH DENOUNCERS OF IT RARE

"There are, of course, foolish people who denounce any care of the Army or Navy as militarism, but I do not think that these people are numerous.

Declamation against militarism has no more serious place in an earnest and intelligent movement for righteousness in this country than declamation against the worship of Baal or Ashtaroth."

LESSONS OF THE CIVIL WAR

(Speech before the Hamilton Club, Apr. 10, 1899.)

"If in 1861 the men who loved the Union had believed that peace was the end of all things, and war and strife the worst of all things, and had acted up to their belief, we would have saved hundreds of thousands of lives; we would have saved hundreds of millions of dollars.

Moreover, besides saving all the blood and treasure we then lavished, we would have prevented the heartbreak of many women, the dissolution of many homes, and we would have spared the country those months of gloom and shame when it seemed as if our Armies marched only to defeat.

We could have avoided all this suffering simply by shrinking from strife. And if we had thus avoided it, we would have shown that we were weaklings and that we were unfit to stand among the great nations of the earth.

Thank God for the iron in the blood of our fathers, the men who upheld the wisdom of Lincoln and bore sword or rifle in the Armies of Grant and Lee! Let us, the children of the men who proved themselves equal to the mighty days—let us, the children of the men who carried the great Civil War to a triumphant conclusion, praise the God of our fathers that the ignoble counsels of peace were rejected; that the suffering and loss, the blackness of sorrow and despair, were unflinchingly faced and the years of strife endured; for in the end the slave was freed, the Union restored, and the mighty American Republic placed once more as a helmeted queen among nations."

PROFESSIONAL NONCOMBATANTS HARMFUL

(From Life of Thomas H. Benton, written in 1887.)

"A class of professional noncombatants is as hurtful to the healthy growth of a nation as a class of fire eaters, for a weakness or folly is nationally as bad as a vice, or worse. No man who is not willing to bear arms and to fight for his rights can give a good reason why he should be entitled to the privilege of living in a free community."

PEACE-AT-ANY-PRICE MEN COST BLOOD AND WEALTH

(From the "War with the United States, 1812-1815," written for the English History of the Royal Navy in 1897.)

"Both Britain and America have produced men of the 'peace-at-any-price' pattern, and in America, in one great crisis at least, these men cost the Nation more in blood and wealth than the political leaders most recklessly indifferent to war have ever cost it."

FEAR GOD AND TAKE YOUR OWN PART

(Letter to Carl Schurz, Sept. 8, 1905, published in Autobiography.)

"I thank you for your congratulations [upon the conclusion of peace between Japan and Russia]. If I had been known as one of the conventional type of peace advocates, I could have done nothing whatever in bringing about peace now, I would be powerless in the future to accomplish anything, and I would not have been able to help confer the boons upon Cuba, the Philippines, Porto Rico, and Panama, brought about by our action therein.

If this country had not fought the Spanish War, if we had failed to take the action we did about Panama, all mankind would have been the loser."

FRIGHTFUL CONSEQUENCES OF AN UNJUST PEACE

"While the Turks were butchering the Armenians the European powers kept the peace, and thereby added a burden of infamy to the nineteenth century, for in keeping the peace a greater number of lives were lost than in any European war since Napoleon, and these lives were those of women and children as well as of men; while the moral degradation, the brutality inflicted and endured, the aggregate hideous wrong done, surpassed that of any war of which we have record in modern times."

PARTIAL DISARMAMENT CALAMITOUS

"Unjust war is dreadful; a just war may be the highest duty. To have the best nations, the free and civilized nations, disarm and leave the despotisms and barbarisms with great military force would be a calamity compared to which the calamities caused by all the wars of the nineteenth century would be trivial."

HIGH PURPOSE WITHOUT POWER USELESS

(In the *Outlook,* September 9, 1911.)

RECORD ON PREPAREDNESS

"Our chief usefulness to humanity rests on our combining power with high purpose; and high purpose by itself is utterly useless if the power to put it into effect is lacking."

TRUE LOVERS OF PEACE

"In the history of our country the peace advocates who treat peace as more than righteousness will never be, and never have been, of service, either to the nation or to mankind.

The true lovers of peace, the men who have really helped onward the movement for peace, have been those who followed, even though afar off, in the footsteps of Washington and Lincoln and stood for righteousness as the supreme end of national life."

WHAT PACIFISM HAS DONE FOR CHINA

(In the *Outlook,* November 14, 1911.)

"A complete absence of militarism in China and China's effort to rely purely on pacific measures in dealing with all foreign powers have not only caused it to lose various Provinces to various foreign powers within the last few decades, but have had not the smallest effect in saving it from tyranny, misgovernment, and the most far-reaching economic misery at home; and, moreover, have had the effect of depriving it of means of keeping order within its own boundaries."

Col. Roosevelt's poor opinion of the usefulness of arbitration treaties when unbacked by force is not the outgrowth of developments of the present war, but, like his opinions on the other vital questions of national policy, is a matter of long-standing conviction:

ARBITRATION TREATIES USELESS UNLESS BACKED BY FORCE

(Address to the graduating class of the Naval Academy, Annapolis, January 30, 1905.)

"The adoption of those (arbitration) treaties by themselves would not bring peace. We are a good many years short of the millennium yet; and for the present and immediate future we can rest assured that the word of the man who is suspected of desiring peace because he is afraid of war will count for little."

RELIANCE OF A FIRST-CLASS FLEET SAFER

(Address, as Assistant Secretary of the Navy, before the Naval War College, June, 1897.)

"Arbitration is an excellent thing, but ultimately those who wish to see this country at peace with foreign nations will be wise if they place reliance upon a first-class fleet of first-class battleships rather than on any arbitration treaty which the wit of men can devise."

(Address at dinner of the Sons of the American Revolution, New York, March 17, 1905.)

"I know one excellent gentleman in Congress who said he preferred arbitration to battleships. So do I. But suppose the other man does not? I want to have the battleships as a provocative for arbitration so far as the other man is concerned.

We have now got our Navy up to a good point. We have built and are building 40 armored ships. For a year or two, or two or three years, to come what we need to do is to provide for the personnel of those ships and to secure the very highest standard of efficiency in handling them, singly and in squadrons; above all, for handling the great guns."

ARMED STRENGTH ALONE MAKES ARBITRATION
SUCCESSFUL

(Annual message to Congress, December 3, 1906.)

"The chance for the settlement of disputes peacefully, by arbitration, now depends mainly upon the possession by the nations that mean to do right of sufficient armed strength to make their purpose effective."

LIMITATION OF ARMAMENTS IMPOSSIBLE

(Annual message to Congress, December 3, 1907.)

"It is evident (from the failure of The Hague conference to take action on the limitation of armament) that it is folly for this Nation to base any hope of securing peace on any international agreement as to the limitation of armaments. Such being the fact, it would be most unwise to stop the upbuilding of our Navy."

NO SAFEGUARD AGAINST VIOLATION

(Address before the Nobel Prize Committee, Christiania, Norway, accepting the Nobel Peace Prize, May 5, 1910.)

"All really civilized communities should have effective arbitration treaties among themselves. I believe that these treaties can cover almost all questions liable to arise between such nations, if they are drawn with the explicit agreement that each contracting party will respect the other's territory and its absolute sovereignty within that territory, and the equally explicit agreement that (aside from the very rare cases where the nation's honor is vitally concerned) all other possible subjects of controversy will be submitted to arbitration. Such a treaty would insure peace unless one party deliberately violated it. Of course, as yet, there is no adequate safeguard against such deliberate violation, but the establishment of a sufficient number of these treaties would go a long way toward creating a world opinion which would finally find expression in the provision of methods to forbid or punish such violation."

NO SINGLE POWER CAN LIMIT ARMAMENTS

"Something should be done as soon as possible to check the growth of armaments, especially naval armaments, by international agreement. No one power could or should act by itself; for it is eminently undesirable, from the standpoint of the peace of righteousness, that a power which really does believe in peace should place itself at the mercy of some rival which may at bottom have no such belief and no intention of acting on it.

Finally, it would be a master stroke if those great powers honestly bent on peace would form a league of peace, not only to keep the peace among themselves but to prevent, by force if necessary, its being broken by others."

NEED OF AN INTERNATIONAL POLICE POWER

"The supreme difficulty in connection with developing the peace work of The Hague arises from the lack of any executive power, of any police power, to enforce the decrees of the court.

Each nation must keep well prepared to defend itself until the establishment of some form of international police power, competent and willing to prevent violence as between nations.

As things are now, such power to command peace throughout the world could only be assured by some combination between those great nations which sincerely desire peace and have no thought themselves of committing aggressions."

WILSON'S LOST OPPORTUNITY

"The combination might at first be only to secure peace within certain definite limits and certain definite conditions, but the ruler or statesman who should bring about such a combination would have earned his place in history for all time and his title to the gratitude of all mankind."

PAPER TREATIES USELESS IF NOT BACKED BY FORCE

(In the *Outlook*, November 4, 1911.)

RECORD ON PREPAREDNESS

"This war (between Italy and Turkey) proves the utter inefficiency of paper treaties when they are unbacked by force; the utter folly of those who believe that these paper treaties accomplish any useful purpose in the present stage of the world's development when there is no force behind them; and, finally, not merely the folly but the iniquity of making treaties which there is no real intention of putting into effect."

WICKED TO MAKE TREATIES SURE TO BE BROKEN

"It would be not merely foolish but wicked for us as a Nation to agree to arbitrate any dispute that affects our vital interest or our independence or honor, because such an agreement would amount on our part to a covenant to abandon our duty, to an agreement to surrender the rights of the American people about unknown matters at unknown times in the future.

Such an agreement would be wicked if kept, and yet to break it—as it undoubtedly would be broken if the occasion arose—would be only less shameful than keeping it."

Even on the subject of hyphenated Americans, the views which Col. Roosevelt has been expressing since the outbreak of the European War are not new. He uttered the same sentiments more than 20 years ago and has reiterated them frequently since.

HYPHENATED AMERICANS NOT DESIRABLE

(From "True Americanism," published April, 1894.)
"We welcome the German or the Irishman who becomes an American. We have no use for the German or Irishman who remains such. We do not wish German-Americans and Irish-Americans who figure as such in our social and political life; we want only Americans, and, provided they are such, we do not care whether

411

they are of native or of Irish or of German ancestry. We have no room in any healthy American community for a German-American vote or an Irish-American vote, and it is contemptible demagogy to put planks into any party platform with the purpose of catching such a vote. We have no room for any people who do not act and vote simply as Americans and as nothing else."

ALL AMERICANS IN ROUGH RIDERS

(Speech at New Mexico, May 5, 1903.)

"There were men in my regiment (in the Spanish War) who themselves were born in England, Ireland, Germany, or Scandinavia, but there was not a man, no matter what his creed, what his birthplace, what his ancestry, who was not an American and nothing else."

GOOD CITIZENSHIP THE TEST

(Speech at Butte, Mont., May 27, 1903.)

"If we are to preserve this Republic as it was founded, as it was handed down to us by the men of sixty-one to sixty-five, and as it is and will be, we must draw the line never between section and section, never between creed and creed, thrice never between class and class; but along the line of conduct, the line that separates the good citizen wherever he may be found from the bad citizen wherever he may be found."

GOOD AMERICANISM NOT A MATTER OF BIRTH

(Message to Congress, December 6, 1904.)

"Good Americanism is a matter of heart, of conscience, of lofty aspiration, of sound common sense, but not of birthplace or of creed. The medal of honor, the highest prize to be won by those who serve in the Army and the Navy of the United States, decorates men born here, and it also decorates men born in Great Britain and Ireland, in Germany, in Scandinavia, in France, and doubtless in other countries also."

RECORD ON PREPAREDNESS

(Speech at dinner of the Friendly Sons of St. Patrick, New York, March 17, 1905.)

"My fellow countrymen, I have spoken to-night especially of what has been done for this Nation of ours by men of Irish blood. But, after all, in speaking to you or to any body of my fellow citizens, no matter from what Old World country they themselves or their forefathers may have come, the great thing is to remember that we are all of us Americans. Let us keep our pride in the stocks from which we have sprung, but let us show that pride, not by holding aloof from one another, least of all by preserving the Old World jealousies and bitternesses, but by joining in a spirit of generous rivalry to see which can do most for our great common country."

Finally, in regard to the Monroe Doctrine and the necessity of upholding it by force in case of need, Col. Roosevelt has for years held and advocated no uncertain views.

THE MONROE DOCTRINE ONLY EFFECTIVE IF UPHELD BY FORCE

(At Augusta, Me., August 26, 1902.)

"The Monroe Doctrine is simply a statement of our very firm belief that on this continent the nations now existing here must be left to work out their own destinies among themselves and that the continent is not longer to be regarded as colonizing ground for any European nation.

The only power on the continent that can make that doctrine effective is, of course, ourselves, for in the world as it is, gentlemen, the nation which advances a given doctrine likely to interfere in any way with other nations must possess power to back it up if she wishes the doctrine to be respected."

BLUSTER WITHOUT FORCE WORSE THAN ABANDONMENT

(Speech at Chicago, April 2, 1903.)

"I believe in the Monroe Doctrine with all my heart and soul. I am convinced that the immense majority of our fellow countrymen so believe in it; but I would infinitely prefer to see us abandon it than to see us put it forward and bluster about it, and yet fail to build up the efficient fighting strength which in the last resort can alone make it respected by any strong foreign power whose interest it may ever happen to be to violate it."

"SPEAK SOFTLY AND CARRY A BIG STICK"

"There is a homely old adage which runs: 'Speak softly and carry a big stick; you will go far.' If the American Nation will speak softly, and yet build, and keep at a pitch of the highest training, a thoroughly efficient Navy, the Monroe Doctrine will go far."